THE KOLA RUN

Vice-Admiral Sir Ian Campbell K.B.E., C.B., D.S.O.
and Captain Donald Macintyre D.S.O., D.S.C.,
Royal Navy

The Kola Run

A Record of Arctic Convoys 1941-1945

Futura Publications Limited

A Futura Book

First published in Great Britain in 1958 by
Frederick Muller Ltd

First Futura Publications edition 1975
Copyright © Sir Ian Campbell and Captain Donald
Macintyre 1958

ISBN 0 8600 71154
Printed in Great Britain by
Hazell Watson & Viney Ltd
Aylesbury, Bucks

Futura Publications Limited
49 Poland Street,
London W1A 2LG

ACKNOWLEDGEMENTS

The plans and appendices contained in this book have been reconstructed from Crown Copyright material made available by the Lords Commissioners of the Admiralty and are reproduced by permission of the Controller, H.M. Stationery Office.

The authors could not have undertaken this work without the ready co-operation of the Admiralty where Lieutenant Commander Kemp and the Historical Section which he heads gave every encouragement and advice. Their thanks are particularly due to Mr. Hurford of the Historical Section and to Mr. Ellmers, and later Mr. Gardiner, of the Records Office. The many calls made on their time and personnel are hereby gratefully acknowledged.

The illustrations are published by the courtesy of the Director of the Imperial War Museum, the help and co-operation of whose Photographic Department have been unfailing and generous.

Much background material and points of interest were sought from many others close to the sources of the events described, foremost among whom were:

Admirals Sir Ernest Archer, Sir Harold Burrough, Sir Douglas Fisher; Rear-Admirals Sir Richard Bevan, M. W. S. Boucher, H. Crombie, R. L. Fisher, H. W. Faulkner; Commodore K. Dowding, R.N.R.; Captains A. D. H. Jay and I. Morton; to all of whom the authors' thanks are due.

CONTENTS

DIAGRAMS

FOREWORD

by

ADMIRAL OF THE FLEET SIR RHODERICK MCGRIGOR,

G.C.B., D.S.O.

This is the story of the Arctic Convoys which fought their way to North Russia through four years of the war. It is told by two officers who had great experience as Escort Commanders.

Vice-Admiral Sir Ian Campbell, as Captain (D) in H.M.S. *Milne*, commanded the 3rd Flotilla, the 'M' class destroyers, from 1942 to 1944 and some of their exploits and experiences will be read in the chapters of this book. Admiral Campbell's period of command began in those early days when every advantage seemed to lie with the enemy.

Captain Macintyre spent most of the war in command of escort forces in the Atlantic. He played a leading part in the long-drawn-out battle against the U-boats.

The authors have a great tale to tell. It is a tale of courage and determination, of seamanship and great endurance in the most adverse conditions of weather and bitter cold and attack by enemy forces, of triumph over disaster and of fighting through, so often theoretically against impossible odds.

The convoy escorts were mainly ships of the Royal Navy with an occasional ship of the Polish, Norwegian or other allied Navies who played their gallant part and fitted so well into the team. The convoys consisted of Allied merchant ships, mostly British and American, whose proud record it is that in spite of all they experienced and endured they never faltered.

I personally did not take part in these convoys until 1944–45, the latter years of the war when we had at last got adequate escorts including aircraft to operate with the convoys from the little escort carriers which accompanied them. It has been an exhilarating experience to read this book and to recapture some of the spirit of those days.

To me it brings back many memories. I see again the crews of Swordfish aircraft in their open cockpits, flying off into the bitter, endless Arctic night to patrol or to attack a suspected U-boat, and their return out of the darkness two or three hours later.

I remember those tremendous gales and seas with the whole length and breadth of the Atlantic behind them, which scattered the convoys and left their legacy of damage and distress; the urgency of reassembling the convoy as soon as the weather moderated enough to allow ships to choose a course to steer, so as to be ready for the inevitable attack by enemy aircraft; and then sometimes just one pair of fighters, all that remained serviceable, taking off to play their intrepid and invaluable part in breaking up the enemy air attack, with the carriers pitching like wild things; and the incredible skill of their return on board after patiently circling the ship until a lull in the motion made this just, and only just, possible.

I picture again the convoy itself, Liberty ships, cargo ships of all sizes, tankers and ammunition ships, manoeuvring under attack like a well-trained fleet; and its escorts, perhaps a small cruiser with destroyers, some modern, some veterans of the first war, and little frigates and corvettes, disappearing and reappearing in huge seas, ever active against the attack of U-boat or aircraft and in helping the merchant ships in trouble or distress.

I gladly take this opportunity of paying my tribute to the Captains, officers and men of those warships and merchantmen. They fought their way through, whatever the odds, during four years of war and made so great a contribution to the final victory.

I trust this absorbing book will attract the wide attention it deserves both in this country and abroad.

PROLOGUE

On 22nd June 1941, the uneasy, false friendship between the two dictators, Hitler and Stalin, dissolved as the legions of Nazi Germany rolled across the Russo-German frontier. The rulers of Germany and Russia had each for long had their eye on the domination of the Old World. An eventual clash was inevitable. But while Hitler had reached the peak of his strength in 1941, Russia, planning to strike when the rest of Europe lay exhausted, whichever way Hitler's war should go, would not be ready for several years to mobilize her full power. Caught unprepared, it soon became apparent that Russia, left to her own resources, would go down in defeat before the splendidly equipped, veteran armies of Germany as she had done twenty-three years before.

Alternatively, if Russia could be kept in the ring, Hitler's defeat was now certain. Military aid by Britain, the only country still in the fight and striving desperately to renew her strength after the disasters of 1940, was out of the question. But, by taking advantage of her one great asset, command of the sea, Britain could, in spite of her own desperate needs, send material help, particularly in the two weapons of which Russia was most urgently in need – tanks and aircraft. Sympathy for a country treacherously attacked by the common enemy combined with self-interest led to an offer of such help, which was readily, though hardly gratefully, accepted.

Thus to the Royal Navy, its resources already stretched almost to the limit by world-wide, unaided responsibilities, an additional burden was assigned – that of opening and protecting a new shipping route which, unlike the trans-Atlantic, was exposed for a great part of its length to enemy-held territory on its flank.

The original understanding was that Russian merchant ships

would carry the cargoes but, in the event, these proved quite inadequate in numbers. Britain's merchant navy, already being decimated by the U-boat attacks in the Atlantic, was called on to make up the deficiency.

The offer made and accepted, no time was lost in getting to work. Less than two months after the German attack on Russia, the first convoy of seven ships sailed for Archangel. This early demonstration of goodwill set the pattern for what was to follow. At tremendous sacrifice in weapons and munitions critically needed by our own forces, at a terrible risk of naval disaster at the hands of the superior air and surface forces deployed in Norway and at a grievous cost in ships and men, convoys were fought through to Murmansk and Archangel for the rest of the war, only pausing for the mid-summer months when continuous daylight made their defence impossible in the face of shore-based air attacks.

With the entry of the U.S.A. into the war six months later, the Americans joined wholeheartedly in the enterprise, American ships in the convoys often outnumbering the British. American material made up the bulk of the cargoes. But the responsibility for the safe and timely arrival of the convoys was solely that of the Home Fleet of the Royal Navy. It entailed their defence against the battleships, cruisers, destroyers and submarines of the German Navy, all of which were brought into play, and against the high bombers, dive-bombers and torpedo planes of the Luftwaffe.

A glance at the map will give an idea of what this involved. Leaving Iceland, a convoy for North Russia would head northeast for the vicinity of Bear Island. The decision whether to pass north or south of that desolate Arctic upthrust of rock depended on how far south was the barrier of solid ice. By the time that nearer, lonely Arctic island, Jan Mayen, had been passed, the convoy route, still some 1400 miles long, was continuously in range of airfields in Norway; its ability to evade the U-boats waiting in ambush was limited by the ice barrier in the north and the proximity of airfields to the east and south-east.

As the convoy approached the North Cape, its dangers were multiplied by the possibility of the enemy's heavy warships, the gigantic *Tirpitz*, the powerful battle-cruisers *Scharnhorst* and *Gneisenau*, the pocket-battleship *Lutzow* and the heavy cruisers *Hipper* and *Prinz Eugen*, slipping out at their own chosen moment from their safe bases in Norway and falling on the convoy and its escort of lightly armed anti-submarine and anti-aircraft ships. These dangers persisted right to the mouth of the Kola Inlet, a bare thirty miles from enemy territory.

Thus the problem for the Commander-in-Chief Home Fleet, with his ships based far away at Scapa Flow, was, having given the convoy a sufficient escort of light forces to drive off U-boat and air attacks, to provide cover against any sortie by the German heavy ships without unnecessarily exposing his own battleships and cruisers to the overwhelming air attack that the enemy could concentrate against them from his shore bases. It was a problem of the utmost nicety. In the story of the Arctic Convoys, we shall see with what success it was met.

We shall see failure to have our covering forces available at the right time and place offset by the gallant repulse of heavy cruisers by a few British destroyers; the loss of British cruisers by U-boat or air attack through their retention with convoys to give protection against surface threats. We shall watch with dismay the annihilation by submarine and air attack of a convoy ordered to scatter in the face of a surface threat when no covering force was available to counter it; and finally we will be able to applaud the successful tactics which lured the mighty *Scharnhorst* to her doom at the hands of the ships of the covering force.

Around the convoys themselves, the picture will be of the never-ceasing probing of the depths by the asdics of the escorts, the rumble of depth charges and the thudding of torpedoes in the bowels of ships; the deafening bedlam of air attacks, the crump of bombs, the crack and chatter of spitting guns. As the story moves to its climax, the curve of losses amongst the merchant ships mounts steadily until a new factor comes to even the odds and then to give victory to the defenders – the escort aircraft-carrier.

But running right through the story is the steadfast gallantry of the men who manned the ships, merchantmen and escorts. The former condemned, defenceless, to grin and bear it, with perhaps a cargo of explosive beneath their feet and the deadly cold of the Arctic seas waiting for them. The latter standing their watches with the freezing spray lashing them, or feeding the guns with shells from which ice must be chipped in order to set the fuses.

Other convoys there were in the Second World War which were fought through, with varying success, against similar hazards, notably in the Mediterranean. But no convoy enterprise was so continuously operated in the face of such heavy losses and in such daunting conditions of weather. Furthermore it was pressed on in spite of an utter lack of appreciation by the ally for whose benefit it was undertaken and an entire absence of his help, even where it was readily available. An occasional growl from the Russian bear at the hold-up of greedily awaited war material was the only acknowledgement of our losses. At the Russian ports of destination, our men were subjected to every petty restriction and inconvenience in grim surroundings. To keep Russia's own waters, in the approaches to Murmansk and Archangel, free of mines and submarines, British minesweepers had to be stationed there. A British minelayer, *Apollo*, had to steam 4000 miles to lay an anti-submarine minefield on the Russians' own doorstep.

But in spite of all discouragement war munitions flowed in a steady stream to Russia, much of it American, but all of it material which we urgently needed ourselves. As Winston Churchill has said, 'The Service departments felt it was like flaying off pieces of their skin.' After one convoy battle, the captain of the aircraft-carrier involved complained in his report that his pilots were having to fight in lightly-armed Hurricanes of an early type while the latest Mark were in the holds of the ships they were escorting to Russia.

In the history of the Second World War as seen by future generations, the Arctic convoys will appear but a minor side-show, except to the serious student of naval strategy. Throughout England's naval history, the passage of mercantile or troop-carrying convoys, her own or her enemy's, has been the backbone to which is attached the more easily visible flesh of the famous battles whose names are household words.

From the first great English naval victory at Sluys in 1340, which was fought to ensure the safe passage of merchant ships across the narrow seas to Flanders, to Trafalgar, which was essentially an attack on the escort without which Napoleon's invasion fleet could not sail, this has been true.

In modern times all the major actions of the Royal Navy in the Second World War developed from the necessity to protect merchant ships – the sinking of the *Bismarck* and of the *Scharnhorst*, the battles of Cape Matapan and Sirte. The accounts of the battles will shine out from the pages of the history books. The dull, pedestrian business of shepherding the convoys through, which is the very fruit and essence of sea-power, will tend to be taken for granted.

This account of how one ocean route was kept open in the face of odds theoretically impossible may serve to fill in the background to the more general picture of the war at sea, which is all that can be contained within the covers of histories of manageable size. Like the story of other theatres of the naval war, it is one which begins with a dogged defence with inadequate and unsuitable forces, inevitable when a nation refuses to pay for the weapons of defence in time of peace. It moves on through a period of increasing success marred by a costly disaster, to the final phase in which forces become available to give the convoys almost complete protection.

Let us launch ourselves therefore on to the broad stream of the story. It will take us through storm and tempest northwards to smoky seas where great icebergs stand watching us go by, to the ice barrier which we must skirt closely to keep as great a distance as possible between us and the enemy's strongholds. Fog and snow will blind us; ice will encase our ship with insidious increase as spray freezes as it falls aboard. There we must meet our ruthless enemy determined that we shall not pass. There too we will meet our ally, surly, suspicious, unappreciative and unhelpful.

These are the ingredients of the Kola Run.

1

FIRST CLASHES

The German High Command was slow to react to the institution of Arctic convoys, perhaps because they were confident that Russia would go down to their Blitzkrieg before Allied aid could affect the issue, perhaps through poor intelligence. Whatever the cause, from August to December 1941 five small convoys reached Russia unscathed, the sixth lost only one ship from U-boat attack.

It was against this convoy, P.Q. 6, that the first warning came that the Germans were deploying their surface ships in north Norwegian harbours whence they could sally forth to attack our convoys with little risk of encountering the Home Fleet covering forces.

The local escort for the last, short lap of the convoy's voyage, into Kola Inlet, consisting of British minesweepers based there, had barely taken over from the ocean escort when from two of them, the *Speedy* and the *Hazard*, gunflashes were sighted out of the gathering gloom to the north-eastward. Silhouetted as they were against the lighter sky to the south-west, the two little ships, mounting but two 4-inch guns apiece, were quickly in the midst of shell splashes from the 5·1-inch guns of German destroyers, whose shapes they could now dimly make out.

With the *Speedy* heavily hit, her mast shot away and both guns out of action, the two minesweepers turned away to the south, making smoke to cover the convoy. But here, in their first encounter with a convoy and its escort, the German surface forces showed a lack of enterprise that was to be repeated on subsequent occasions. Faced by these two lightly armed, slow ships, whom they could have wiped from the face of the sea with a few salvoes, they broke off the action, leaving P.Q. 6 to reach harbour unscathed.

Thus, at the turn of the year, there was good reason for confidence. In the long hours of darkness, with a brief twilight around mid-day, the enemy seemed unable to locate the small convoys that were still the normal, and to bring his U-boats into action in any numbers. His aircraft were similarly impotent. The escorts were rewarded for their interminable voyages in gloom, darkness and incessant, screaming gales by the satisfaction of seeing their charges safely into harbour with their priceless cargoes.

But such immunity could not last. The days were inexorably lengthening. There was no telling how things would go when aircraft could detect and shadow the convoys, calling U-boats up to lie in wait and bombers in to the attack. Yet through January and February 1942, only by lying in ambush off the Kola Inlet were the U-boats able to make contact with the convoys attacking them as they were manoeuvring to enter harbour. Even here they managed to sink only one merchantman and one destroyer from P.Q. 7, 8, 9, 10 and 11.

The loss of the latter, the big Tribal Class *Matabele*, provided an ominous example of what could be expected in those icy seas by crews forced to take to the water. Though her consorts were quickly on the scene to rescue survivors, only two out of a ship's company of some 200 were found alive.

It was deplorable that, after coming 2000 miles from Iceland unscathed, the convoy should be attacked by U-boats operating with impunity in the restricted waters off Kola Inlet. This was something far short of collaboration on the part of the Russians. Our hard-worked flotilla of minesweepers could not be expected to ensure the defence of the Russians' own waters. Rear-Admiral Burrough, in his flagship *Nigeria* at Murmansk, struggled throughout February, with small success, to persuade the Russians to take an interest in their own behalf.

Meanwhile, already in January 1942, the first stir in the German fleet had been detected, as the great battleship *Tirpitz* was reported moving north. Strangely enough, however, it was not the lure of the Arctic convoys that had brought her from safe retreat at Kiel, but Hitler's 'intuition' that Norway was about to be invaded. 'Every ship,' he cried, 'which is not stationed in Norway is in the wrong place!' But until the *Scharnhorst*, *Gneisenau* and *Prinz Eugen*, bottled up in Brest, were extricated, he had not many ships to deploy in the north. Even the mighty *Tirpitz* could not operate safely, alone and unscreened.

It was therefore not until the *Admiral Scheer* and the *Prinz Eugen* sailed north on 20th February with three destroyers to join the *Tirpitz* that a serious threat was appreciated. Now, even when the *Prinz Eugen* had been torpedoed and damaged by Commander Sladen's submarine *Trident*, a force existed which could bring disaster to the two convoys, outward and inward, P.Q. 12 and Q.P. 8, which were assembling.

In the war room at the Admiralty and in the operations room of Admiral Tovey's flagship at Scapa Flow the question was asked a dozen times a day, 'Any news of the *Tirpitz*?' The Royal Air Force was entrusted with the task of keeping watch on the German squadron, but in the wicked weather and long hours of darkness of those latitudes, aerial reconnaissance alone could not be relied upon. Backing it were our submarines stationed along the Norwegian coast, their lonely, monotonous patrols only made bearable by the thought of some day having the *Tirpitz* or one of her consorts in their sights.

The *Trident* had already had that rewarding experience and had made good use of it; but for the remainder there had been nothing but day after day and week after week of storm and cold and blank horizons till their hearts were ready to break. It was therefore a tremendous moment for Lieutenant R. F. Raikes, captain of the submarine *Seawolf*, when on the evening of 6th March the masts and fighting top of a large warship hove over the horizon.

The news spread quickly through the ship's company as the *Seawolf* steered at her utmost speed to try to achieve an attacking position. But it was not to be. Though Raikes got close enough to identify the enemy ship, she swept by at high speed, far out of range of his torpedoes. But as the enemy vanished again over his limited horizon, from the *Seawolf* went out the vital message, '*Tirpitz* is out!'

With this important news a situation of great complexity faced Admiral Tovey, the C.-in-C., Home Fleet. Over a period of days, the two convoys would be approaching each other and then, having passed on opposite courses, would be drawing away from each other again. Only for a brief spell would they be near enough for one force to cover them both. If he divided his fleet, one portion might be met and defeated by *Tirpitz* and *Scheer* who would then be free to work havoc in the convoy they had been covering.

However, defence of the convoys was not uppermost in Tovey's mind. He believed that his principal objective must be to bring the *Tirpitz* to action. The only place in which he could be sure of doing this was on her line of eventual retreat to her base at Narvik. He therefore decided that while the battleship *Duke of York*, the battle-cruiser *Renown* and the cruiser *Kenya* covered, as best they could, both convoys, he, in the *King George V* with his only carrier, *Victorious* and the cruiser *Berwick*, would be free to range at will in search of the *Tirpitz*.

But these dispositions did not please the Admiralty at all. They had developed a healthy respect for what shore-based bombers could do to warships without fighter cover. They ordered the Commander-in-Chief to keep his ships concentrated so that *Victorious*'s fighters could cover them all.

The widespread game of blind-man's-buff which ensued between these ships and the German squadron is no part of our story. It is sufficient to say that in the mist and smother of those smoky seas, they advanced and retreated and passed on opposite courses without ever meeting each other, as though in some vast maritime minuet. Meanwhile the two convoys moved on towards each other.

The outward bound P.Q. 12, meeting pack-ice, was forced further south than had been planned and, at noon on 7th March, passed Q.P. 8 on an opposite course. Barely eighty miles to the southward, the *Tirpitz* and her three destroyers were casting north-westward on the trail of the defenceless prey they sensed was somewhere near at hand. Not far to the westward, Tovey, unable to operate his aircraft owing to thick weather and severe icing, was also blindly groping for his opponent.

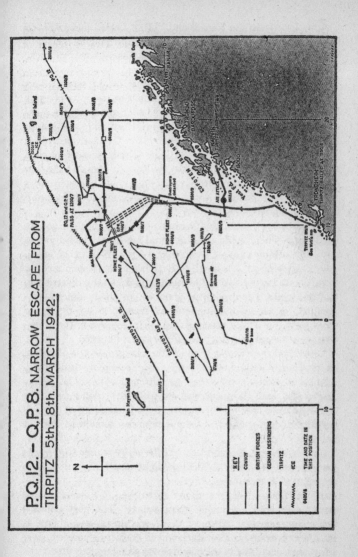

P.Q.12. – Q.P.8. NARROW ESCAPE FROM TIRPITZ 5th–8th MARCH 1942.

KEY
CONVOY
BRITISH FORCES
GERMAN DESTROYERS
TIRPITZ
ICE
0400/6 TIME AND DATE IN THIS POSITION

A clash between the *Tirpitz* and Q.P. 8 seemed inevitable – a clash which must have led to a fleet action as soon as the alarm was flashed to Tovey. But in those days of early, primitive radar sets, the weather was still the master at sea.

Lieutenant-Commander Seymour of the *Hazard*, senior officer of the escort of Q.P. 8, which consisted of but two minesweepers and two little corvettes, never knew that at one moment, ten miles ahead of his convoy in the murk, the great battleship was sweeping past; while astern of the convoy, the German destroyers, similarly screened by the northern mists, were passing so close that they encountered a straggler, a Russian ship, which they quickly sank. Any one of these enemy units could have wiped out the weak escort. But they drove on unsuspecting and the inward convoy was saved.

Foiled in his search, the German Admiral Ciliax pressed on northwards where sound reasoning told him he might still fall in with the outward convoy. By the narrowest of margins he failed. P.Q. 12, hoping to pass north of Bear Island, had again recoiled from the ice barrier and been forced to make a long diversion to the south which took it once again within eighty miles of the questing *Tirpitz*. Contact there would have spelt catastrophe for the convoy, for Tovey was hundreds of miles away to the south-west, bent on intercepting the enemy as he returned to Narvik. But luck and the weather were on the convoy's side. It ploughed on, unalarmed and unaware of the danger so closely threatening.

Another Arctic convoy had got through without loss. How narrow had been its escape was not realized by either side. The Germans were now awakening to an understanding of the importance of this traffic and were determined to stop it. Bomber squadrons were sent to the northern airfields of Banak and Bardufoss, U-boats were concentrated and the heavy cruiser *Hipper* was sent to join the *Tirpitz*. With daylight lengthening they were confident of success.

On the British side, the immunity enjoyed in spite of meagre escorts had bred an unwise complacency. The next outward convoy, ominously numbered P.Q. 13, was already assembling, as was the homeward Q.P. 9. Each was to consist of nineteen merchant ships. The size of the convoys was going up, but that of the escort force allotted to them was not. It was quite inadequate in the face of the mounting threat. Destroyers and frigates were desperately needed in half a dozen other war theatres. Calculations of the risk influenced by the availability of escorts resulted in one cruiser, two destroyers and two trawlers being considered sufficient for the job. Against a moderate U-boat attack, this was the minimum required. A minor thrust by surface craft could also be taken care of with luck. But a combination of the two, or air attack, would find the defending forces woefully deficient.

It is a melancholy fact that British warships designed and built before the war were armed with little thought to the menace of air attack. The main gun batteries were suitable for surface engagement only, their maximum elevation insufficient to engage any but low-flying aircraft. The deadly German dive-bomber technique came as an ugly eye-opener and many a sharp lesson had it delivered in the Norway campaign and at Dunkirk. A remedy was neither easily nor quickly to be found and so, in the early months of 1942, these Arctic convoys were being sailed, through waters dominated by the enemy air force, virtually defenceless against the dive-bomber and the torpedo plane.

The cost was bound to be heavy. How heavy was not at first appreciated, and it was only after a series of calamitous experiences and the happy advent of suitable anti-aircraft ships that escorts capable of fighting the convoys through were provided.

Let us look at the sort of ships that were used for escort at this time. With each convoy went a cruiser whose battery of 6-inch guns could be relied upon to beat off attack by destroyers and at least to hold enemy cruisers at bay while the convoy escaped. The cruiser could also put up a barrage that might daunt any dive-bombers or torpedo planes from pressing their attacks in to a killing range.

But, chained to the slow, plodding convoy, she was a tempting and vulnerable target for U-boats and too valuable to risk in this way. We shall see two of them being lost very shortly. After that, any escorting cruisers were held aloof from the convoy itself, where they were clear of U-boat concentrations and free to manoeuvre widely so as to offer as difficult a target as possible. If surface attack threatened, they could come swiftly to the rescue, but their value as anti-aircraft ships was lost.

Then there were the fleet destroyers of pre-war vintage, with four 4·7-inch guns and eight torpedo tubes. The crews of these weapons were out in the open, unshielded from the icy penetrating wind or the spray that would freeze as it flew through the air to land as ice on the decks or lash their shrinking flesh. The guns themselves would often fail to function in the bitter cold, the torpedoes would freeze in the tubes or run erratically when launched.

Not much, it might seem, against the 8-inch or 6-inch guns of the German cruisers or even the five 5·9-inch guns of a big German destroyer of the Narvik class. But in this role they were in fact to prove themselves highly effective against an enemy determined not to risk his limited force of ships too much.

But it was in their endurance and their anti-aircraft capabilities that they were most at a disadvantage. On the long haul from Iceland to Murmansk, though oilers from which they could refuel were included in the convoy, something less than a gale was necessary for them to do so at sea. But, as gale followed gale in the raging, inhospitable Arctic, the destroyers were forced to husband their precious oil supply. Every high-speed rush after a U-boat or on the endless missions of encouragement and shepherding around the convoy was undertaken at a risk of running down to a stop in mid-ocean, the most ignominious as well as dangerous situation for any ship of war. Furthermore, as fuel ran low, stability became less and might fall below the safety level at which a ship could ride the tremendous seas of the far north.

The anti-aircraft armament of these ships was usually no more than a single 2-pounder pom-pom or a four-barrelled 0·5-inch machine-gun – of little use against a determined dive-bomber or torpedo plane.

More up-to-date destroyers were coming into service with dual-purpose guns and control systems that made them reasonably effective against aircraft. Their guns were housed in spray-proof turrets, too, which gave the crews protection from the weather. But such ships were few and far between as yet.

The backbone of any convoy escort, so far as anti-submarine

protection went, was the corvette of the 'Flower' class. The design of these little ships of 1010 tons displacement was adapted from that of the whaler and was one of the most happy results of the labours of the Corps of Naval Constructors. Chunky, broad-beamed, solidly constructed and able to ride the worst storms the northern seas could generate, their names were redolent of an English garden dreaming under a summer sun – *Poppy, Gentian, Calendula, Clematis, Honeysuckle, Bluebell* and a hundred others. Those manned by the Free French followed this rule – *Roselys, La Malouine, Aconit* and so on.

But designed for mass production, the Flower class were driven by simple reciprocating steam engines which could not thrust them along at better than fifteen knots; so they could not be sent far afield or they might take a day or more to rejoin their convoy. With their small size, too, they were limited in the equipment they could carry and were thus restricted to a specialized anti-submarine function. One 4-inch, low-angle gun and a brace of machine-guns was the total of their gun armament, which gave them little value against air attack.

Sharing with the corvettes the hundred and one domestic chores in and around the convoys were the trawlers. These were fine, deep-sea craft and sterling sea-boats which could ride out any weather. Their low freeboard made them excellent rescue ships. Their endurance, given good coal, was ample. But they were comparatively slow, they had no room for the many devices which went to make up an effective anti-submarine equipment and their armament was restricted to a single 4-inch gun forward and, perhaps, a couple of Oerlikon 20-millimetre machine-guns. In spite of these limitations, they and their R.N.V.R. and R.N.R. Patrol Service crews did wonderful work of which examples will be found interspersing these pages.

The older destroyers, corvettes and trawlers mentioned above formed what were known as the 'through' escorts. Joining the convoys at their assembly ports, they remained with them till their arrival some twelve days later. Besides these there were the 'local' escorts – minesweepers based either in the Orkneys and Shetlands or in North Russia. Of the latter we shall hear much in this story. Originally two flotillas – as a result of losses they were later amalgamated into one – they probably had the grimmest assignment of any body of ships in the war. Besides their primary task of keeping the channels into Murmansk and Archangel clear of mines in the awful weather conditions of those latitudes, they would accompany the homeward convoys on the first few days of their voyage and meet the incoming ones, joining the escort for what was often the toughest part of their journey. For months on end, between their spells of duty they lay in the dismal surroundings of the White Sea ports and the Kola Inlet, in winter suffering the aching monotony of the long nights and few hours of grey twilight, in summer the equally hateful eternal daylight in which enemy bombers from bases close by roamed at will with little opposition from the Russians.

At long intervals these little ships would go, one at a time, to England to rest and refit, joining up with the through escort of a convoy for the passage. The unglamorous nature of their work, virtually defenceless against aircraft or surface attack as they were, brought them little fame or credit except amongst those who welcomed their timely arrival with many a hard-pressed convoy, the first sign that its ordeal was nearing its end. Their only reward was the knowledge of many a wounded merchant ship brought safely to port and many a survivor gathered from the scant shelter of open boats or rafts.

It was of such ships, and pitifully few of them, that convoy escorts were being made up in the spring of 1942 when, with P.Q. 13, the curtain rose on the second act of the drama of the Arctic convoys, an act which was to show British fortunes in this story at their lowest ebb and to lead the enemy to premature jubilation which, in the long run, would prove to be unjustified.

In that grim spring of 1942, indeed, British fortunes were at their nadir everywhere. Blow after blow had shaken the whole war structure to its foundations. In the Far East the Japanese were everywhere successful. Singapore, Java, New Guinea, told an unbroken tale of Allied defeat. Our latest battleship and a battle-cruiser had gone down before the Japanese Fleet Air Arm. In the Middle East the German armies had swept forward 300 miles in North Africa. In the Mediterranean the *Ark Royal* and the *Barham* had been sunk, the battleships *Valiant* and *Queen Elizabeth* put out of action. The Battle of the Atlantic was at its grimmest stage and every available escort was needed to fight the vital convoys through.

It was with affairs at this crisis that the Joint Services Mission in Washington gave priority to the task of keeping Russia effectively in the war.

So nineteen deeply loaded ships, carrying tanks, aircraft and vehicles for the hard-pressed Russian armies sailed from Iceland as Convoy P.Q. 13 on 20th March 1942. A similar number sailed empty from Kola Inlet westbound as Q.P. 9. Q.P. 9's story illustrates the anomaly that success leaves little or nothing to tell. The first U-boat to attempt an attack, *U655*, was detected, depth-charged to the surface and rammed to destruction by the mine-sweeper *Sharpshooter* of the close escort. No other enemy cared to provoke so boisterous a welcome. The convoy arrived intact at its destination having been screened by thick weather for the whole voyage.

The laden, valuable ships of P.Q. 13 were too attractive a bait to be let by so easily. Yet they had a through escort of only two destroyers, *Fury* and *Eclipse*, and two trawlers, while the cruiser *Trinidad* provided close cover, in company with the convoy by day to give anti-aircraft support, standing away by night when U-boat attacks on the convoy were most likely.

With the convoy also were three small warships, *Sulla*, *Sumba* and *Silja* – Norwegian whalers being delivered to Russia for use as magnetic minesweepers. But these were to prove of negative value, if not a positive menace. Carrying insufficient oil for the journey, they would have to be towed for at least forty-eight hours to conserve fuel.

It was a force totally inadequate for the task ahead of them, had they known it. Still, it was thought, other convoys had got by with no more. But, alas, conditions were not the same now. By the end of March there was no real darkness in the far north to shroud the convoy from the shadowing planes, only a few hours of semi-darkness.

For the first four days, in fair weather, P.Q. 13 pounded steadily north-eastward, making good progress. But it was too good to last. On 24th March a violent gale came down out of the west, mounting steadily in fury. During the next four days, huge seas and thick weather combined to scatter the unwieldy vessels. Not yet equipped with radar, there was little the escorts could do, enveloped in black darkness, flying spray and whirling mists, to keep them together. When the Arctic day reluctantly came to life south of Bear Island on the 28th, a blank, empty waste of tumbling rollers was all that could be seen from the bridges of the escorts. The convoy was scattered far and wide, impossible to screen or defend by the meagre escorts. As the day wore on, the weather moderated and some of the ships were able to gather in small groups, with one of which, of six ships, the *Eclipse* made contact. The rest of the convoy was strung out over 150 miles of storm-tossed ocean.

As they plodded eastward thus, they were sighted and reported by the first enemy reconnaissance plane, and soon the bombers were streaming out from Banak and Bardufoss. Within an hour they had found their prey, and for the rest of the day the gunners in the ships were continuously at action stations, driving them off as best they could with the inadequate weapons to hand. With the *Trinidad* unable to come to the help of so dispersed a target, the opposition that the enemy pilots had to face was comparatively slight. Yet they were singularly ineffective. Until late in the day they failed to score a single hit. But then a straggler was set upon and sunk, and at 7.30 in the evening also, the escorts heard the last signal of the *Empire Ranger*, away ahead of the remainder, as she reported herself sinking and the crew abandoning ship.

Many of the aircraft arriving on the scene were lured to the bait of the valuable cruiser, but the *Trinidad*'s guns drove off attack after attack and she remained unscathed.

Then on the evening of that day, 28th March, came the news of a new threat. Three German destroyers had sailed from Kirkenes in the far north and were searching for the scattered convoy. With the *Fury* in company, Captain Saunders of the *Trinidad* took the two ships on a wide sweep to the southward during the night so as to be in a position to cut off the enemy whichever of the two main portions of the convoy he should attack. As dawn approached, all was still quiet, however, and, knowing that the destroyer *Oribi* and two Russian destroyers, which had been despatched from Kola to reinforce the escort, would soon be joining, Saunders led round to the north-eastward to meet them. This would also bring him in contact with the leading group of the convoy.

It was not long before, on the radar screen, three contacts duly appeared; but they could be either *Oribi* and her consorts or the enemy. Alarm bells clanged as the crews tumbled to their action stations, the guns' crews of the destroyer clumsy in their layers of clothing against the icy blast streaming along the upper deck. But as dim grey shapes loomed out of the east, a signal light winked, giving the current British challenge.

The newcomers were a splendid addition and enabled Saunders to leave them to reinforce the *Eclipse* escorting the rear group of ships, while he turned eastward again with the *Fury* to close the leading group. This portion of the convoy, originally six in number, was now reduced to four. The S.S. *Ballot*, sailing under the Panamanian flag, had been so shaken by near misses during the previous day's attacks that she had dropped astern and lost touch. The *Induna* had gallantly taken in tow the whaler *Silja*, running short of fuel. These two also had dropped astern and, running into ice floes, had lost contact with their group.

Meanwhile there had been no news of the German destroyers since they had sailed. But they were already on the scent of the convoy having found, on the previous evening, the laden boats of the *Empire Ranger*, and taken her crew prisoner. They knew they must be roughly on the convoy route therefore. Sweeping along it they had fallen in with the *Bateau* around midnight. Shells and a torpedo from the flotilla leader, *Z.26*, had sent her to the bottom, the crew being taken aboard the destroyers.

A wide sweep round the area brought them no further success, and at 8.30 in the morning of the 29th the Germans were again searching westwards along the convoy route. The unpredictable Arctic weather had been clear and bright since dawn with the visibility extreme. But now ahead of them black clouds almost down to sea level were rolling eastwards before a rising gale. Hidden in the murk, *Trinidad* and *Fury* were plunging along at

20 knots to a meeting with the enemy. Neither side was aware of the other's presence.

Once again radar gave the first warning to the British. This time there was no doubt. The shapes that hove in sight were clearly identifiable as three big, Narvik class destroyers, *Z.26*, *Z.25* and *Z.24*, making for the rear group of ships of the convoy. The guns of the *Trinidad* roared out and shells were at once slamming into the leading destroyer, setting her ablaze amidships. In shocked surprise, the German leader, swerved away into the cover of the snowstorm and faded out of sight.

The two rear destroyers, turning to avoid torpedoes which they thought had been fired at them, lost touch with their leader in the mist and snow. The *Z.26*, damaged and on fire, was alone, and soon *Trinidad* and *Fury* were in contact with her again and surrounding her with shell splashes as she zigzagged desperately in her efforts to escape. But further hits struck home, and the German's end must have been certain in a short time when sudden disaster altered the whole picture.

In haste to deliver the *coup de grâce*, Saunders gave the order for torpedoes to be fired from the *Trinidad*. As the sights came on, one after the other, the firing levers at the tubes went over, but only from one of them did the torpedo launch. The special anti-freezing oil needed in that climate had been unavailable when the *Trinidad* sailed and the torpedoes were frozen in their mountings. The one torpedo which got away failed to run true, no doubt for a similar reason. It circled back and was seen as it broke surface heading for the cruiser! It was too close to avoid. With a detonation that shook the ship from stem to stern, it burst against a boiler room, flooding that big compartment and bringing her to a standstill with a heavy list.

Reprieved for the moment, *Z.26* made off to the south-west, where a heavy snowstorm gave her cover, with the *Fury* in chase. Her course led her close north of the rear portion of the convoy, and now the *Eclipse* got a glimpse of her as she loomed momentarily out of the mist; but, unable to identify her, *Eclipse*'s captain, Lieutenant-Commander Mack, could not engage her. Almost at the same moment the *Fury* came tearing out of the snow, mistook *Eclipse* for the enemy and got two salvoes off at her before realizing her mistake.

For some minutes chaos reigned as destroyers sped past and round each other in the increasing thickness until Lieutenant-Commander Campbell of the *Fury*, seeing that other forces were available to carry on the chase of the *Z.26*, turned to rejoin the *Trinidad*, while the *Eclipse* swung round to investigate the strange ship, still unidentified, that had been seen to slip away to the west. As Mack wrote later, 'There seemed altogether too many destroyers around the convoy.'

He was quite right. Following up a radar contact, he saw a grey shape loom up at 800 yards. A brief moment of peering doubt and he knew it was the enemy. There followed a crazy running fight through the swirling, blinding snowstorm. Gunnery conditions were about as bad as they could be – decks sheathed in ice, freezing spray making binoculars useless and a heavy sea rolling the *Eclipse* gunwales under.

But the German was in no condition for battle after his treatment at the hands of the *Trinidad*. When six times the *Eclipse*'s 4·7-inch shells had hit her, the *Z.26* was brought to a halt. But now the tables were to be turned once more. Shaping up to torpedo the *Z.26*, Mack was confronted by the sight of her two consorts clearly in view as the snow-smother suddenly lifted. No match for the two heavily armed Germans, *Eclipse* turned to run for cover in the retreating snowstorm; before she could gain it, she had been heavily hit, her hull holed and her aerials shot away.

But the Germans did not follow up their success. Turning to help their comrades, they left *Eclipse* to limp away to safety while they rescued the crew of the now sinking *Z.26*.

When the *Fury* rejoined the *Trinidad*, she found her lying with a 17-degree list. But her crew were struggling desperately to make emergency repairs, shoring up bulkheads, pumping out what compartments they could and flooding others to reduce the list, isolating the shattered boilers and getting steam to the engines from the remainder. At last, painfully, she got slowly under way, while *Fury* circled her. For now U-boats were gathering to ravel further the already confused situation. One found the crippled cruiser, but before the submarine could get a torpedo away it was pounced on by the destroyer and sunk, a brilliant little action in the grim conditions prevailing.

But others had found easier targets amongst the merchant ships. The *Induna*, with the *Silja* still in tow, had broken free of the ice during the afternoon. Then, during the night, in the renewed gale, the tow had parted and she had had to go on alone. She deserved better than the fate that met her when, early the next morning a U-boat's torpedo slammed into her side. Her crew, left to the scant mercy of the raging Arctic sea, suffered untold miseries in their boats before the survivors were rescued three days later by a Russian minesweeper.

Another U-boat found the S.S. *Effingham* and sent her, too, to the bottom, leaving her crew in their boats. The remainder of the convoy plodded grimly on, largely devoid of the protection by men-of-war they were entitled to expect, wondering what new form of nemesis was coming to them. But the *Effingham* was the last casualty, for help was on its way from Kola.

There, four ships of the 6th Minesweeping Flotilla, *Harrier*, *Gossamer*, *Speedwell* and *Hussar*, based in the drab misery of North Russia, had been waiting to sail to take over the convoy on its last lap into Murmansk. On 28th March they left harbour as the first news of the fighting was coming in. They knew that the *Harpalion* had been bombed but might be still afloat, that the *Empire Ranger* had signalled that she was sinking 180 miles north of Cape Kanin, that the rest of the convoy was widely scattered. All else was conjecture.

Detaching *Speedwell* to search for the damaged ships or survivors, Commander Jay in the *Harrier* led the remainder along the convoy route to round up and escort any ships they could find. Then came the news of the surface actions and *Trinidad*'s torpedoing, at which the *Harrier* left to find and help her. As dusk was falling, feeling her way blindly through smothering, swirling snowstorms, she found the cruiser and joined her escort.

Next morning, the gale, which had shown signs of moderating, regathered its fury. The seas mounting up astern were making it more and more difficult for the *Trinidad* to steer at her best speed of only four knots. Peering through the falling snow at her, Jay of the *Harrier* saw a great wave seize the cruiser's stern and swing

34

it in a crazy arc to turn the ship beam-on to the run of the sea, where she lay, unable to recover or regain her course. She had broached-to. Taking his ship close in, Jay sent over a wire hawser with the aid of which the cruiser was hauled back, stern on to the seas.

Soon afterwards, with *Trinidad* under the lee of Kildin Island and riding more easily, the *Harrier* was off again to search for lost ships. She came across the whaler *Silja* out of fuel in spite of the *Induna*'s tow, and wallowing helplessly. So the *Harrier* took her in tow again and when, at 4 o'clock in the morning of 31st March the two ships reached shelter off the port of Polyarnoe at the entrance of the Kola Inlet, the *Harrier* pumped five tons of fuel into the *Silja* and then left at once to join *Speedwell* and *Hussar* on their tireless work of search and rescue.

That afternoon they were rewarded. In a break in the incessant snowstorms, a look-out sighted a red sail. It proved to be that of a lifeboat from the *Effingham* and was the visible evidence of a tale of grim endurance and courage. When their ship was torpedoed and sunk, this boat, containing the Chief Officer, one other officer and thirteen of the crew had got safely away in spite of heavy seas. With fine seamanship they had got the boat clear and their sail hoisted and, while the officers navigated, the remainder huddled as best they could to keep life in their bodies in the bitter cold and the wild tossing of their boat. The first miserable day was followed by the long Arctic twilight in gale and snow. Hope was low as the dawn disclosed nothing but grey, leaping waves and the ceaseless swirl of snowflakes. Only a steadfast refusal to give in kept life in the frozen little company. In spite of the cheerful encouragement and leadership of the Chief Officer, as the day wore on five of the crew slipped quietly out of life before the blessed sight came of their rescuers.

The survivors were quickly got aboard the *Harrier* where their frozen bodies were revived. For one more it was too late, but the remainder, in spite of frost bite and other injuries, recovered.

That day the last of the surviving ships of the convoy reached harbour. P.Q. 13 had arrived!

2

LENGTHENING ODDS

P.Q. 13 had certainly arrived. But it was hardly the 'safe and timely arrival' which the escorts were bidden to ensure. Out of nineteen ships, five had been sunk – more than 25 per cent – and, though the enemy had lost one destroyer and two U-boats, a valuable British cruiser and the destroyer *Eclipse* had been severely damaged and would be out of action for months. The long record of immunity of the Arctic convoys had been broken.

There were two main reasons for this, the increasing period of daylight, which enabled the enemy's reconnaissance planes to detect the convoy and call in submarines, aircraft and surface ships to the attack, and the meagre escort which had been allocated to the convoy.

It was perhaps understandable that, so long as the convoys were getting through without great loss, as they had been up to now, in the desperate shortage of destroyers and frigates of that time it should have been considered a fair risk to send so small an escort force. But P.Q. 13 made it clear that such arrangements could not continue. Admiral Tovey appealed for more destroyers and corvettes to be allocated. They could not come from the Home Fleet whence no more could be spared. Other commands would have to be drawn on.

His professional knowledge told him also that, even with more escorts, as days lengthened towards the summer conditions of perpetual daylight, the dice were too heavily loaded against the convoys to make their continuation a practical operation of war. He could give no protection against the enemy's heavy ships during the last part of the outward passage. His battleships were the only remaining units capable of meeting the *Tirpitz* should she break out into the Atlantic. To risk them without fighter cover within easy range of the Norwegian airfields was out of the question. The convoy escorts available were unsuitable for defence against air attack. Furthermore, U-boats could operate with comparative impunity in the northern waters owing to the loss of efficiency of the asdic there.

If the Russians would give fighter cover from their northern airfields or give real assistance with their anti-submarine vessels, the odds might be lessened, the risk made acceptable. But appeals to them brought little response; our tale of losses was received with scant sympathy and renewed complaints at the resultant slowing down of supplies.

But as the Commander-in-Chief anticipated, his representations were of no avail. President Roosevelt pressed Winston Churchill to persist with aid to Russia; Winston Churchill brought his influence and authority to bear on the Defence Committee in opposition to the First Sea Lord's dire warnings. The convoys were to continue. Indeed they were to be stepped up in size.

P.Q. 14, which sailed from Reykjavik on 8th April, comprised twenty-four ships, but the impending show-down was delayed in this case through the convoy running into heavy pack-ice. By the time it had broken clear, only eight ships remained concentrated and fit to continue, the remainder turning back. Even this little convoy did not escape unscathed, losing one of its number to a U-boat's torpedoes.

The corresponding return convoy, Q.P. 10, of sixteen ships, gave another warning of what could be in store, though the enemy never deployed the same strength against the empty, return convoys as they did against those outward bound with the tanks, aircraft and vehicles for Russia which they were determined to intercept.

Between Kola and Bear Island was the most dangerous part of the voyage, as the map shows. Throughout it, during the winter and spring, the convoys, pressed southwards by the pack ice, were continuously in easy range of the enemy airfields, the nearest, at Petsamo, being barely sixty miles from Kola itself. From

Kirkenes, another forty miles along the coast, German destroyers could sally forth and be amongst the convoys within twelve hours of sailing. For the U-boats, the problem of finding the convoys was simplified by the constricted waters available south of the ice barrier.

It seems incredible that the enemy, so perfectly placed to harry the route from above, below and on the surface of the sea, was unable absolutely to prevent the passage of the convoys. The German Fuehrer raged to his naval staff about the 'employment of every available means to paralyse the hitherto almost undisturbed sea communications between the Western powers and Russia in the Arctic and to eliminate the enemy's mastery of the sea, which extends right into our coastal waters'.

He was right to rage. But it was not the German dispositions that were wrong. It was the Luftwaffe pilots, the U-boat and destroyer captains who were at fault. 'Sea communications' or 'routes' cannot be attacked. It is ships which are the target, and, time and again, the enemy showed himself incapable of getting his attacks home on the ships though he completely dominated the eastern end of the route.

The Luftwaffe pilots were astonishingly ineffective if they met any opposition. U-boat captains' reports were full of such expressions as 'Unable to attack because of very strong escorts' or 'Striving to attack but driven off by escorts just before getting into position.' As for the surface ships, hamstrung by Hitler's anxiety to avoid any risks, they either skulked in harbour or allowed themselves to be driven off by greatly inferior forces.

But even if the lack of skill and determination of the enemy's forces, sea and air, could have been foretold, the unanimous naval opinion, that passage of convoys from April onwards was not a reasonable risk, was sound. Overridden by political considerations, efforts to provide a stronger and more suitable escort for the summer convoys were being pressed on at a high priority. But meanwhile Q.P. 10 had to be got back with what escorts were available at Kola. These were five destroyers, *Oribi*, *Punjabi*, *Marne*, *Fury* and *Eclipse*, the last-named temporarily patched up after her damage in action, the minesweeper *Speedwell* and two trawlers *Blackfly* and *Paynter*. As close cover there was the

38

cruiser *Liverpool*, which would stand away during the brief hours of twilight when aircraft could not attack, and rejoin the convoy by day to provide anti-aircraft support.

Commander John McBeath of the *Oribi*, senior officer of the close escort, was not one to suffer dismay at the task facing him, but he must have welcomed this addition to the force, for only the *Marne* amongst his destroyers mounted more than a single 3-inch or 4-inch gun that could elevate sufficiently to serve as an anti-aircraft gun. Good station-keeping by ships of the convoy so as to keep in a compact body from which concentrated fire from their guns could be directed at attacking aircraft was likely to be their best defence; but this takes iron nerve and a cool head when every bomber plummeting down seems to be aiming at your particular ship.

It was not long before the convoy had its first test. With Kola only twenty-five miles from enemy territory, its departure on 10th April was known at once to the Germans. At first light the Ju. 88s arrived, but, for some reason, in small formations only. With bitter winds from the Pole bringing sub-zero weather even at sea, they no doubt had their problems of operation and maintenance. Against these attacks the merchant ships showed their metal by shooting down two aircraft and damaging several others. But three Ju. 88s concentrating on the *Empire Cowper* scored their first success, sending her to the bottom.

By the evening, the ships, ghostly white in their covering of snow, were threading their way between icebergs, which continued to be in sight all the next day between the incessant snow squalls. The weather kept all but a few of the aircraft from making contact and all in the convoy blessed the soft snowflakes screening them. But the proximity of the ice was inducing large variations in the sea temperature which affected the efficiency of the asdics in the escorts, deflecting the sound beams with which they probed the depths. This was serious, for U-boats were known to be gathering round.

As the Arctic day gave way to twilight, McBeath stationed his ships as best he could to guard against this new hazard. Sleepless vigilance in the escorts was the only defence against these sinister, slinking craft. Commanding Officers prowled restlessly on their cramped bridges or sat huddled in layers of clothing behind their compass binnacles, while look-outs peered forth, scrutinizing their allotted sectors of sea, cursing the snow and the cold which fogged their binoculars. At the asdics, operators crouched with earphones on head, trying to coax information from the 'ping, ping', which was maddeningly deadened by the bad water conditions.

But around 1 o'clock, a U-boat succeeded in getting close enough undetected to attack. The distress rocket soaring up from the *Kiev* and a dull concussion through the deck under his feet told McBeath that a torpedo had got home in the convoy. Half an hour later it was the turn of the *El Occidente*. With escorts standing by the stricken ships as they sank, to pick up their crews, the screen had got dangerously thin, when contact with the attacker was momentarily gained by the *Oribi*. Her depth charges were not enough to destroy the U-boat, but they discouraged it from further attacks. By sunrise the escorts were back in station ready for the Ju. 88s which would surely come.

This time the enemy had gathered a strong squadron together and, at 6 o'clock, twenty of them came screaming down out of the sun. But the convoy was well together and ready for them. From the heterogeneous collection of weapons in the merchant ships, as well as from those of the escorts, such a volume of fire went skywards that the German pilots were daunted and sent their bombs wide. Not a single ship was hit.

Twenty minutes later they were back again. No more inclined to face the gunfire, they hurled their bombs wildly amongst the columns of ships but, even so, four of them were shot down into the sea. Unfortunately one ship, the *Harpalion*, which had survived the attack on P.Q. 13, was so damaged by a near miss that she could not go on. There was no help for it but for an escort to take off the crew and sink her.

For all their greater effort, the Luftwaffe had received a rude shock and a bloody nose. In three days they had disposed of but two empty ships at a cost of six of their aircraft shot down and many more damaged. John MacBeath gave full credit to the masters and gunners of the merchantmen when he reported: 'The behaviour of the merchant ships was beyond praise. They kept perfect formation despite air and U-boat attacks. Their control of fire and its accuracy was exemplified in their many successes in shooting down aircraft.'

The worst was over for the convoy for ahead stretched a rolling bank of fog. Blessed fog! The bugbear of the mariner in times of peace and kindly shelter from attack in war! By mid-day the ships were slipping silently through the enveloping brume. The westerly gale of which it was the forerunner was sending warmth ahead of it and the ships were thawing out. A week of heavy weather was all that the convoy had to put up with for the rest of the voyage, and without further loss it reached Reykjavik on 21st April.

Yet for all its success against aircraft, the hard fact remained that a quarter of its number had been sunk before the fog came to its rescue, an unacceptable rate of loss. The belief was held at that time that large convoys were more vulnerable than small, owing to their unwieldiness and the large number of escorts required effectively to screen them. Later this was shown to be a fallacy, the fact being that for any given attack that got home, the same number of ships was likely to be sunk, so that the bigger the convoy, the smaller the percentage losses. Arctic convoys steadily grew in size, but there was a limit in this direction imposed by the poor unloading facilities at the Russian ports.

The problem facing the Commander-in-Chief Home Fleet had grown in complexity since his near encounter with the *Tirpitz* in the mists and darkness of March. The *Tirpitz* was still there, in spite of repeated efforts by the Royal Air Force to eliminate her. So were the *Hipper*, *Scheer* and *Lutzow*, separately or together constituting a threat which could only be met by the heavy ships of the Home Fleet.

The Luftwaffe in the north had been heavily reinforced. This, with the increasing hours of daylight, would make the deployment of Tovey's irreplaceable battleships where they could give cover against surface attack all the more risky. Though not known to us yet, the Germans, spurred by the example of their allies and the ineffectiveness of their bombers, had developed a torpedo-bomber which would soon be sent against the convoys.

It has to be remembered that always the Admiralty and the C.-in-C. had to take into consideration the predicament they would be in if a battleship or their only aircraft carrier were to be crippled in the far north in waters infested by U-boats, a thousand miles from its base.

Against these advantages to the enemy could be set the handicap presented to the U-boats by the absence of darkness in which they preferred to attack. By the beginning of May, the season would have arrived when the sun shone for twenty-four hours a day in the latitude of North Cape.

The threat by aircraft and surface ships had therefore become the predominant consideration. Against the former, new defensive devices were slowly coming on the scene, the first being the C.A.M. ship (Catapult Aircraft Merchantman), from which a single Hurricane fighter could be catapulted, the aircraft being 'ditched' on completion of its flight. The next was the merchantman specially converted as an anti-aircraft ship. These were manned by the Royal Navy and flew the White Ensign. Against surface attack the cruiser, attached whenever possible as close cover, was relied upon to back the lightly armed destroyer escorts.

Lightly armed indeed they were. After the experiences of P.Q. 13 and Q.P. 10, the Western Approaches Command had been called upon to provide additional escorts. But Western Approaches destroyers had had their gun and torpedo armament cut down in order to make room for greatly increased depth-charge equipment. They were excellent anti-submarine ships, as were the little Flower class corvettes which came with them, and all were manned by veterans of the Atlantic battle, but, on paper at least, they were quite out of their class when confronted by the big German destroyers.

They could not seriously be considered in such a role by those allocating a convoy's defences. Yet, as we shall see, there is more to be considered when forecasting results in a sea fight than the number and size of guns on each side.

So with this help from the Western Approaches and improved anti-aircraft defence, the Home Fleet faced the coming crisis with a stout heart but against its better judgement as orders from the summit came down that nothing must halt the flow of supplies to Russia.

3

TRIUMPH AND DISASTER

Thus when, on a crisp Icelandic spring morning, the twenty-five masters of the ships forming P.Q. 15 assembled in Reykjavik for the customary convoy conference before sailing, their somewhat gloomy forebodings of the, by now, notorious Kola Run ahead of them were offset to some extent by the size and composition of the escort as explained to them by its senior officer, Captain J. H. F. Crombie of the minesweeper *Bramble*.

Besides his division of four minesweepers bound for a spell of duty in North Russia, there would be four trawlers and six destroyers. True, three of the latter were Western Approaches ships, good anti-submarine craft but little else, but there were also two fleet destroyers, *Somali* and *Matchless* and one of the little 'Hunt' class with six 4-inch guns on high-angle mountings, most effective against aircraft. Then came the very welcome news that one of the new, specially equipped anti-aircraft ships, H.M.S. *Ulster Queen*, would be there. No longer would enemy aircraft have only machine-gun fire to face if they got in amongst this convoy.

Looking at the sheet of paper which showed the convoy formation and details of the ships in it, the masters saw 'C.A.M.' after the name of the *Empire Morn*. As they wondered idly what it could stand for, they heard Crombie explaining about the Hurricane fighter which might be sent off to knock down the shadowing aircraft before it could send off the message that would bring the bombers streaming out against them.

It was a much more cheerful body of master mariners who left the conference room than had come in. The master of the *Cape Corso* wryly grinned his satisfaction at such a strong escort, as he thought of the cargo of high explosive in the holds of his ship. But the Kola Run was the Kola Run still — no joking matter!

The next day, 26th April, the *Botavon*, flying the blue St. George Cross flag of the Commodore, Captain H. J. Anchor, led the way out of harbour. As the last ship cleared the swept channel he hoisted the signal 'Form Convoy', and for the next few hours the twenty-five ships manoeuvred cumbrously into station in six columns. Another Arctic convoy was on its way.

For four days it made steadily north-eastwards, unmolested and unalarmed. On the 28th two oilers joined and from them the destroyers topped up their fuel tanks while the weather held fair. The same day, though unknown to the crews of the merchant ships, a strong Anglo-American force led by the Commander-in-Chief and Rear-Admiral Giffen, U.S.N., in the U.S.S. *Washington* sailed from Scapa Flow to cruise to the southward of the convoy route and give cover against any foray by the *Tirpitz*. On 30th April Rear-Admiral Harold Burrough, by now a veteran of these operations, joined with the cruisers *Nigeria* and *London*.

It was a timely arrival, for that evening, when the convoy was 250 miles south-west of Bear Island, the first German reconnaissance plane found and reported it. The misty weather with frequent snow showers was not suitable for launching the Hurricane on its first-and-last flight from the C.A.M.-ship, but it also gave the convoy considerable cover. Twenty-four hours went by with no further sign of the enemy and when at 10 o'clock on the evening of 1st May, six Ju. 88s appeared, they were met by such a volume of fire from the strong escort and the ships of the convoy that they sent their bombs wide in a ragged, ill-coordinated attack.

But the time was approaching for the cruisers, too valuable to be risked in areas where the U-boats concentrated, to leave for their covering positions whence they would only return at a threat of enemy surface attack. The *London* left at midnight, but Admiral Burrough held on with the convoy until 10 o'clock the next morning.

All through 1st May news had been coming in of stirring events

44

around the homeward-bound Q.P. 11, which would soon be passing on an opposite course. When it came in sight, Captain Crombie ordered the *Somali* to close it and get in contact with its escort. Her captain, Commander Jack Eaton, was soon back, bringing a gloomy forecast of what might be expected further east. The pack-ice was unseasonably far south, German destroyers were in the vicinity and U-boats were concentrated in the area. One of them had torpedoed the cruiser *Edinburgh* which was now struggling back towards Kola. He also brought news of a brand new type of threat. For the first time, German torpedo-bombers had been encountered.

Eaton had barely passed this news to Crombie when the enemy shadowing aircraft arrived. Soon, too, on the radio direction finders fitted in the Western Approaches destroyers, signals from U-boats were intercepted. In the escorts a tense feeling of anticipation was growing. It was bitterly cold around the guns where the crews crouched, trying to shelter from the wind. But 2nd May passed without incident until at 8 o'clock in the evening, the destroyer *St. Albans* and the minesweeper *Seagull* were seen to be investigating a submarine contact. For once water conditions for the asdics were good and, as they ran in to drop their depth charges, they knew that their attacks were accurate. As the last of a pattern detonated and sent up its white pillar of water, the excited crews let out a sudden cheer as they saw a submarine come to the surface in a boil of foam. But then their jubilation died away into a dismayed silence. On the conning tower was the number. *P.551*. It was a British submarine!

The crew abandoned their sinking craft and were picked up by the two escorts. They were found to be Poles manning a British submarine. Unable to fix their position for several days, due to low visibility hiding sun and stars, they had been some 100 miles from their allotted patrol area. Crestfallen, the escorts resumed their station on the convoy, steadily ploughing its way eastward.

Midnight passed. The middle-watchmen coming on duty found a gloomy Arctic twilight with ships barely visible at four miles – less in the direction of the frequent patches of haze. But all was peaceful. The radar screens were clear of aircraft contacts. Then suddenly from the starboard side of the convoy there was a roar of engines and six Heinkel IIIs came streaking out of the murk almost at water level. From their bellies fell the torpedoes to start on their short run to their targets, while the aircraft zoomed up over the ships of the convoy where the startled gunners swung their guns to try to follow them.

It was a skilful and very bold attack. The pilots indeed, paid for their temerity as three of them crashed into the sea shattered by gunfire; but their skill sent three of their torpedoes speeding true for ships of the convoy. The Commodore's ship, *Botavon*, and another, the *Jutland*, shuddered as torpedoes exploded in their sides and they stopped in a sinking condition. But the *Cape Corso*, similarly hit, disintegrated in one tremendous thunderclap as its deadly cargo exploded.

The new German weapon had made a dramatic entry on to the stage and, though Commodore Anchor and 137 survivors were rescued from the sunken ships, the fearful end of the *Cape Corso* could not but cause awe and dismay amongst the merchant crews. But the price had been a relatively heavy one for the enemy. Out of only twelve torpedo-bomber crews they had trained at this time, they had lost a quarter in this one attack. It was no doubt for this reason that P.Q. 15 saw no more of them. But the devastating possibilities of this form of attack was not lost on the senior naval officers concerned with the direction of these Arctic operations and were, no doubt, in their minds as they one and all protested against their continuation during the summer months.

However, except for an abortive bombing attack which cost the enemy one Ju. 88 on the evening of the same day, P.Q. 15 covered the remainder of its voyage unmolested, reaching Kola late on 5th May. Their ordeal was not over when they dropped anchor. Baulked of their prey at sea, the Germans tried hard to make up for it by sending their bombers over on every clear day of the fifteen that were spent discharging cargo at Murmansk. The *Ulster Queen*, berthed amongst them to give anti-aircraft cover, was in action almost daily, but it did not prevent her imperturbable captain, D. S. M'Grath, from organizing a most successful regatta in order, as he put it, 'to divert highly loaded minds from air to muscle'.

But we must leave the sorely-tried crews of P.Q. 15 as they lie, longing for their release from the drab misery of Murmansk, and turn to find out how the corresponding homeward-bound convoy had fared. And a strange and stirring tale it was.

Q.P. 11 had sailed from Kola on 28th April, thirteen ships, for which a through escort of four Western Approaches destroyers, *Bulldog*, *Beagle*, *Beverley* and *Amazon*, with their much reduced gun armaments, two fleet destroyers, *Foresight* and *Forester* which had also had had one of their 4·7-inch guns removed, four Flower class corvettes and a trawler. Four minesweepers and two Russian destroyers sailed as local escort. This force, commanded by Commander Maxwell Richmond in *Bulldog*, was quite adequate to deal with any U-boat attacks which might be expected, but none of the escorts was suitably armed against air attack, nor could they be reckoned capable of engaging enemy destroyers on anything like equal terms.

However, as close cover there was the cruiser *Edinburgh*, in which Rear-Admiral S. S. Bonham-Carter, commanding the 18th Cruiser Squadron, was flying his flag. She could be expected to bring her strong anti-aircraft armament into action at the right moment and to protect the convoy against surface attack.

Inevitably the departure of Q.P. 11 was known almost at once to the enemy and on the first day out there was the familiar sight of the German reconnaissance plane, circling endlessly at a safe distance. U-boats, too, were heard reporting the convoy's position and course. A westerly gale was making things difficult for the lightly loaded merchantmen as they thrashed along with their propellors half out of the water. They were making good only five knots when the minesweepers of the local escort left to return to Kola. But no aircraft attacks developed during the first two days and U-boats, seeing the ring of weaving escorts, kept their distance.

But one of them, *U456*, had gained a position directly ahead of the convoy on the afternoon of the 30th and was lying in wait, hoping a gap in the screen might give a chance to get in amongst the merchant ships. But the first thing that came in sight was not the forest of mastheads of the convoy coming up over the horizon but a lone cruiser, the *Edinburgh*. She was zigzagging at nineteen knots and would be a very difficult target; but there was no screen round her to worry about, and she was the sort of fat prize every U-boat commander dreamt about. Kapitän-Leutnant Max Teichert of *U456* decided to attack.

With frequent observations through his periscope he tried to forecast the irregular zigzag of the cruiser so as to get his boat into a good attack position. Luck was with him. As the distance came down to a suitable range for firing, he saw his target swing round to a new course. She would be sure to stay on it for several minutes. In brief, staccato tones, the U-boat captain passed the course and speed and range to the officer manipulating the calculating device which would give the correct course on which the torpedoes must run to hit. In a moment all was ready. With a last look at the target, Teichert gave the order, 'Los!'

In the *Edinburgh* there was no warning of disaster. The first torpedo hit her on the starboard side, forward, blasting a huge hole and flooding several compartments. Immediately afterwards another hit her right aft, tearing off her stern and wrecking her rudder and the two inner propeller shafts. The ship came to a shuddering stop with a heavy list.

From the convoy fifteen miles behind, a great column of water and smoke was seen to rise up from beyond the horizon in the direction in which *Edinburgh* had last been seen. Grimly certain of what must have happened, Commander Richmond at once ordered Commander Salter of the *Foresight* to take the *Forester* and the two Russian destroyers with him to investigate. They soon came up with the cruiser, listing heavily, but under way again, using her two outer propellers with which she could make some eight knots.

But the tangled wreckage of her stern and the two shattered shafts, hanging down, made her quite unmanageable. Every time she got way on her, she swung head to wind. At once the destroyers got to work. While three of them circled the stricken ship to screen her from further attacks, the *Forester* passed a tow and, with this help, the *Edinburgh* tried once again to get under way. But again her bow swung irresistibly away from her course, snapping the heavy wire tow-rope like cotton.

That method was evidently no good, so it was proposed to try a tow-line aft, which might help the *Edinburgh* to steer. But at this moment, four miles away, a U-boat was sighted on the surface; Teichert had been unable to resist coming up to get a look at his handiwork. Rescue operations had to be broken off while the U-boat was put down and kept from closing to deliver a *coup de grâce*.

As soon as this danger was under control – though *U456* managed to get away to claim the reward for his spirited attack – Salter returned and passed a wire tow-line from *Foresight* into the *Edinburgh* right aft. This was more successful, and by the evening the little force was making three knots in the direction of Kola, helped by a cessation of the gale, which had given way to a bitter Polar breeze bringing intermittent snow and low visibility. There were reasonable hopes of getting the *Edinburgh* back to Murmansk, some 240 miles away.

But at six o'clock the next morning, 1st May, hopes were dashed by a signal from the Russian destroyers. They were running short of fuel and must return to harbour to replenish. There was nothing for it but to let them go. With only two destroyers remaining, the Admiral decided that both must be used to screen against U-boats which were clinging to their trail and hoping to get in an attack. So the *Foresight*'s wire was cast off. At once the *Edinburgh* started her antics again and progress was reduced almost to nothing.

However, a Russian tug was on its way, sent by the Senior British Naval Officer, North Russia, in company with the minesweepers, *Harrier, Niger, Hussar* and *Gossamer*, who had just got back from the convoy. Hope was by no means dead, even though the Russian destroyers, who could have brought massive assistance in the events that were to come, had announced that, as it was May Day and a national holiday, they would not be available for sea until the 4th May – this in spite of the vital intelligence that had come in that three German destroyers had sailed from Kirkenes during the early hours of the 1st.

But we must leave the *Edinburgh* for the time being, making her painful progress towards harbour, as, at about the time the Russian destroyers were leaving, the hitherto unmolested passage of the convoy was about to be interrupted. At 5.40 a.m. on 1st May, four He. IIIs swept in to make the first German torpedo-bomber attack of the war. But they did not show the same skill and courage as those that were to attack P.Q. 15 a little later, as has been related. The corvette *Snowflake*, with her single 4-inch gun and two machine-guns, was sufficient to put them off their stroke and they loosed their torpedoes ineffectively at long range without facing the fire of the merchant ships.

The convoy was now closely beset. For besides air attack, which was likely to continue now that the airmen knew their exact position, information from the radio direction finders indicated at least four U-boats hanging on to its coat-tails waiting for a suitable moment to attack. One of them had been sighted from the *Amazon*, hovering on the horizon. But Richmond could not afford to send escorts out to deal with them and so reduce the anti-aircraft defences of the convoy. He kept the screen close in and defied the U-boats to get through it.

To add to the worries of the senior officer of the escort, heavy pack-ice was now sighted ahead with large drifting masses extending twenty miles to the southward of the route. The north-westerly course which had been ordered so as to put the U-boats astern in hopes of shaking them off had to be abandoned for one of west, on which course the convoy was closely skirting the edge of the ice barrier from which was coming a deathly cold, cutting wind and incessant snow flurries.

It was with affairs in this anxious state that startling news reached Commander Richmond in his station on the starboard bow of the convoy. First, the *Snowflake* reported at 1.45 p.m. three unidentified radar contacts to the southward. Almost immediately afterwards, from *Beverley*, came the signal 'Enemy in Sight. Three destroyers.'

This was a threat that must take precedence over any others. Streaking across the front of the convoy, Richmond called for his three remaining destroyer consorts to join the *Bulldog* at full speed. By 2 o'clock his four ships were in line ahead and steering between the enemy and the convoy. Seven minutes later guns flashed out on either side. It was the beginning of a series of actions which should, on paper, have resulted in annihilation of the British force, followed by a massacre of the defenceless merchantmen. Six 4·7-inch and three 4-inch guns on the British side, with antiquated control systems, were pitted against the five 5-inch and six 5·9-inch guns of the most up-to-date German ships.

But a paper analysis would fail to show two overriding modifications of the result – on the British side an appreciation and determination that the convoy must be defended no matter what the cost; on the German, the crippling influence of the instructions, originating from the Fuehrer himself, that no risks must be run with Germany's precious ships. The two added up to an excess of morale in the British force which was to achieve an astonishing result.

As the two lines of destroyers steered at high speed on parallel courses, all guns firing, both sides loosed torpedoes at their opponents. None found a target, though the *Bulldog* was closely missed. But after three minutes of this cannonade, in which they were not once hit, the Germans suddenly broke off the action and turned away.

On the British side, the *Amazon* had been twice hit by the heavy shells of the enemy. With her wheelhouse shattered, the main and auxiliary steering positions unusable, she was careering wildly along at twenty-eight knots out of control until her captain, Lieutenant-Commander Lord Teynham, using manoeuvres of the engines to steer, brought her back into the line at the rear. But her capacity to fight had been sorely reduced. Her forward gun was out of action with many of its crew wounded, the starboard pom-pom gun amidships was destroyed and its crew killed or wounded, as were some of the after gun's crew and that of the 3-inch high-angle gun.

But the enemy must know nothing of all this. In spite of a slight wound, Lord Teynham somehow managed to keep *Amazon* in the line, an apparent threat still, as Richmond led his ships back under a smoke screen to a position between the convoy and the circling German destroyers.

Meanwhile there had been an unexpected outcome of the exchange of torpedo fire. One of the German torpedoes, continuing its run after passing through the British destroyer line, found a straggler from the convoy, a Russian freighter, across its path and claimed a victim for which it had not been intended. It was a bonus the enemy did not deserve.

Slowly circling the convoy in time with the German flotilla, Richmond sighted them again at 2.33, coming in from the south-south-east. At once he boldly steered for them and seven minutes later both sides opened fire at long range. This time neither flotilla was hit, yet the enemy would risk nothing and, after five minutes, turned away once more, the German wolves driven off by the defiance of old and toothless hounds.

When Richmond got back to the convoy this time he found it well in amongst the ice floes. With the probability of air attacks being renewed still in his mind, he led his ships through whatever lanes of open water he could find which would take him near enough to give anti-aircraft support. But with one eye he watched that there was always a free channel open in case the enemy destroyers returned. It was as well he did, for an hour later they were detected approaching, this time from astern of the convoy.

Again the unequal combat was joined, as with an air of utter confidence the destroyer escorts went pelting towards their enemy. For a time the *Bulldog* was rushing along through a forest of shell splashes as her range was accurately found. But she escaped serious damage and, as the enemy once more turned away, the escorts rejoined the convoy. If the Germans could have brought themselves to force their way through Richmond's dogged but flimsy defence, they would have found a rich and easy target. The twelve remaining merchant ships were strung out in a single line some seven miles long as they picked their way gingerly through the ice.

Yet, though twice more the enemy destroyers probed towards the convoy, each time they came up against the escorting destroyers in line and ready to fight to a finish rather than let them through. What must have been a growing sense of shame and frustration amongst the German crews was brought to an end when, at 5.45, they received orders to abandon their efforts and go to what they hoped would be a softer target in the shape of the crippled *Edinburgh* 200 miles to the eastward. Richmond's outrageous bluff had worked. It was with grim appreciation of his leader's success that Lieutenant R. A. Price of the *Beverley* signalled to him, 'I should hate to play poker with you.'

The convoy was saved, for neither U-boats nor aircraft molested it further. Breaking clear at last of the ice, it passed P.Q. 15 the next morning on to whom, and the luckless *Edinburgh*, the enemy directed all his further efforts. To the latter we, too, must return to hear the end of the story.

4

A HEAVY FORFEIT EXACTED

We left the crippled *Edinburgh* making progress by means of brief spurts ahead, each followed by a reversal of her engines to get her back on to the course for harbour, on which she was making good only two knots. It was an exhausting and barely worth-while process, but for twenty-four hours it was kept up. At least it dispelled that most unnerving of all feelings in a ship in U-boat waters, that of lying, a 'sitting duck'. Throughout the day and night, *Foresight* and *Forester* steamed tirelessly round her to scare off the U-boats.

During the afternoon of 1st May, there came the first news of Q.P. 11's encounter with the German warships. To be ready for any eventuality, Admiral Bonham-Carter instructed his destroyers as to their tactics should the enemy come up with them. They were to act independently, taking every opportunity to defeat the enemy, without undue risk to themselves in defending the *Edinburgh*. They were thus released from the handicap of having to concentrate on a purely defensive role.

At 6 p.m., a Russian escort vessel, the *Rubin*, arrived to augment the screen and at midnight hopes ran high as the four minesweepers hove in sight with the long-awaited tug. But these hopes were soon dashed by the discovery that the Russian tug had insufficient power to tow the cruiser. The best it could do was, by means of a tow-line on the *Edinburgh*'s starboard bow and aided by another from the *Gossamer* on the port quarter, to keep her roughly on a course for Kola at the miserable speed of three knots. By 5.30 in the morning this arrangement had been completed and, with the now strong anti-submarine escort circling, slow progress was again being made when, at 6.27, the flash and thud of gunfire from the *Hussar* announced the opening of a new phase of the situation.

With her two 4-inch guns, the little minesweeper was defying the same group of heavily armed destroyers which had been foiled by Commander Richmond's bold bluff. But as shell splashes straddled her, it was time to seek support and the *Hussar* fell back towards the *Edinburgh*. There, at the first alarm, the tows had been cast off and the cruiser went on to her full speed of eight knots. She could only circle round to port in an irregular curve, but this seemed better than remaining stopped.

There followed a wild, crazy, intermittent fight as the destroyers played a deadly game of hide-and-seek in and out of the snow showers and the banks of funnel smoke laid by both sides. The Germans were no more inclined to make a fight of it than they had been on the previous day. Their lack of stomach was intensified very early in the action by a brilliant piece of gunnery by the *Edinburgh*.

Nine minutes after the first contact, the *Hermann Schoemann*, suddenly running out of the shelter of a snowstorm, was engaged by the *Edinburgh*'s only serviceable turret. The first salvo fell within 100 yards of the destroyer. Like a scalded cat, the German swung away at full speed and tried to hide behind her own smoke screen. But it was in vain. The second salvo landed squarely on to her. With both engines heavily damaged and all control instruments wrecked, the *Schoemann* came to a stop, completely out of action.

This changed the complexion of things entirely. What little offensive spirit the Germans had possessed was replaced by a single-minded desire to rescue the crew of the crippled ship and get away to safety. Even the attainment of this unambitious object was held up by the attentions of *Foresight* and *Forester*. Each time the *Z.24* or *Z.25* shaped course to get alongside the *Schoemann*, they came up against one or the other of the British destroyers.

At the moment when the *Schoemann* was hit, *Foresight* and *Forester* were steering northward independently to seek out the enemy amongst the snow flurries. Out of one of these, Salter saw the *Z.24* emerge, steering straight for him. He swung the *Fore-sight* to starboard to bring all his guns to bear but in the smother of smoke and snow he only had brief glimpses of the German destroyers. *Forester*, on the other hand, a little to the westward of him, stood on to the north and thus Lieutenant-Commander G. P. Huddert, her captain, found himself in a good position to fire torpedoes at the advancing *Z.24*.

But as he did so the full fury of the German's greatly superior armament fell on his ship as three 5·9-inch shells hit. The first, plunging into the forward boiler-room, killed the stokers there and brought the ship to a stop in a cloud of smoke and escaping steam. Then a hit near the bridge wrecked 'B' gun, just below and in front of it, made a shambles of the bridge and killed Huddert himself. A third shell struck aft, putting the after gun also out of action.

As she lay there, while the engineers strove amidst the wreckage to isolate the shattered boiler room and get steam to the engines from the other, while the first-aid parties did what they could for the wounded and the 1st Lieutenant, J. Bitmead, assumed command in place of his dead captain, it seemed that the final moment had come for the *Forester* as torpedo tracks were seen heading directly for her vitals. The tracks reached them and there was a moment of frozen immobility as all hands waited for the shattering explosion that would be the end of them. But nothing happened. The tracks were seen extending their faint straight lines beyond the ship. Breaths were suddenly expelled in relief and wonderment. The torpedoes had passed underneath and on.

As realization of their escape flooded through them, the crew of the *Forester* plunged with renewed enthusiasm into the work of repairing the damage and getting under way again. The sole remaining gun flamed into action whenever an enemy appeared in sight.

Commander Salter, meanwhile, seeing the plight of his flotilla mate, had brought the *Foresight* back and was also engaging the German destroyers as they appeared momentarily from time to time. But while this was going on, the German torpedoes were continuing their course. They were nearing the end of their run, for they were beginning to splash on the surface and lose speed.

But as luck would have it, the *Edinburgh*, in the wild gyrations which were all she was capable of, was slowly crossing their path. One of them, porpoising along, could be seen making straight for her. There was nothing that Captain Faulkner could do to avoid it. For the third time his ship lurched and shook at the rending explosion.

It was the death blow for the *Edinburgh*, for it had struck on the port side opposite where the first torpedo from *U456* had hit. She was consequently almost cut in two and was plainly doomed. But while the enemy remained in sight, her guns remained in action, wringing a wry testimony from the captain of the *Z.24*, who described her shooting, even at this stage, as 'extraordinarily good'.

Let us leave her thus for the moment and see how the smaller ships were faring. It was on *Foresight* and *Forester* that the brunt of the fighting was falling, but the minesweepers also played a gallant part, lunging forward like terriers at every opportunity, to bring their puny armament into play. Little did they realize that amidst the fog of battle their fearless action was leading the enemy to identify them as big destroyers of the 'Tribal' or 'Jervis' class and to treat the British force with a respect that their actual strength did not by any means warrant.

Thus, with *Forester* and *Edinburgh* both lying dead in the water, the enemy could still not bring himself to close in for the kill. The *Forester* indeed was in dire straits, the centre of a storm of fire. Seeing it, Salter drove forward in the *Foresight* in the nick of time to take his ship between *Forester* and the enemy, laying a smoke screen to cover her and drawing the fire on to himself. But, boldly closing the enemy to fire torpedoes at the *Schoemann*, Salter now himself ran into a devastating concentration of fire. Desperately he turned away at full speed and made smoke, but he was too late. Four shells hit his ship bringing her to a standstill, causing heavy casualties and leaving her with one gun only fit for action. Besides the 1st Lieutenant, R. A. Fawdrey, and seven ratings, there was also killed Captain Stone, master of the *Lancaster Castle*, who was taking passage in the destroyer.

There was now nothing but the little group of minesweepers to prevent the Germans from annihilating the whole force at their leisure. But the prohibition against taking any unnecessary risks and the belief that there were still modern destroyers present and unaccounted for stayed their hand. Even the *Foresight*, lying helpless under their guns was saved as the *Forester*, her wounds temporarily patched, got under way. Coming upon his leader sore beset, Lieutenant Bitmead repaid his debt by zigzagging between him and the enemy and laying down a smoke screen.

It was the end of the action. The Germans, frustrated and anxious to get away without further damage, at last got alongside the *Hermann Schoemann*, took off 200 survivors and scuttled the ship before making off at high speed to the north-west, being finally lost to view by 8.20.

Meanwhile the *Edinburgh* had been dying. Her list had increased to seventeen degrees and steam could no longer be maintained in the boilers. The time had come to abandon ship. The wounded had already been transferred to minesweepers and now the Admiral called the *Gossamer* and *Harrier* alongside to take off the remainder. The *Edinburgh*'s crew had done all that men could do to save her. As their captain wrote of their ordeal later, 'Emergencies were met with such confidence and calmness that they ceased to be emergencies.'

Now they watched as the *Foresight*, once again under way on one engine, put her last torpedo into their ship which thereupon broke in half. The stern rolled over while the bows rose high in the air as though in salute before sliding quickly down to the depths. With that, the remainder of the force set off sadly, but yet proudly, for Kola.

It was the end of a gallant story. The quaint tribute that came from the captain of the only Russian ship present, the *Rubin*, is worthy of record.

'Dear Sir,
   Soviets seamen was witness of heroic battle English seamen with predominants powers of enemy. English seamen did observe their sacred duty before Fatherland. We are prouding of staunchness and courage English seamen – our allies.'

The escorts of the two convoys could be well satisfied with the way they had got their charges through. Out of thirty-eight merchant ships involved, only four had been lost. But the cost in warships and the vulnerability of convoys to the new air weapon as shown by the loss of three ships to the one skilfully executed attack on P.Q. 15 underlined the repeated warnings of the senior naval officers concerned that the time had come to call a halt until autumn should shorten the hours of daylight.

*   *   *

Another heavy loss was to be sustained before the next convoys sailed. When Admiral Bonham-Carter reached Murmansk, he found another of his squadron there, the damaged *Trinidad*, which had come out of dry-dock on 2nd May. Temporary repairs to make her seaworthy were still being made but on the 5th, Bonham-Carter hoisted his flag in her with intentions of sailing for England on the 9th. Then intelligence reports came in of a northward move of the German pocket-battleships from Trondheim. Until their whereabouts were established by air reconnaissance, a move would be unwise.

However, by 13th May, the situation was cleared up. Only the *Scheer* had left Trondheim to move to Narvik, where she was not a serious threat. The *Trinidad* therefore set off, escorted by the destroyers *Somali, Matchless, Foresight* and *Forester*, the last two also temporarily repaired after their action damage. Waiting west of Bear Island to cover their passage was a force of four cruisers and four destroyers.

But between Kola and Bear Island was, as always, the most dangerous stretch. However, Russian air escort for the first two days had been promised. With the fairly high speed of which the force was capable there seemed no reason for anxiety, even though its position was reported by a reconnaissance aircraft early on the 14th. Murky weather with low cloud and snow showers shrouded it at first as it slipped along at twenty knots in a calm sea.

But then, as the afternoon and evening of the 14th wore on, the weather cleared considerably, the presence of ice forced an alteration of course unhealthily close to the enemy coast, shadowing aircraft clung on tenaciously and continuous homing signals could be heard. There were all the signs of a large-scale attack being imminent. The promised Russian fighter escort failed to materialize.

At 9 p.m. came the first warnings from the radar operators. Formations of aircraft at fifteen, thirty, forty-five and sixty miles were showing on their screens. The Admiral headed his force for the protection of patches of thicker weather, but they seemed to dissolve as he reached them, while low cloud served only to screen the planes as they made for their attack positions.

For the next three-quarters of an hour, at the guns, in the control positions and on the bridges of the ships, men could only wait with tense patience for what was in store. When at last, out of the clouds, the first Ju. 88s snarled down, it was almost a relief to the taut-strung nerves. During the next hour there was hardly a moment when there was not an attack in progress, the scream of dive-bombers' engines, the crump of bomb bursts and the frenzied cacophony of the guns. The destroyers were selected as targets as often as the *Trinidad*.

But not a hit had the bombers scored – though there had been many near misses – when at 10.30 the torpedo-planes appeared, skimming low over the ice to the northward. Met by a fierce barrage from the cruiser, they swerved away and circled to come in from astern. There, they had to face the fire of the *Foresight* and *Forester*, a wall of flashing shell bursts. It was too much for them. Three hurriedly dropped their torpedoes at long range on the starboard quarter of the *Trinidad* while the remainder flew on in a wide circle to come in from the other side.

Turning directly away from the torpedoes to 'comb the tracks', *Trinidad* had no difficulty in avoiding them. But, while all eyes were watching the second group of planes to see where they would drop their torpedoes, out of the low clouds above the cruiser suddenly plummeted a lone Ju. 88 to loose a stick of bombs.

It was the end of the road for the *Trinidad*. One bomb, bursting on the waterline on the starboard side, blew in the temporary patch that had been welded on in Murmansk, flooding a magazine and the compartments around it. Another, missing the bridge by inches, plunged down through two decks before bursting on the lower mess deck, wiping out the whole of the forward damage control party stationed there and starting a raging fire.

The ship listed over until she was lying over at an angle of fourteen degrees. But she was still capable of twenty knots and her steering was unaffected. It was just as well, for now the last of the torpedo-bombers had reached their dropping positions on the port side. Once again Captain Saunders swung his ship round to comb the tracks successfully. But he was in a considerable dilemma. The wind of his progress was fanning the flames of the fire ever more fiercely. If he stopped, he would present a sitting target to the bombers. He deemed it best to keep moving and hope to master the fire later.

At last, thirty minutes after the bombs had hit, the radar screens showed the welcome picture of all enemy aircraft retiring, their attacks completed. Gratefully, Saunders rang down 'Stop engines.' But it was already too late. The fire was quite out of control. While the *Forester* came alongside to take off the wounded and the passengers, the Admiral considered the situation. The expert, so far as damage control was concerned, was Constructor Commander Skinner. Arriving on the bridge, smoke-grimed and red-eyed, he had no difficulty in giving his opinion of the possibilities. 'Sir,' he said, 'it would take the whole Glasgow Fire Brigade to put it out.'

For the second time in a month, Bonham-Carter was faced with the necessity of giving the order to abandon his flagship. With U-boats hovering round – one had already been sighted on the surface astern of the *Trinidad* – and with the 'snooper' aircraft still in contact to bring on further air attacks, there was no alternative. One by one the destroyers were called alongside to embark survivors and finally the Admiral and Captain Saunders climbed over the side on to the deck of the *Somali*, whence the former sent orders to the *Matchless* to put two torpedoes into the cruiser.

She went quickly to the bottom. With her went one officer, sixty ratings and twenty merchant seamen passengers who had been killed by the bombs.

* * *

The loss of these two valuable cruisers did nothing to reconcile naval opinion to the continuance of operations in the far north, operations considered inherently unsound. With the skies dominated by the enemy air force, and U-boats concentrated in the area, the Admiralty was adamant that our heavy ships – the only guard against a break-out into the western ocean by the *Tirpitz* and her powerful consorts – must not be sent to the eastward of Bear Island. Sooner or later, therefore, the Germans must surely wake up to the fact that they could operate their big ships with impunity in the Barents Sea.

But even if they did not, with the season of perpetual daylight now beginning, the threat to the convoys was beyond the limit which naval opinion was prepared willingly to accept. Admiral Bonham-Carter stated his views in no uncertain terms.

'I am still convinced,' he wrote, 'that until the aerodromes in Northern Norway are neutralized and there are some hours of darkness, the continuation of these convoys must be stopped. If they must continue for political reasons, very serious and heavy losses must be expected. The force of the German attacks will increase and not diminish. We in the Navy are paid to do this sort of job, but it is beginning to be too much to ask of the men of the merchant navy. We may be able to avoid bombs and torpedoes with our speed, a six- or eight-knot ship has not this advantage.'

Political reasons for the continuation of the convoys there were, but whether they should have overridden unanimous naval opinion we shall be able to judge as the story unfolds. From America were coming urgent appeals from the President to step up the size and frequency of the Arctic convoys. Ships loaded for Russia were waiting in ever-increasing numbers. Any further delays would have 'a most unfortunate effect' on Russian opinion and, indeed, already growls from the Russian bear could be heard. There can be no doubt that a cessation of convoys at this time would have alienated the Russians with their inherent lack of appreciation of naval problems. It is doubtful whether American naval and political opinion were yet educated up to an understanding of the facts of the situation – America had been less than six months in the war at this time.

Cabling a detailed explanation of our difficulties to President

Roosevelt, Winston Churchill secured agreement that any increase in the number of Arctic convoys was just not within our power. But the ones already planned would go on. It was the Prime Minister's view that failure to make the attempt would weaken our influence with both our Allies. The operation would be justified if half got through. He shared the misgivings of the Chiefs of Staff, but felt it was a matter of duty.

That was probably the sentiment of the naval officers entrusted with the escort, of the masters of the merchant ships assembling at Hvalfiord, near Reykjavik, and of the ratings and merchant seamen who cursed as they learnt that it was the Kola Run again for them.

5

NIGHT NEVER FALLS

It was now the season of perpetual daylight on the Kola Run
– the season in which, in time of peace, the travel agencies lure
tourists to Norway to enjoy the midnight sun. Strolling on
the promenade deck of a pleasure steamer, revelling in the beauty
of the glassy waters of the Norwegian fiords in which the steep
sides are mirrored, is no doubt a wonderful experience. The day
is never too long. But to the crews of ships sailing under the
threat of air attack, never-ending daylight brings a feeling of
depression, a longing for a few hours of rest from ceaseless
scanning of the sky and a hate of the pale sun moving endlessly
round the horizon.

To have, perhaps, the hours off watch from 8 p.m. to midnight
broken by recurrent clanging of alarm bells and the call to action
stations, the blast of gunfire and the crump of bombs and, maybe,
the sight of a neighbouring ship hit and sunk, and then to come
from a darkened cabin or mess-deck for the middle watch to
find the sun still shining brought a feeling of despair at the never-
ending nature of the ordeal. Day and night ceased to have any
meaning. Sleep was taken in cat-naps as opportunity offered.

As the days went by, fatigue ate imperceptibly into the facul-
ties. It became difficult to make a quick or logical decision. Yet
it was the masters of the merchant ships, the captains of the
escorts and, above all, the escort force commanders who had to
be ready to make such decisions yet could least afford to take
time off to sleep.

In addition, even in May, there would be the effect of the cold.
For the convoys would keep as far north as the ice barrier would
allow. From it would come the glacial polar winds which, com-

bined with the wind of their own ships' motion, brought conditions in which only in layers of heavy, fatiguing clothing could a man survive.

Winter or summer, the Kola Run was no picnic. But experience was to show that the summer was the more deadly of the two. Indeed, British naval opinion already appreciated this and, if it had not been for great pressure from our Allies, there can be little doubt that P.Q. 15 would have been the last convoy to be run until the following autumn. Though the destruction of two of the Germans' limited number of destroyers had greatly reduced the threat by these craft, the force of heavy ships still lay in the Norwegian fiords, ready to sally forth and take the convoy in the flank. As the First Sea Lord wrote to Admiral King, the C.-in-C. of the United States Navy, 'the whole thing is a most unsound operation with the dice loaded against us in every direction'.

Admiralty opinion was that, were the positions reversed, they could guarantee that not a single ship of a convoy would be allowed to reach Russia. But, good as our intelligence was with regard to the whereabouts and movements of enemy ships, there was one vital piece of information that the Admiralty did not have – Hitler's almost hysterical prohibitions against any risks being run by his surface ships. Even had this been appreciated, however, there would still have been, at this time, a deep reluctance to run the gauntlet of the enemy's massed air power; but at least there would not have been the constant, nagging preoccupation with the disastrous consequences likely if the German heavy ships got in amongst the convoy and its lightly-armed escort – a preoccupation which was to lead to a decision which will always be a subject of bitter controversy owing to the catastrophe which followed it.

But before that day comes, we must follow one more convoy as it fights its way through the Barents Sea to Russia.

P.Q. 16 was the biggest Arctic convoy so far to sail – thirty-five ships. With the seasonal opening of the port of Archangel in the White Sea increasing the unloading facilities, one of the objections to larger convoys had been eliminated. Once again the close escort was a strong one against U-boat attack but very weak in the anti-aircraft role. They were backed up, however, by the anti-aircraft ship *Alynbank* and the presence of a C.A.M.-ship, the *Empire Lawrence*.

Commodore Gale in the *Ocean Voice* led them out of Hvalfiord on 21st May with a local escort of the minesweeper *Hazard* and the trawlers *St. Elstan, Lady Madeleine, Retriever* and *Northern Spray*. From Seidisfiord, the fuelling base on the east coast of Iceland, came forth the 'through' escort to join the convoy. Led by Commander Richard Onslow in the fleet destroyer *Ashanti*, they comprised one other fleet destroyer, the *Martin*, three Western Approaches destroyer-escorts, *Achates, Volunteer* and *Garland* (the last named under the Polish flag), and four Flower-class corvettes, *Honeysuckle, Starwort, Hyderabad* and *Roselys* (of the Free French Navy).

Early on the 25th, Admiral Burrough joined with his cruiser squadron to assume his familiar role with his flagship *Nigeria*, the *Kent, Norfolk* and *Liverpool*, with the destroyers *Onslow, Oribi* and *Marne*. Stationing his cruisers in pairs between the convoy columns and sending his destroyers to join the convoy screen, he was ready to bring his powerful anti-aircraft armament into action.

As usual, his arrival was nicely timed, coinciding as it did with that of the first German reconnaissance plane which from then onwards became a permanent feature of the summer sky as it droned round the horizon. But the enemy was in no hurry to attack. He knew that for the next five days the convoy would be in range. Meanwhile in fair weather the destroyers of the escort were able to top up their fuel tanks and dismiss the two fleet oilers to return to Iceland.

Soon after noon, the homeward Q.P. 12 hove in sight. The Hurricane from their C.A.M.-ship *Empire Morn* had been launched to shoot down the first shadower to arrive, and they had had no further trouble. But the pilot of the Hurricane, Pilot Officer Kendall, had been tragically lost owing to his parachute failing to open in time. The escort reported, however, that a U-boat had been sighted early that morning. P.Q. 16's passage from now on was unlikely to be as peaceful as it had been.

* * *

An hour later, from the bridge of the *Martin*, stationed out on the starboard side of the screen, the black dot on the horizon is sighted which can be nothing else but the conning tower of a submarine. A report goes off to the senior officer of the screen while the *Martin* is already gathering speed in the U-boat's direction. Richard Onslow cannot spare another destroyer to co-operate as the expected air attack may materialize at any moment. Long before the *Martin* can reach the U-boat's position, it has dived and, by herself, the destroyer has little chance of getting it in her asdic beam. But the U-boat is put down and kept down while the convoy steams on. It will be harmless for a long while, until it can make a great circle round the convoy, beyond the horizon, and get ahead of it.

But in the convoy, tension is increasing. It is many hours since the 'snooper' plane reported its position. The bombers will be arriving soon. In the merchantmen, thrusting steadily forward in nine columns, making a great rectangle five miles broad and two deep, the guns' crews are gathered under shelter near their guns, swapping reminiscences of other ships and other convoys. If they have been on the Kola Run before, there will be a tense look about them and they will not be saying much.

In the *Ocean Voice*, the Commodore is on the bridge with his Yeoman of Signals, ready to hoist the Air Warning signal, to be followed perhaps by that for an Emergency Turn which will bring all ships of the convoy round together to 'comb the tracks' of any torpedoes that may be loosed at the convoy from the Heinkel IIIs.

The escorts weave endlessly back and forth in their stations round the outside of the convoy, sweeping below the surface with their asdics, with their radar the sky above. The cruisers, with their big, powerful radar sets are likely to give the first warning of high-flying aircraft. But only the eyes of the watchful look-outs will detect the torpedo-bombers skimming low over the water.

Hour after hour has gone by thus. The first watch – 8 to midnight – has come on duty but there will be no darkness to bring respite. The sun still hangs in a clear sky. Look-outs stamp on the deck and beat their gloved hands together in vain search for warmth.

Then the loud-speakers of the radio telephones crackle and a voice from which all emotion has been banished, broadcasts in homely accents the brief words that tell of enemy aircraft approaching. A flag signal at the masthead of the *Nigeria*, repeated by the escorts and the Commodore's flagship, gives the warning to the merchant ships. With a roar and a sheet of flame from the catapult, the Hurricane is launched from the C.A.M.-ship as the bunch of black specks in the distant sky are sighted.

*   *   *

So began a running fight which was to last for five consecutive days with short intervals. On this first day, the advantage lay with the British force. With the four cruisers adding their massive fire power to that of the escorts, the enemy were flying through a tremendous storm of bursting shells before ever they came into the concentrated machine-gun fire which they had to face to deliver their weapons with any accuracy.

In this first attack, of the six Ju. 88s that dived on to the convoy, two were shot down, while out of the seven torpedo-planes, Pilot Officer Hay in the C.A.M.-ship's Hurricane shot down one in flames and sent another staggering away heavily damaged and unlikely to reach its base. Not a bomb or torpedo found its mark, though a near miss had immobilized one ship, the *Carlton*, which had to be sent back to Iceland in tow of the trawler *Northern Spray*. Pilot Officer Hay, though wounded, successfully baled out of his aircraft and was picked up by the *Volunteer*.

Two hours later, out of the midnight sun, came another attack by twelve dive-bombers; but again the gunfire was too much for them. As they turned for base, the convoy still steamed on in good formation, its numbers unreduced.

But there was more than air attack to be dealt with. During the middle watch, a U-boat, aided by the usual bad water conditions for the asdic, crept, submerged, close enough to get in a long shot into the convoy. One of its torpedoes found its mark in the *Syros*, which went quickly to the bottom. Though the trawlers were smartly on the spot to pick up the crew, so sudden had the ship's end been that nine men were missing when the roll was called.

It was a warning which the cruisers could not ignore. They were too valuable to be risked where U-boats were concentrated and Admiral Burrough's orders laid it down that at this stage of the voyage his ships must leave the convoy and cruise at a distance with their screen of destroyers, prepared to return only to intervene at any threat of surface attack. At 3.30 on the morning of the 26th, they parted company together with their three destroyers.

It was as well they did for throughout that day U-boats were seen skulking on the horizon. The escorts were kept busy dashing out to scare them off. There was little more they could do, for always there was the necessity to be back again soon with the convoy ready for the next air alarm. The strong anti-submarine screen was too much for the submarines to venture an attack, but if there had been the lure of four fat cruisers in the convoy, they would hardly have allowed themselves to be so easily discouraged.

But Richard Onslow could have no illusions as to the vulnerability of his convoy from the time the cruiser force passed out of sight beyond the horizon. Except for *Alynbank* and the *Martin*, one of the new fleet destroyers coming into service with 4·7-inch guns on mountings which gave them sufficient elevation to be used as high-angle guns, he had no ship which could engage dive-bombers with any efficiency before they committed themselves to their dive and so came within range of machine-guns. Though the only attack on the 26th, by a mixed force of torpedo-bombers and Ju. 88s was effectively dealt with without loss to his force, there were still four more days to go, each taking him into closer range of the enemy airfields.

By the 27th, the diminished strength of the convoy's defence had been appreciated by the enemy. They began an all-out air attack at 3.20 that morning which continued almost without a break for the next sixteen hours. Cloud, which had now spread across the sky at a height of 3000 feet, and a layer of filmy haze at half that height provided ideal cover for the aircraft. Only for the last few seconds of their attacks were they under fire. The consequences were shattering for the convoy which had up to now so successfully defended itself.

The first to suffer was the freighter *Alamar*, hit by two bombs, set on fire and abandoned in a sinking condition. Five minutes later the *Mormacsul*, close missed by two bombs, her hull burst asunder, was also sinking. The survivors from these two ships were still being picked up by the escorts when a fresh onslaught began. A concentration of Ju. 88s picked on the C.A.M.-ship *Empire Lawrence* and, with five direct hits sent her to the bottom. At the same time the Russian freighter *Stari Bolshevik* was hit and a fire started in her fore hold. The *Empire Baffin* and the American *City of Joliet* were damaged by near misses, the latter having finally to be abandoned the following day.

For the merchant crews, the scream of aircraft engines, the sight of bombs curving so gracefully and with such deadly menace, each one apparently aimed at the beholder, the deafening pandemonium of the guns and the shuddering of the ships under their feet as the bombs burst around them, all added up to a nightmare all the more terrifying through their inability to fight back as the guns' crews could. They had helplessly to endure, taking what shelter they could behind flimsy deck superstructures and pray for an end to their terrors.

Accounts which have been written based on the impressions of these men, particularly in American freighters where the crews were new to this sort of thing at that time, give a picture of utter confusion in the convoy, with ships weaving wildly to and fro in their efforts to avoid bombs, while the sea around them was criss-crossed with the tracks of torpedoes from U-boats amongst the columns.

The masters would tell a different story for the most part. In spite of all the enemy's efforts, there was, in fact, amazingly little confusion. Grimly the course was maintained, except when Emergency Turns were ordered during torpedo-bomber attacks. In preservation of the convoy formation lay the chief defence and the masters knew it. The formation once broken, the enemy's task would be enormously eased as he picked off individual ships no longer having to run the gauntlet of cross-fire from their neighbours.

As the main attack of that day, the 27th, died away at 2.30 in the afternoon, the convoy could be seen still ploughing steadily ahead. Three had sunk. The *Stari Bolshevik* had dropped somewhat behind as her crew fought with frantic energy the fire raging in her hold. The *City of Joliet* had stopped, abandoned prematurely by her crew who would shortly return aboard and get their ship once more under way and in station. Further astern, corvettes and trawlers were picking up the last of the survivors of the sunken ships – 74 officers and 397 men.

But the German air commander who would shortly be listening to exultant accounts by his bomber pilots of the near annihilation they had wreaked on the convoy would have been disheartened to see that more than thirty fine merchantmen still drove defiantly eastward in good order.

In the escorts, as scalding tea and cocoa went the rounds of the tired guns' crews, empty cartridge cases littering the decks were being cleared away and fresh ready-use ammunition supplied. In one of the destroyers, the Polish-manned *Garland*, tragedy had struck. A group of four bombs had fallen close alongside. The first, bursting on impact with the water, had evidently detonated the other three in mid-air. A devastating storm of jagged splinters had swept her decks and pierced her hull. Twenty-five men lay dead and forty-three more wounded. Both her forward guns and one boiler room were out of action. She could be of no further use in defence. At the escort commander's orders, she left at her best speed for Murmansk where her wounded and her damage could be attended to.

Another of the escorts, the French *Roselys*, was now sent to see what she could do to help the *Stari Bolshevik*. In spite of her fire, her cargo of high explosive and damage to her fire-fighting gear, she was still plugging along gallantly, trying to catch up, while her crew, women sailors amongst them, fought the flames. With nice seamanship, Lieutenant Bergeret brought the *Roselys* close alongside the Russian, passed fire hoses across with which, as both ships steamed along together, the fire was gradually brought under control.

The afternoon of the 27th passed in comparative quiet with but one dive-bomber attack which failed to do any damage. With leisure to look around, Onslow saw that the edge of the ice was trending away to the north. He could now alter the convoy's course to the north-east, taking it further from the enemy shore and heading for conditions of thicker weather and low cloud that he could see in that direction. But before the day was out another massive onslaught by dive-bombers and torpedo-aircraft descended.

Some of the merchant ships were running short of ammunition for their guns. The guns' crews were shaken and tired. The defence was losing some of its zest though Onslow, steering his ship from time to time amongst the columns, did much to encourage the weary men whose steadfastness he praised without stint. But masters and captains could not help wondering how long their men could stand up under the continuous strain. Exhausted automatons, craving only sleep and peace, could not fight effectively.

The enemy pressed their attacks well home. A bomb hit the ammunition ship *Empire Purcell*, setting her on fire. The crew had barely time to abandon ship before she blew up. A torpedo hit the *Lowther Castle* and sank her. The Commodore's ship *Ocean Voice* received a bomb which set her on fire and tore a huge hole in her side. But in spite of it the master and crew stuck to their ship, fought the fire and held their station in the convoy, eventually to reach port with much of her precious cargo intact.

Once again the rumble of aircraft engines died away and the harassed escort commander had time to survey the situation. His convoy had been further depleted. One of those still afloat, the *City of Joliet*, was getting steadily further down by the bows and could not survive much longer. The *Ocean Voice* and the *Stari Bolshevik* were both pouring smoke from their riven hulls and might have to be abandoned at any moment. Ammunition was running low. Three more days of their ordeal still lay ahead. In his report, Commander Onslow recorded how he felt at this time:

'With another three days to go and twenty per cent of the convoy already lost, I felt far from optimistic. The question of ammunition began to worry me badly. I ordered all ships to exercise strict economy and restricted controlled fire in *Ashanti* to one mounting at a time. We were all inspired however by the parade-ground rigidity of the convoy's station keeping, including *Ocean Voice* and *Stari Bolshevik*, who were both billowing smoke from their fore holds.'

During the night, the corvette *Hyderabad* was able to go alongside three American freighters who had run out of ammunition and give them a fresh supply. But at last the weather was coming to the aid of the tormented ships. Low cloud and mist shrouded them and occasionally the drone of frustrated bombers could be heard overhead searching for them. Ice began to gather on masts and rigging, giving the ships a ghostly appearance. Decks became dangerously slippery. Ammunition had to be continually wiped dry or the fuses would be iced up. But anything was better than the constant alarms in the clearer weather. Snatches of sleep could be taken.

During the forenoon of the 28th, three Russian destroyers joined the escort, a welcome sign that the end of the voyage could not long be delayed. Only one feeble and unsuccessful attack by four Ju. 88s took place on that day – another day nearer port without further loss.

But there was no real respite yet. Early on the 29th, with a clearance of the weather, the torpedo-bombers and Ju. 88s came in again; but with guns' crews reinvigorated by a few hours' rest without alarms, the escort drove them off. The enemy, too, was losing his zest, attacking these seemingly tireless and imperturbable ships. However, when that evening, after Captain Crombie's minesweepers had arrived and, with the *Alynbank* and the *Martin*, led away the six ships destined for Archangel, the two sections of the convoy came under the heaviest attack yet as eighteen Ju. 88s pounced on the Murmansk section and fifteen on the Archangel ships. The enemy recoiled in surprise at the reception they got. Not a bomb found a target.

Nor did it during the next day when three separate attacks were beaten off at a cost to the enemy of two more of his aircraft. Exultant as the guns' crews were at their success, they were many of them near the end of their tether. It was with many a weary groan that they went to action stations that afternoon when yet another formation of aircraft was sighted. Then, in the escorts and the Commodore's flagship, the signal ran up, 'Cease Fire'. It was Russian Hurricane fighters which had arrived at long last to give the convoy cover. Red-eyed, unshaven, gaunt-faced men slapped each others' shoulders and laughed crazily together as they realized what it meant. The long ordeal was over.

At 4 o'clock on the afternoon of that day, 30th May, the Murmansk section passed Toros Island at the entrance to the Kola Inlet under the admiring eyes of its escort commander, Richard Onslow, 'reduced in numbers, battered and tired, but still keeping perfect station'.

In spite of the loss of one-fifth of the convoy, Onslow had every reason to be proud of the outcome of the operation considering the forces pitted against him. The Luftwaffe knew full well the extent of their failure but, not daring to admit it, they claimed to have totally destroyed the convoy. Even Doenitz, ever jealous for the reputation of his U-boats but disappointed at their showing on this occasion, accepted the Luftwaffe's claim and recommended that aircraft, instead of submarines, should be used against any future summer convoys.

On the British side, Admiral Tovey commented, 'This success was beyond expectation.' Onslow, too, was not deluded into thinking that such good fortune could be relied upon so long as the anti-aircraft defence of the Arctic convoys was so weak. More C.A.M.-ships, more anti-aircraft ships were essential, he insisted. Even better would be an escort aircraft-carrier, the first of which were expected in service soon.

As in other theatres of the war, these ships, makeshift substitutes for the carriers the Navy had shortsightedly failed to build at their leisure in the years between the wars, were eventually to reverse the odds in the Arctic battles. But so much in demand were they everywhere that it was not to be for many months yet that any could be allocated to that theatre. Not for the first or last time in the history of the war, it is heartbreaking to count the losses that might have been avoided if the Navy had entered it with a sufficiency of aircraft-carriers and the aircraft and air crews to put in them.

The experience of P.Q. 16, correctly interpreted, might well have been sufficient to drive home the lesson that, until adequate defence could be provided, summer convoys were a game not worth the candle. But it was to take a catastrophe to do this – a tragedy the actors in which were assembling in the wings even as Onslow thankfully berthed his ships in Kola Inlet.

6

CONVOY SCATTER!

It is not surprising that the story of the hazardous voyages of the Arctic convoys, growing ever more so with each one, should have begun by now to play on the nerves of the staff officers responsible. At the Admiralty and in the operations room of the Home Fleet flagship the progress of every one was watched with deep anxiety as the symbol representing it crawled so slowly across the wall maps. Intelligence of U-boat concentrations and of impending air attack would come in. Tidings of how the convoy was coping with them would be awaited, if not with fear, certainly with misgivings.

Beyond all reasonable expectations, these two forms of menace had, up to now, failed to achieve any great measure of success. The dogged determination of the masters of the merchantmen not to be intimidated into breaking formation had contributed largely to the defeat of both of them. So long as the convoy remained a compact body, the enemy airmen and U-boat captains had to face a formidable, concentrated defence in order to press home their attacks. This, more often than not, they jibbed at doing.

If these had been the only threats confronting the convoys, the future could perhaps have been regarded with reasonable confidence. The escorts available were increasing in number. New types designed for anti-aircraft defence were coming into service at last. But always, a gnawing anxiety to the naval staffs, were the German heavy ships in Norwegian harbours. It was inexplicable that, except for the *Tirpitz*'s abortive sortie against P.Q. 12 in February and the two unimpressive attempts by the German destroyers, the enemy had not tried to cut up a convoy in the Barents Sea. To the Admiralty there seemed to be no defence against such an attack except by our submarines who were maintained on patrol off the Norwegian coast. But the chances of one of these being lucky enough to bring off an attack against a German force sweeping by at high speed were too remote to be counted upon.

The heavy ships of the Home Fleet, which alone could meet the available force of German heavy ships, had the primary task of preventing a break-out into the Atlantic. If, to cover a convoy, they passed into the Barents Sea without sure knowledge that they would find the enemy there, they would be leaving the door wide open behind them. They could only wait in the background until it was known that the *Tirpitz* and her lesser consorts were committed and then hope to intercept them as they retired to their bases.

The Home Fleet cruisers, on the other hand, could not stand up to the greatly superior power of the *Tirpitz* and the pocket battleships. West of Bear Island, they could, if they accepted the risk from U-boats' torpedoes, give anti-aircraft support to the convoys and cover them against attack by cruisers or destroyers. In the Barents Sea they seemed, on paper, to be a hostage to fortune and to run an unreasonable risk.

Such was the strategic position as it appeared to the anxious naval staffs. It was, said Admiral Tovey, 'wholly favourable to the enemy'. Knowing, as we do now, that the German surface fleet was labouring under such restrictive instructions from Hitler that it was virtually impossible to take it into action, it is tempting to criticize this appreciation. But the Admiralty had no such knowledge. Certainly they had seen the lack of stomach for a fight displayed by the German destroyers on two occasions. They had also previous examples of German unwillingness to risk their ships in battle during the Atlantic excursions of the *Hipper*, *Scharnhorst* and *Gneisenau*. All these were typical of the tactics of a weaker naval power following the strategy of maintenance of a 'fleet in being'.

But the Admiralty could not bring themselves to base their strategy on such an assumption. A Nelson, with the nerve to follow his 'hunch' as he did when he followed the French fleet to Egypt or across the Atlantic, might have done so. But Nelsons come few and far between. The naval staff's caution, wise or excessive as the reader may judge for himself, is the key to events that were shortly to unfold.

While the ships that were to form P.Q. 17 were assembling in Hvalfiord, a new German Commander-in-Chief, Admiral Schniewind, had hoisted his flag in the *Tirpitz*, lying with *Hipper* and four destroyers at Trondheim. At Narvik, further north, were the *Scheer* and *Lutzow* with six more destroyers. The 'new broom' was full of ideas for taking his force out to intercept the next Arctic convoy. But even as he laid his plans, orders came down from the Fuehrer further restricting the freedom of movement of the fleet. Not unless and until the Home Fleet's aircraft carriers had been located and attacked by the Luftwaffe might he leave harbour. By then it would certainly be too late, if he remained at Trondheim, to get at a convoy. He planned, therefore, as soon as the next convoy was known to have sailed, to move *Tirpitz* and *Hipper* to Vestfiord and the *Scheer* and *Lutzow* to Altenfiord in the far north. Operation 'Rosselspring' (Knight's Move), he called it.

In order that he should get the necessary intelligence as early as possible, Admiral Schniewind sent three of his ten available U-boats to patrol the north-east sector of the Denmark Strait as early as the 5th June. In view of this German zeal in reconnaissance, it was disappointing for the British that a dummy convoy of four colliers and five large minelayers, which sailed from Scapa on 29th June to induce the Germans to commit their forces prematurely, was never sighted by the enemy in spite of trailing its shirt for a few days.

However, the position, from the Admiralty's point of view, was no worse than it had been. A careful watch was kept by aircraft of R.A.F. Coastal Command on the enemy's ships and any movement should be detected at an early stage. Preparations for the sailing of P.Q. 17 and its opposite number, Q.P. 13, went ahead. The outward convoy was to comprise thirty-six ships, twenty-two of them American, led by Commodore J. C. K. Dowding, R.N.R., no newcomer to the Kola Run, though he had not so far experienced a summer convoy.

As for previous convoys, a very large naval force was to be deployed, consisting of a 'Covering Force' of battleships, an aircraft carrier and destroyers led by the Commander-in-Chief in the *Duke of York*, a 'Support Force' of cruisers, two British and two American, under the command of Rear-Admiral Louis Hamilton, besides the close escort. The covering force, however, was to cruise well to the west of Bear Island whence they would only move on receipt of definite intelligence which would enable them to intercept the *Tirpitz*. Hamilton's cruisers would cruise in support to the northward of the convoy route, their task being to engage any surface forces, other than the *Tirpitz*, which threatened. Their role as anti-aircraft ships would be taken on this occasion by two of the specially equipped vessels, *Palomares* and *Pozarica*.

In command of the escort sailed Commander J. E. Broome in the destroyer *Keppel* with a strong anti-submarine force consisting of six destroyers, four corvettes and two submarines. These last had been tried before, with the idea that should enemy forces succeed in intercepting the convoy, the submarines might be able to get into position to attack them. It had not, so far – indeed it never did – work out that way in practice.

With the convoy sailed also three Rescue Ships, *Rathlin*, *Zaafaran* and *Zamelek*. These craft, the need for which experience in the Atlantic had shown, were small passenger steamers in which a medical staff was carried, sick bays and extra accommodation fitted. Their low freeboard and the 'scrambling nets' which could be lowered over the side and up which men in boats and rafts or swimming could clamber, enabled them to embark survivors with the least possible delay. They thus relieved the escorts of this responsibility, leaving them free to concentrate on their duties of defence. They also saved them from the heart-breaking and all too common experience of having to leave men struggling in the water while they dealt with an enemy U-boat or aircraft.

The rescue ships played a heroic and largely unsung part in the convoy battles in the Atlantic as well as the Arctic. It took iron nerve and cool courage to lie immobilized in the middle of an attack, an easy target for torpedo or bomb, while survivors were helped on board, often a long and difficult business in rough weather and icy seas.

So it was a well-balanced force that sailed as P.Q. 17 from Hvalfiord on 27th June. 'Jackie' Broome was an experienced escort force commander and he looked forward to the voyage with quiet confidence. The route was a great deal longer than on previous occasions as the withdrawal of the edge of the ice-barrier allowed the convoy to reach far up into the Arctic before turning eastwards to pass north of Bear Island. The destroyers would consequently need to refuel at least once, so three tankers sailed with the convoy. The *Grey Ranger* and the *Douglas* would transfer to the homeward Q.P. 13 when it passed, but the third, the *Aldersdale*, would go all the way with P.Q. 17.

All went smoothly and well for the first few days. In fine, calm weather, the convoy settled down under Commodore Dowding's leadership and made good progress. Lonely Jan Mayen Island had been passed, far out of sight over the horizon, on 1st July, when the enemy first discovered that P.Q. 17 was at sea, U-boats on patrol reporting it that day. Some of these were sighted on the surface and destroyer escorts drove them off. But the damage was done and at noon the inevitable reconnaissance aircraft arrived.

At German naval headquarters in the north, great excitement prevailed. Ten U-boats were sent instructions to concentrate to shadow and attack, while the *Tirpitz* and the pocket battleships were brought to short notice for steam, ready for the first moves of 'Rosselspring'. At the same time the Luftwaffe prepared to launch their first attacks on the following day by which time the convoy would be well within range.

The 1st July thus passed quietly in P.Q. 17. Taking advantage of the fair weather, all destroyers filled their fuel tanks before the two tankers should leave early on the 2nd to join the approaching Q.P. 13. The homeward convoy, favoured by thick weather throughout their voyage, had not been molested at all. At noon on the 2nd, it passed by on opposite course, leaving P.Q. 17 the sole object of the enemy's attentions.

That evening he made his first attempt with nine torpedo-planes. They had a very warm reception, its vigour enhanced by the fire of the American destroyer *Rowan* which had come from Admiral Hamilton's cruiser force to the convoy to fuel from the *Aldersdale*. The *Rowan* repaid this hospitality by shooting down one of the attackers. The remainder of the Heinkels fought shy of trying to penetrate the convoy screen and loosed their torpedoes ineffectively at long range.

'Jackie' Broome had reason to be pleased with this first showing of the escort under his command. The situation was further improved that night when the convoy slipped into a sheltering mantle of thick fog. He was not to enjoy the resultant immunity for long, however. For, during the following forenoon, the weather cleared and, though 'Snooper Joe', the shadowing aircraft had apparently been thrown off the scent, it was not long before it was evident that U-boats had clung to his trail. The afternoon was spent driving off any that came too close. But another day had gone by and the convoy still drove on, its numbers complete.

That evening, Admiral Hamilton's cruisers, hovering over the horizon to the north, were also sighted by the enemy and reported. At this time, too, Hamilton received the first news that the German heavy ships were on the move. These movements had begun on the previous afternoon when, in anticipation of the Fuehrer's permission for a sortie, Schniewind had given orders for the *Tirpitz* and *Hipper* to leave Trondheim for the Vestfiord with their escort of four destroyers. At the same time the *Scheer* and the *Lutzow*, with their six destroyers weighed anchor to move from Narvik to Altenfiord.

Misfortunes befell the Germans almost at once. The *Lutzow*, negotiating a narrow fiord, ran aground, receiving such damage that she would have to return to Germany for repairs. Then, when the *Tirpitz*'s force reached Vestfiord, three of its destroyers making up the Ofot Fiord to Narvik also grounded and were put out of action. The German force was still, however, a formidable one. Operation 'Rosselspring' could go ahead. As soon as Admiral Tovey's fleet was located and his carrier successfully attacked by the Luftwaffe, the way would be clear for the *Tirpitz* and her consorts to sail. Perhaps then some action experience would re-vitalize the drooping morale of the German crews chafing and discontented at the soul-destroying monotony of life aboard their harbour-bound ships.

All that was known to the Admiralty, however, was that the *Tirpitz* and *Hipper* had left Trondheim. Bad weather in the north had prevented air reconnaissance of the Narvik area. Anxiety began to mount in London. The four heavy German ships might be anywhere at sea. In fact, during the night of the 3rd, the *Tirpitz* had moved on from Narvik to join the *Scheer* at Altenfiord. So that, when at last the weather cleared sufficiently on the 4th for a clear view of Narvik from the air, that harbour, too, was seen to be empty.

The situation had arisen which the British naval staff had long foreseen and feared. With a valuable convoy just entering the Barents Sea accompanied by an Anglo-American cruiser squadron which would be outclassed in an encounter with the German fleet, Schniewind's ships had vanished into the blue. Even if the Admiralty and the Commander-in-Chief had been prepared to take the only British battleship and the only available aircraft carrier into the U-boat-infested and Luftwaffe-dominated waters of the Barents Sea, where a lucky torpedo hit might leave one of these valuable ships crippled with no destroyer screen owing to lack of fuel, they could not do so until location of the *Tirpitz* made it clear that it was against the convoy that she was steering.

In this moment of crisis the First Sea Lord, Admiral Sir Dudley Pound, called a staff meeting at the Admiralty on the evening of 4th July to consider what should be done.

* * *

At sea, 3rd July had passed quietly. Doenitz's U-boat commanders were writing in their logs, 'Unable to close to the attack owing to powerful escort.' The Luftwaffe was hanging back, unwilling to risk another dose such as had been administered to their torpedo squadron on the previous day. At midnight American Independence Day began. In the light of the midnight sun, seen through breaks in the fog, large Stars and Stripes unfolded at the mastheads of this predominantly American convoy. Sixty miles due south lay Bear Island. Soon, according to his orders, Admiral Hamilton's squadron would be leaving, after which P.Q. 17 would be on its own.

But all hands were in good heart, confident that though not without some loss, they could fight their way through to Archangel in the face of anything the Luftwaffe or Doenitz could do. Even when, through a hole in the fog, a single torpedo-bomber suddenly dropped down to put a torpedo skilfully into the *Christopher Newton*, just before 5 a.m., confidence remained firm. When the crew had been taken aboard a rescue ship, an escort sent the immobilized freighter to the bottom. The convoy plugged doggedly on.

By mid-day, however, the growing anxiety felt in London was making itself evident in an increasing number of signals to Admiral Hamilton from the Admiralty. The cruisers had instructions not to go further in company with the convoy than the meridian of twenty-five degrees East. But at noon, Hamilton was given leave to stay longer, subject to any contrary orders from the Commander-in-Chief. Admiral Tovey, fretting, not for the first time in his tenure of command, at such interference by the Admiralty with the operational control of his forces, intervened at once with a signal to Hamilton instructing him to leave on reaching twenty-five degrees East unless the Admiralty could assure him that he could not meet the *Tirpitz*.

At this, Hamilton replied that he would withdraw to the westward at 10 p.m. when the refuelling of his destroyers would be completed. Barely had this decision been communicated when from the Admiralty came the order to remain with the convoy pending instructions as further information might be available shortly.

Taken in conjunction with the earlier news that the German heavy ships had been stirring from their long inactivity, this seemed to indicate to both Hamilton and Broome that the time had come to consider what their tactics would have to be if enemy surface forces were met. Neither of them lacked confidence that, by skilful use of smoke screens and torpedo threat, they could hold off an enemy who had before now shown himself unwilling to 'mix it' in a sea fight.

While his destroyers went, one by one, to the *Aldersdale* for oil, Hamilton's squadron zigzagged to and fro across the line of advance of the convoy some ten to twenty miles ahead of it. The

4th July wore on without incident until 7.30 that evening when an ill-coordinated attack by bombers and torpedo-planes achieved nothing. The United States destroyer *Wainwright*, arriving to fuel, gave an impressive demonstration of long-range controlled anti-aircraft fire which did much to lower the enemy's zest. Bombs and torpedoes all went wide.

So far the vaunted Luftwaffe had been singularly unsuccessful. It may be that scathing criticism from on high had served to put some back-bone into the next squadron that attacked, or it may simply be that it was the 'First Eleven' which was now being brought into play. It is possible, too, that the success they now achieved was due entirely to the resolute courage of their leader. For when twenty-five torpedo bombers came streaking in, fast and low, from the starboard quarter, the leading aircraft, ignoring the tempest of fire from all around, held on till he was well into the convoy before dropping two torpedoes aimed at point-blank range at the *Navarino*. A moment later it crashed in flames just ahead of the escort leader *Keppel*.

His followers were not so bold. Jackie Broome, giving credit to a gallant foe, said later, 'Had they kept with him, dividing and generally embarrassing the A.A. fire, many ships would have been sunk.' But, meeting the wall of shell bursts and the deadly streams of tracer shells, they split up, jinking like a wisp of snipe, unable to aim their torpedoes with any accuracy. Only two more ships were hit, the *William Hooper* and the Russian tanker *Azerbaidjan*. The *Navarino* and the *William Hooper* had to be sunk by the escorts, but the Russian was found by Broome, when he closed to see how she was getting on, to be 'holed but happy and capable of nine knots'. She regained her station in the convoy and was eventually to reach harbour safely. Three aircraft destroyed and at least one damaged was the price the enemy paid for this success.

After this heavy and unusually well-led attack, Broome was supremely confident that he had the measure of the enemy. As he was to write later, 'My impression on seeing the resolution displayed by the convoy and its escort was that provided ammunition held out, P.Q. 17 could get anywhere.'

But even as the gunfire died away, as the convoy got into its stride again and every gunlayer in the force was gleefully claiming the destruction of one of the crashed planes, a decision was being taken at Admiral Pound's staff conference that was to lead to repercussions whose echoes would take many a year to die away and to recriminations which are still repeated to this day.

* * *

As we have seen, on the afternoon of the 4th, the Admiralty was bereft of all information as to the whereabouts of the *Tirpitz* and *Hipper*. The air reconnaissance which might have discovered them where they lay at anchor at Altenfiord, awaiting Hitler's permission to sail, had again failed to materialize, though from photographic reconnaissance our intelligence was able to say that it was 'tolerably certain' that *Scheer* and *Lutzow* were in Altenfiord. But by the evening the *Tirpitz* had at last been located. Confronting the First Sea Lord's staff meeting was the knowledge that she could be amongst the convoy by 2 o'clock on the morning of 5th July.

Such a situation with a convoy in the wide waters of the Atlantic was catered for and had been successfully met in the past. When an attack by superior forces was known to be imminent and unavoidable, the technique was for the escort to engage the enemy, if possible screening with smoke the convoy, which thereupon scattered. This was a pre-arranged manoeuvre in which each ship had a course to steer differing from that of its neighbours. Thus, on the order to scatter, the convoy would open like the petals of a symmetrical flower. By the time the raider had dealt with the escort, the ships of the convoy would be steering away to every point of the compass, making it a lengthy business for the raider to round them up one by one and sink them.

This, in fact, was how it had fallen out when, in November 1940, the *Scheer*'s topmasts hove over the horizon in sight of Captain Fegan of the Armed Merchant Cruiser *Jervis Bay*, the sole escort of an Atlantic convoy of thirty-seven ships. Giving the Commodore the order to scatter the convoy, Fegan steamed gallantly into action against hopeless odds, to his death and a posthumous Victoria Cross. When the *Jervis Bay*'s last gun had been silenced and the *Scheer* could turn her attention to the convoy, most of the ships were disappearing over the horizon in every direction. Six of them only could the *Scheer* dispose of before fear of being trapped by avenging British forces forced her to scurry away to another part of the ocean.

Such were the tactics which Sir Dudley Pound was considering ordering P.Q. 17 to carry out now. But in what different circumstances from the *Jervis Bay* incident! There, the decision was taken by the man on the spot, the enemy plainly in sight and bearing down on the convoy. Now it was to be taken by an authority remote from the scene who could not have the latest information of weather or of air or U-boat threat, nor, indeed, of the surface threat either.

Jervis Bay's convoy had the whole wide Atlantic in which to scatter and in which a sparsely distributed U-boat force was the only other danger to face. P.Q. 17 was restricted to the north by the ice barrier and to the south by an enemy-held shore. Ahead and astern U-boats were concentrated and enemy aircraft roamed at will in large numbers.

Yet when the First Sea Lord put his proposal to the staff meeting, there seems to have been no voice raised in disagreement; only a comment by the Vice-Chief of the Naval Staff, Vice-Admiral H. R. Moore, that if the convoy was to scatter it must do so soon or it would have no sea room.

So the die was cast. The convoy would be ordered to scatter. Whether the decision was right or wrong – and here it must be said that Admiral Tovey, Rear-Admiral Hamilton and Commander Broome all deemed it disastrously wrong – is a question of high technicality and hedged with imponderables. Schniewind did eventually sail to attack the convoy and might have, as planned, wiped out the escort with one half of his force while the other half massacred the convoy. But some of the many British and Russian submarines on patrol in the area might have got home an attack on the German ships first – the Russian *K.21* did, in fact make an unsuccessful attack. Rear-Admiral Hamilton's cruisers, boldly handled under cover of smoke screens, as he planned to use them, might have outmanoeuvred Admiral Schniewind in whose ears rang Admiral Raeder's damping warning words that a naval reverse at that time would be particularly unfortunate.

Let us leave the question of right or wrong at that, remembering how Nelson once wrote, 'Nothing is certain, in a sea fight above all others.' What is sure, however, is that the decision once taken, lack of imagination on the part of the naval staff in drafting the necessary signals gave those at sea an entirely false impression of the situation. Let us transport ourselves to the bridge of H.M.S. *Keppel* and stand beside 'Jackie' Broome as he read the signals which came in.

7

'... DIVIDED WE FALL'

Broome was in an exuberant mood for he had just seen his force deal very adequately with as weighty an air attack as had so far been mounted against the Arctic convoys. He and Commodore Dowding 'were sharing', as he wrote later, 'the wave of confidence which swept the convoy and escort after the air attack. The tails of P.Q. 17 were well up!'

Broome and Rear-Admiral Hamilton had been expecting a signal from the Admiralty giving the 'further information' which they had said might be available shortly. Instead, came the first message drafted by the Admiralty staff following on the First Sea Lord's conference: 'Most Immediate. Cruiser force withdraw to westward at high speed.' Only on occasions of the utmost urgency could the priority indication 'Most Immediate' be used.

The message therefore seemed to indicate that some force in overwhelming strength was moving to entrap Hamilton's cruisers. The next signal heightened this impression. 'Immediate. Owing to threat of surface ships, convoy is to disperse and proceed to Russian ports.' It seemed quite clear now that surface attack was imminent. The orders were categorical no matter how much Hamilton and Broome disliked receiving them. The Admiralty must have information denied to the two sea commanders.

When, a few minutes later, a further signal came in drafted by someone in the Admiralty who realized that the wrong terminology had been used in telling the convoy to 'disperse', which is quite different from 'scattering', it sounded like a despairing, warning shriek. 'Most Immediate. Convoy is to scatter.'

This last signal more than either of the others gave the impression that the enemy's mastheads might appear over the horizon at any moment. A fleet action was imminent! Broome naturally felt that in that case there was little that his destroyers could do amongst the scattering convoy, but that his torpedoes would be a considerable access of strength to Admiral Hamilton's force in the coming action. Sore at heart, therefore, but confident that he was doing right, having passed the order at 10.15 p.m. to an astonished Dowding that his convoy was to scatter, he ordered the remainder of the escorts to proceed independently to Archangel. With that, he called in his destroyers and steered to join Hamilton's cruisers which had just turned to the westward and would shortly sweep past the convoy at twenty-five knots. 'In the eyes of all who did not know the full story,' as Hamilton said, 'running away, and at high speed.'

At this stage none of the escorts thought they were running away. On the contrary, they thought that a desperate fight lay ahead of them as an exchange of signals between the *Keppel* and one of the submarines shows. Ordered to proceed independently, the submarine sent the informatory signal to the *Keppel*, 'Intend to remain on the surface as long as possible.' With grim wit, Jackie Broome replied, 'So do I.'

Alas, though owing to the Admiralty's deceptive signals Hamilton did not realize it, running away is exactly what he was unwittingly doing. 'Had I been aware', the Admiral went on, 'that the Admiralty had no further information of the enemy heavy units than I myself possessed, I would have remained in a covering position until the convoy was widely dispersed when I could have parted company in a less ostentatious manner.'

But once the convoy had scattered, the presence of the cruisers would have made little difference. By simply shifting her anchorage the *Tirpitz* had done what massed U-boats and aircraft had failed to do. She had broken the cohesion of the convoy, the principal defence against both those methods of attack. Even had Broome's destroyers been sent back when it became clear that there was, in fact, no danger of an immediate surface attack, there was little they could have done. Perhaps a few ships might have been saved, but losses would still have been calamitous. The following day the wolves descended on the scattered flock which they had hardly dared to attack while the shepherd was there to guard and the sheepdogs snarled round the outside of the fold.

*   *   *

To Commodore Dowding, even less 'in the know' than the escorts as to what was going on, the order to scatter came as a fearful shock. Disbelieving at first, he asked for the signal to be repeated. When Broome's last signal came to him, 'Sorry to leave you like this. Good luck. Looks like a bloody business', he knew it was only too true. The necessary signal was hoisted in the Commodore's flagship, *River Afton*, left flying for a short time until its import had been taken in by the masters and then hauled down. P.Q. 17 had ceased to exist.

In its place was a disorganized body of ships steering so as to put the greatest possible distance between themselves and their neighbours in the shortest possible time, and a handful of escort corvettes with orders to proceed independently to Archangel. That the convoy scattered exactly as laid down in the signal book speaks much for the fine discipline of the masters, for it meant that some had initially to steer to the west or south-west, away from their hoped-for destination and in the direction whence an enemy might be expected to arrive.

Once the manœuvre of scattering had been completed, however, some of the merchantmen wisely joined up with others to make small groups round each of which gathered a few escorts to give what protection they could. One group, the rescue ship *Rathlin* and two merchantmen, steered boldly on a direct course for Archangel and arrived safely on 9th July, having driven off attacks and shot down an enemy aircraft on the way.

Most groups, however, decided that their best chance of safety lay in making for shelter in Novaya Zemlya and waiting there for escort. The majority of those which set off alone were pounced upon on 5th July and either sunk in short order or so damaged that their crews took to the boats, perhaps sometimes rather prematurely. The temptation to get away, without haste, while all boats were in sound condition must have been strong to crews demoralized by the desertion of their escort, the blank loneliness of the Arctic scene, the freezing breath coming off the ice, the endless daylight, exposing their defencelessness to U-boats and aircraft alike. It was a weird, terrifying world to most of the crews, made worse by the effect of the mirage by means of which they could sometimes see their late convoy companions mirrored in the sky from over the horizon, being bombed.

One or two crews thus decided they would rather submit to the hazards of a boat trip of several hundred miles than stay aboard, trying to keep their slightly damaged ships afloat, to await their apparently certain end at the hands of aircraft or U-boat. Strangely enough those that took this line, favoured by fair weather, either succeeded in reaching Novaya Zemlya, where they were taken aboard ships which had already got there, or were picked up in good shape by escorts searching for survivors. One crew which had taken to the boats actually refused to be picked up by another merchant ship which found them. They reckoned they were safer where they were, and perhaps they were right for their would-be rescuer was later torpedoed.

The majority of the crews, however, stuck to their ships with great gallantry and were often left with only rafts on which to get away. One of these was the Commodore's *River Afton*. For more than three hours Dowding, a steward and a deck boy shared four barrels lashed together, in water not far above freezing level. He has related how he saw other survivors drifting around in boats and on rafts and most of them amazingly cheerful though chances of rescue seemed very faint. Even in such a pitiable situation, Dowding's sense of humour did not desert him and he derived grim amusement from the sailor in charge of one of the rafts whom he could hear abjuring a particularly sodden, shivering and complaining shipmate not to be 'so bloody wet'!

In hope of rescue, smoke floats were lighted but in the flat calm the smoke drifted away low along the surface and it seemed unlikely that it would do much good. But, twenty miles away, in the corvette *Lotus*, searching for survivors, it appeared, owing to mirage, as a dense column in the sky. Thus, an hour later, Dowding and the master and crew of the *River Afton* joined the many

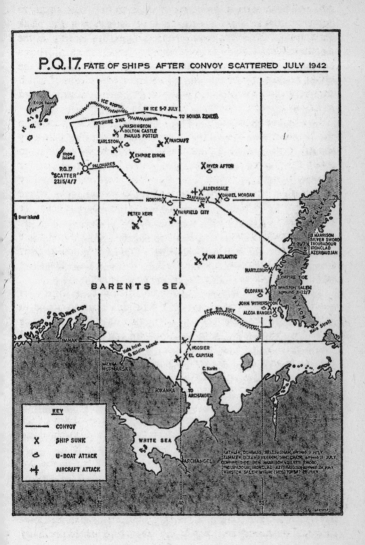

P.Q.17. FATE OF SHIPS AFTER CONVOY SCATTERED JULY 1942

ICE EDGE
IN ICE 5-7 JULY
TO NOVAYA ZEMLYA
AYRSHIRE 3 M.V.
WASHINGTON
BOLTON CASTLE
PAULUS POTTER
EARLSTON
PANCRAFT
Hope Island
EMPIRE BYRON
P.Q.17
"SCATTER"
2215/4/7
PALOMARES
RIVER AFTON
ALDERSDALE
ZAAFARAN
HONOMU
DANIEL MORGAN
Bear Island
PETER KERR
FAIRFIELD CITY
J.K. HARRISON
SILVER SWORD
TROUBADOUR 2 M.V.
IRONCLAD
AZERBAIDJAN
PAN ATLANTIC
HARTLEBURY
EMPIRE TIDE
BARENTS SEA
OLOPANA
WINSTON SALEM aground 2-22/7
JOHN WITHERSPOON
ALCOA RANGER
ICE 9th JULY
North Cape
BANAK
HOOSIER
Kola Inlet
EL CAPITAN
Kildin Islands
C. Kanin
MURMANSK
IOKANKA
TO ARCHANGEL

WHITE SEA

ARCHANGEL

KEY
—— CONVOY
X SHIP SUNK
U-BOAT ATTACK
AIRCRAFT ATTACK

RATHLIN, DONBASS, BELLINGHAM arrived 9 JULY
ZAMALEK, OCEAN FREEDOM, SAMUEL CHASE arrived 11 JULY
EMPIRE TIDE, BEN. HARRISON, SILVER SWORD,
TROUBADOUR, IRONCLAD, AZERBAIDJAN arrived 24 JULY
WINSTON SALEM arrived (MOLOTOVSK) 28 JULY

other survivors aboard the *Lotus*. The corvette continued with her rescue work as she steered towards Novaya Zemlya and was repeatedly aided by this mirage. The inverted image of a ship, hanging in the sky on the horizon, would suddenly be surrounded by bomb splashes but, of course, stretching downwards to the horizon instead of upwards into the air!

Some of the most splendid examples of devotion to duty were given by the guns' crews of the merchant ships. In British ships – and in some of the American freighters also at this time – these were gunners belonging to the D.E.M.S. (Defensively Equipped Merchant Ship) service. In other American ships they were naval reservists under the command of young Ensigns and were known as the Armed Guard.

More than one of the masters paid glowing tribute to their guns' crews for rallying the demoralized ships' companies when they wanted to abandon ship prematurely. In one American ship, when the crew panicked and made to abandon ship, the matter was referred to the leader of the British D.E.M.S. gunners who answered roundly, 'It is our duty to stand fast and take defensive action until the ship sinks.' This stout-hearted rejoinder put an end to the panic and restored morale.

By the end of 5th July, six ships had been sunk by bombs, another six by U-boats' torpedoes. On the next day one more ship was sunk by air attack. Between the 6th and the 8th, U-boats accounted for four more. There is no space here to recount the adventures of the survivors from all these ships, which is a pity, as the resource and dogged endurance which they displayed constitute a bright gleam against the sombre background of the story. We must follow instead the fortunes of those which escaped the first onslaught of the enemy as he found, to his incredulous delight, that the impenetrable phalanx from which he had recoiled in attack after attack had broken up into defenceless units.

The shelter for which most of these ships made was the deep inlet on the west coast of Novaya Zemlya known as Matoschkin Strait. Here, by 7th July five had arrived, as had many of the escorts, including the *Lotus* with Commodore Dowding aboard, and the anti-aircraft ship *Palomares*. After a conference in the last-named, a convoy was formed and sailed that evening. Fog and drift ice off a harsh, inhospitable coast made a nightmare voyage at first. One of the ships, the *Benjamin Harrison* lost touch and returned to the shelter of Matoschkin Strait. From time to time boatloads of survivors were sighted and the occupants taken on board the escorts. When the weather cleared on the 9th, the little convoy found itself off the southern point of Novaya Zemlya faced with pack ice which forced an alteration of course to the westward along its edge. By the evening they had rounded it and were heading south for the White Sea. A bare sixty miles from the Russian coast, forty high-level bombers arrived and for four hours made repeated leisurely attacks undisturbed by sight or sound of a Russian fighter. Though four of them were believed to have been shot down, when the attackers finally drew off at 2.30 on the morning of the 10th, two more ships had been sunk by near misses.

Even the imperturbable Dowding was in low spirits as he penned his first report. His bitter understatement, 'Not a successful convoy! Three ships brought into port out of thirty-seven'! contained a note of heartbreak. But then he heard of the arrival of the *Rathlin* and two others on the 9th and, when news began to come in of others sheltering in Novaya Zemlyan waters, he roused himself. Dowding was not the man to rest while there were any more of his convoy to be brought in. He demanded transport to go out and join them, and escorts to bring them in.

On the 16th, therefore, he left Archangel in the corvette *Poppy* in company with the *Lotus* and the Free French *La Malouine*. The calm weather had broken, and it was after three stormy days that the first sheltered bay on the coast of Novaya Zemlya was reached, Byelushya Bay, where twelve survivors from the torpedoed *Olapana* were found ashore and taken aboard. Searching northwards along the coast, they first came upon the American *Winston Salem* aground on a sandbank. Without tugs there was little they could do for her for the time being. Reporting her position they passed on up the cruel, ice-bound coast.

The next inlet was Moller Bay where they found the C.A.M.-ship *Empire Tide* at anchor and swarming with survivors from other ships. Promising to pick her up on their way south, the little force pressed on to Matoschkin Strait and were cheered by the glad sight of five more merchantmen from the convoy, a Russian ice-breaker *Murman* and a trawler the *Kerov*. Proudly ruling this flotilla was the trawler *Ayrshire* commanded by Lieutenant L. J. A. Gradwell, R.N.V.R.

While the Commodore is arranging to embark in the *Murman*, from which he intends to lead this new convoy southward, we should listen to the tale of Gradwell, a barrister turned sailor 'for the duration', for it is not without interest and charm.

When the convoy scattered on the evening of 4th July and the various escorts picked on ships or groups of ships to shepherd, Gradwell took under his mantle the three American ships *Silver Sword*, *Ironclad* and *Troubadour*. They were already heading northwards in accordance with the orders for scattering. Gradwell persuaded them that the further they could go in that direction the better until the first fury of the enemy attack had spent itself. So, northwards they continued until they came to the ice-packs when, for a time, they turned eastwards.

But the *Ayrshire*'s radio was full of S.O.S. messages from ships being attacked not far to the south of them. Gradwell therefore led his little convoy boldly up the lanes in the pack-ice until he had put some twenty miles between it and the open sea. This made them safe against U-boat attack. But against the gleaming white of the ice, the black and grey ships stood out like sore thumbs and must soon be seen by roaming aircraft. Very well! All hands paint ship! As the *Ayrshire* slowly converted herself to a yacht-like appearance, the merchant captains caught on to the idea and soon all were a stark white.

The ruse was entirely successful. For the next two days the four ships lay undisturbed in the ice. As the hubbub on the radio died away and Gradwell judged that the enemy were satisfied that there were no more targets for them – in the northern part of the Barents Sea, at any rate – the convoy got under way again and headed for the Matoschkin Strait. There they safely arrived on 11th July. After a brief stay there, Gradwell decided that it was time to move on to Archangel. But, with no charts of that dangerous coast, the *Ironclad* ran twice aground and was refloated with the help of the *Ayrshire*. When the *Troubadour* then did the same, and was with difficulty extricated, Gradwell judged it would be better to await assistance.

Feeling his way carefully up the strait, he led the merchantmen twenty miles up it and there the party anchored, well camouflaged in their white paint and overlooked by several reconnoitring enemy aircraft.

The praises of Britain's amateur sailors who manned the vast majority of her little warships have been sung by many authorities on many occasions. But the conduct of the pair of legal lights who formed the Captain and Executive Officer of the *Ayrshire* stands high as what Admiral Tovey described as 'a splendid example of imagination and initiative', an opinion which was warmly endorsed by the masters of the ships the trawler led so skilfully to safety.

But now Commodore Dowding has transferred to the *Murman*. After a conference on 20th July, all the ships in Matoschkin Strait followed the *Murman* out to sea and down the coast. The *Empire Tide* with her load of survivors joined as the convoy passed Möller Bay. The voyage to Archangel was unmolested, which was just as well judging from Dowding's experience with the Russian staff in the *Murman*. When well into the White Sea, two Russian aircraft appeared right ahead and dropped a single smoke flare, obviously some form of recognition signal, and then flew back whence they had come.

At once there was tremendous excitement amongst the Russians. 'Turn the convoy, Commodore', they shouted. 'The aircraft has attacked a submarine.' The alarm bells clanged at which every man on board donned a steel helmet. Nothing would disabuse the Russians of their idea nor would they agree that the strong force of British escorts could well deal with the U-boat, if U-boat there were. On the other hand nothing was going to persuade Dowding to make a fool of himself by turning the convoy. As the Russians' excitement reached fever pitch, they suddenly rang down for full speed and swung away to port until they had put several miles between themselves and the convoy.

Dowding signalled to the senior officer of the escort to disregard the Russians' antics and, as the convoy sailed serenely on without further alarm, the *Murman* was brought finally back to rejoin it. It was not surprising, if this was typical of the Russian naval mentality and efficiency, that the approaches to Kola and the White Sea were a happy hunting ground for German U-boats at times.

The long agony of P.Q. 17 was nearly over. With the salving of the *Winston Salem* under the superintendence of the American Naval Attaché, who flew to Novaya Zemlya in a Catalina flying boat, the last survivor reached port, making a total of eleven out of the thirty-seven which had originally sailed. Besides the twenty-four freighters lost, the faithful *Aldersdale* had gone and the rescue ship *Zaafaran*.

As for the *Tirpitz* which had caused all the trouble she did eventually sail on the afternoon of 5th July. With *Scheer, Hipper* and seven destroyers she steered north-eastwards into the Barents Sea for a few hours; but, on the sighting reports of the Russian submarine *K.21* and the British *P.54* being intercepted, the German naval staff at once began to get cold feet. Calculations showed that Admiral Tovey could get close enough to launch an air attack from his carrier on the German force before it could get back to harbour if it continued with the operation. In any case the scattering of the convoy had delivered it into the hands of the Luftwaffe and the U-boats. Soon after 9.30 on the evening of 5th July, the *Tirpitz* turned back to harbour.

The disaster to P.Q. 17 was not the only bad news in that month of July 1942. Calamity had also befallen the homeward Q.P. 13 at the very time that the ships of P.Q. 17 were being sent to the bottom. Arriving off the north-east corner of Iceland after a quick and uneventful passage, the convoy of thirty-five ships divided, as had been planned. Sixteen ships bound for the United Kingdom turned south down Iceland's east coast led by Commodore Gale. The remaining nineteen, bound for Reykjavik, continued along the north coast led by Captain Hiss, master of the *American Robin*, to whom had been delegated the duty of acting-Commodore for this last leg of the voyage.

The thick weather which had accompanied them for most of the voyage now ceased to be a comforting shroud and became instead a cause for anxiety. With no astronomical observations possible for several days past, the convoy's position was only roughly known. Now it had to make its way through a narrow stretch of water between an allied minefield off the north-west corner of Iceland and the steep, iron-bound coast itself.

It was a wild evening with a north-easterly gale, low cloud almost down to the sea level and heavy rain reducing visibility to no more than a mile. It must be remembered that radar, if fitted at all, was still something of an unreliable toy at that time, particularly in the minesweepers, corvettes and trawlers which formed the escort of this portion of the convoy.

Around 7 p.m. the senior officer of the escort, Commander Cubison of the minesweeper *Niger*, requested the acting-Commodore to reform his ships from five columns into two for the narrow passage. Then, having obtained his estimated position from soundings, which indicated that the North Cape of Iceland had been passed, he ordered a south-westerly course. To confirm his position, Cubison now went ahead to try to make a sure landfall and obtain an accurate 'fix'. Feeling his way through the murk, he sighted nothing until 10 p.m. when a steep cliff loomed up out of the smother which Cubison thought must be the North Cape. The convoy had evidently altered course too soon, it seemed. Cubison signalled Captain Hiss to bring the convoy back to a westerly course again.

He had hardly done this when, in a temporary clearance of the weather, it was suddenly apparent that what had been taken for the North Cape was, in fact, a large iceberg. Hastily Cubison signalled his mistake to Hiss. The convoy must be altered back again at once or it would be in the minefield. But it was too late. At 10.40 the *Niger* herself blew up on a mine and sank with heavy loss of life, including that of Cubison. In the convoy, wild confusion broke out as ship after ship was shaken by heavy explosions. Other mines exploding nearby threw up sudden leaping columns of water like shell splashes. In the tumbling seas and low visibility, some of the masters and crews of the merchantmen, ignorant of the existence of the minefield, thought they were being shelled by a raider; others thought it was a U-boat attack. None knew what to do or which way to turn.

Four ships sank, leaving their crews struggling in the icy water or clinging to rafts and boats. The remainder by good fortune escaped. Escorts were quickly on the scene disregarding the danger from the mines to carry out rescue work. But it was a slow business in the gale that was blowing and many died in the bitter cold before they could be embarked, amongst them being a number of survivors from the *Edinburgh*. The trawlers *Lady Madeleine* and *St. Elstan* picked up sixty between them, but the Free French corvette *Roselys*, boldly and brilliantly handled by Lieutenant Bergeret, saved more than 170 during the six and a half hours that she remained amongst the mines, quartering to and fro in search of survivors to earn, as Vice-Admiral Braynard, the American task force commander at Argentia later told Bergeret, 'the respect and gratitude of the United States Navy'.

With these two convoys, P.Q. 17 and Q.P. 13, the story of the Arctic convoys passed its grimmest phase. Wild fights and tragic losses there were still to be in the smoky seas of the north, but from now onwards, success was to fall more and more on the side of the Allies. As in the Battle of the Atlantic, increasing numbers and better-equipped escorts and above all the advent of the escort carrier to give convoys their own air cover would soon turn the tide.

8

THE CONVOYS MUST GO ON

As that summer of 1942 wore on, Britain's fortunes at sea were showing little improvement over the disastrous events of the spring. Everywhere she was standing desperately on the defensive. In the Mediterranean she was fighting against heavy odds to keep Malta supplied and defended, with the central basin of that sea dominated by the enemy air power, and was suffering heavy losses. In the Indian Ocean, the Japanese, demonstrating the hitting power of a fast carrier squadron to the Royal Navy, which had invented the aircraft carrier but failed adequately to develop it, had driven the fleet back to East African bases with the loss of two cruisers, an aircraft carrier and several destroyers.

In the Pacific, Britain and her allies had been heavily defeated in the Battle of the Java Sea. In the Atlantic the U-boats were enjoying the 'Happy Times' off the coast of America, sinking more than a million tons of shipping a month. Finally in the Arctic the convoys to Russia were losing a high percentage of their numbers and two cruisers had been sunk during operations to defend them. The prospect was one of unrelieved gloom in every direction, it might seem.

But in fact the night of sorrow was at the black hour before the dawn. For nearly three years the superior forces of the enemy had been held off while in the background strength was gathering for the counter-attack. It was not only the quantity of British forces that was growing but the quality of the weapons was improving, the technical equipment with which to control them was being developed at a bewildering pace and the right type of ship was being built and sent to sea.

The nature of naval warfare had drastically changed with the advent of air power. Those who went to war in the destroyers of pre-war construction were soon bewailing the fact that they were almost defenceless against air attack. Their guns could not elevate sufficiently to engage any but the lowest-flying aircraft. The Ju. 87, the dreaded Stuka, and the Ju. 88 dive-bomber were their master – or should have been if the Luftwaffe pilots had been trained in the art of shipping attack.

In the Norwegian campaign British destroyers, hemmed-in in the land-locked fiords, had been condemned to a largely passive role under air attack, relying upon their agility in dodging rather than on the fire-power of their meagre equipment of machine-guns of doubtful reliability. Only the inability of German pilots, trained for land warfare, to hit moving ships, which requires a different technique, saved them. At Dunkirk, however, and later in the Mediterranean, losses had been heavy.

But now coming to join the fleet were the little 'Hunt' class destroyers mounting four 4-inch dual-purpose guns, some of the 'O' class similarly armed and, best of all, the 'M' class with six 4·7-inch guns in three twin turrets which could elevate to fifty-five degrees. Furthermore efficient close-range weapons such as the Oerlikon 20 millimetre and the Bofors 40 millimetre were being mounted. Merchant vessels, too, were getting these guns so that a convoy was becoming a very prickly hedgehog indeed for an airman to attack.

Besides the improved destroyers, cruisers re-armed as anti-aircraft ships and merchant ships converted for the same purpose were coming to sea as convoy escorts.

For all these reasons confidence in the face of air attack was increasing. But of course the great advance which had occurred since the early days of the war was the installation of radar. Most of the new fleet destroyers had by now a gunnery-control set and an air-warning set. Not very good either of them, but a great asset all the same.

What was still lacking was a surface warning set. This was the equipment which was to play the leading part in the defeat of the U-boats in the following year, for it destroyed their ability to approach undetected on the surface by night. In

1942, however, the Home Fleet destroyers had still to make do without it.

Not only did this weaken their defence against the U-boats but it withheld from them the ineffable boon of being able to keep station on the screen at night in safety without being able to see the convoy. Instead, when darkness came down, the screen had to be drawn in close enough for anxious eyes peering through binoculars to get a glimpse from time to time of the dim, black bulks of the merchant ships in the wing columns. This restricted their movements and absorbed much of the attention of officers of the watch, attention which could otherwise have been concentrated wholly on guarding against the stealthy approach of a U-boat.

In the long, black nights of winter, collision was a peril always threatening. Added to the threat of torpedo attack, it brought a grinding strain on captains and officers of the watch. The resultant fatigue, amounting sometimes to exhaustion, was an important factor in favour of the enemy, particularly towards the end of a voyage.

But in spite of the improved armament of the escorts now on the Kola Run, it was still utterly against the odds to think of running convoys through to Russia during the period of perpetual daylight when a combination of submarine, surface and air attack could be brought against them. After the disaster to P.Q. 17, the Navy would undoubtedly have preferred to postpone further convoys to Russia until late autumn. But political forces pressed inexorably. Plans were laid for P.Q. 18 in September. This time, however, its defence was to be in far greater strength and organized on quite different lines. Two principal innovations were involved.

The first was the inclusion in the escort of the auxiliary carrier *Avenger*, carrying twelve Hurricane fighters and three anti-submarine Swordfish. Here, at long last, was the master-touch which was to show the way to the defeat both of the U-boats and the bombers. Three years of tribulation on our convoy routes had been the result of failure to have escort carriers available earlier. Though experience in the First World War had clearly demonstrated that a combined surface and air escort was the answer to

U-boat attack on merchant convoys, the lesson had been forgotten.

The auxiliary carrier was to be a make-shift substitute – and a very successful one – for the properly designed carriers we lacked.

The second innovation planned for the defence of P.Q. 18 was the provision of a strong 'Fighting Destroyer Escort'. Realization of the German unwillingness to face a powerful torpedo threat on their few, and therefore highly valued, surface ships, led to the decision to rely upon such a defence in place of the mis-named 'battleship covering force', which had been shown to be incapable of providing cover east of Bear Island.

But the Navy was not to be left to deal with the problem on its own. The Royal Air Force was at last reaching a stage of expansion and development in which, in spite of its world-wide commitments, it could divert more of its strength to its Coastal Command. At the merger of the R.N.A.S. in the newly-formed R.A.F. in 1918, it had always been envisaged that the Navy would be able to rely upon the R.A.F. for its long-range air requirements. The test of war, however, had shown that the function of naval co-operation was inevitably neglected in favour of the more spectacular, independent tasks of Bomber and Fighter Commands.

Not until late in 1942 were the R.A.F. shore-based squadrons able to bring that support in the reconnaissance, anti-submarine and anti-shipping roles which the Navy was entitled to expect. So far as the Arctic convoys were concerned, the requirements, in default of Russian air support, were for air reconnaissance of enemy warships and anti-submarine patrols over the Russian end of the route and an airborne torpedo threat against enemy surface craft operating out of north Norwegian harbours. Both these requirements were now for a time to be met.

Much patient persuasion of our surly and unhelpful ally at last resulted in arrangements for a squadron of Catalina long-range reconnaissance flying-boats to work from Lake Lakhta near Archangel and Grasnaya in the Kola Inlet. In addition, two squadrons of Hampden torpedo-bombers were to be based in Vaenga on the shores of Kola Inlet. Early in September both these forces were established. The ground crews and stores for the

Hampdens were transported to Kola in August in the United States cruiser *Tuscaloosa*. An indication of the lack of Russian goodwill was given on this occasion when a medical unit, also conveyed in the *Tuscaloosa*, to bring comfort and aid to the wounded and sick from convoys and escorts being treated in the primitive Russian hospitals, was refused permission to land and had to return to England.

The Hampdens themselves had what was for those days a flight of considerable hazard to reach their base. Setting off, thirty-two strong, from Sumburgh in the Shetlands, their route took them over the mountainous territory of northern Norway which was in enemy hands. Their first destination was an airfield at Afrikanda, on Kandalaksha Bay, an inlet of the White Sea, as Vaenga was too close to the front lines.

With the scanty navigational aids of those days it was perhaps not surprising that some of the aircraft should have met misfortune. The losses, however, were severe. Six crashed in Norway or Sweden, three others lost their way and eventually made forced landings, out of fuel. Yet another, arriving over Kola during an air raid, was shot down. The final number which were made ready for operations was twenty-four.

The sailing date for P.Q. 18 was fixed for 2nd September from Loch Ewe on the west coast of Scotland where its assembly would not be so exposed to premature discovery as at Reykjavik. An opposite convoy, Q.P. 14, would sail, composed largely of survivors from P.Q. 17, on the 13th. But, before it could do so, a supply of ammunition and provisions had to be delivered to them. This was done by the destroyers *Marne, Martin, Middleton* and *Blankney*.

It was to lead to a minor success during their return journey. For meanwhile, the Germans, well knowing that an Arctic convoy operation was in the offing, were making preparations. Indeed, one of the features of the actions which were to develop around P.Q. 18 was the complete knowledge of all British plans with regard to it owing to the German ability at this time to read our cyphered messages.

The enemy therefore sent out U-boats, destroyers and an auxiliary minelayer to sow mines in likely areas off the coast of

Novaya Zemlya and at the entrance to the White Sea. Thus it was that the *Marne* and *Martin*, in company with the *Onslaught*, which had been one of *Tuscaloosa's* escort, fell in with the auxiliary minelayer *Ulm* on the 24th August, south-east of Bear Island, and sank her.

By the end of August, the opposing sides had completed their preparations. For both, the coming operation was to be a real trial of strength. The Germans had been greatly elated by their success against P.Q. 17, particularly their air force, which had claimed, quite erroneously, the credit for the scattering of that convoy. They were burning to repeat their triumph and had little need of the stringent orders being passed down from Hitler's headquarters for a great effort to be made. Their torpedo-bomber force had now reached a new total strength of ninety-two aircraft, while their bombers numbered more than 130. The knowledge that an aircraft carrier would be with the convoy added zest and provided a valuable target which could be singled out for attention.

A large force of U-boats was at sea also and the German naval command was avid to use some, at least, of their big ships to attack the homeward Q.P. 14.

On the British side, a force prepared to accept the challenge had been assembled. Besides the through escort under Commander A. B. Russell of two Western Approaches destroyers *Malcolm* and *Achates,* two anti-aircraft ships, *Ulster Queen* and *Alynbank,* four corvettes, three minesweepers, four trawlers and two submarines, there was to be the fighting escort of sixteen destroyers under the command of Rear-Admiral Bob Burnett, flying his flag in the new anti-aircraft cruiser *Scylla*, and the auxiliary aircraft carrier *Avenger* with her personal escort of two destroyers. In the background would be the covering force of cruisers, while off the Norwegian coast would be our submarines lying in ambush for the enemy surface ships.

The *Scylla*, commanded by Captain Ian Macintyre, was a splendid addition to the force. Originally designed as a 6-inch gun cruiser, she had been armed instead with eight 4·5-inch guns as an anti-aircraft ship. These smaller guns, mounted in the turrets intended for 6-inch guns, gave her an odd appearance and earned her the nickname amongst the sailors of 'The Toothless Terror'. She was to gain a very different reputation amongst the pilots of the Luftwaffe and was to become a familiar figure on the Kola Run.

It will be seen from the size of the escort, none of the destroyers of which could complete the voyage without re-fuelling at least once, that even with tankers waiting in Spitzbergen, careful organization was needed if the convoy was not to find itself bereft of part of its escort at the moment when the enemy chose to launch an attack. The through escort of anti-submarine vessels which must accompany the merchant ships to their destination had first call on the tankers with the convoy. To reduce their requirements, it was arranged that a local escort would bring the convoy as far as the Denmark Strait where Archie Russell's escort group would take over on 7th September.

Then, on the 9th, the *Scylla* and half the destroyer force, known as Force 'B', would join, while the other half, Force 'A' would have gone ahead to Spitzbergen so as to join, with tanks full, on the 13th. Half of Force 'B' would also re-fuel at Lowe Sound on 12th September. Thus, when the most hazardous part of the convoy's journey began on the 13th, the escort would be at full strength. On the other hand there would be a period between the 11th and the 13th when, in spite of this somewhat intricate arrangement, the escort would be at its weakest. It was felt, however, that this was acceptable as, during that time, only U-boat attack was likely. The whole scheme relied, of course, on reasonable weather permitting the convoy to keep up to schedule, never a very safe bet in the Arctic.

So it was all arranged. Force 'A' under Captain H. T. Armstrong of the *Onslow*, included the *Onslaught*, *Opportune* and *Offa* of the 17th Flotilla and *Ashanti*, *Eskimo*, *Somali* and *Tartar* of the 6th. Force 'B' came under Captain Ian Campbell, Captain (D) of the 3rd Flotilla in the *Milne* with the *Marne*, *Martin* and *Meteor* and *Faulknor*, *Intrepid*, *Impulse* and *Fury* of the 8th. The convoy sailed on time and was duly met, north of Iceland by the through escort.

* * *

At Scapa Flow, in the intervals of gunnery, torpedo and anti-submarine practices, there were planning and briefing conferences. As August drew to a close, a feeling of excited anticipation permeated these meetings and everyone concerned began to look on this summer convoy as a challenge. They knew that it was being run at the insistence of the politicians and against the considered judgement of the C.-in-C., but were not going to let that dismay them. The escort was to be stronger and more suitable for the task than any that had gone before. There were no illusions that the convoy could get through without losses if the enemy launched his aircraft against it *en masse*, but a quiet confidence was felt that he would be made to pay dearly for any successes – dearly enough to make him realize that he was making a bad bargain.

So the escorts lay, swinging to their buoys in Gutta Sound in perfect late summer weather. Soon they would be skirting the polar ice-pack and perhaps chipping the accumulation of ice off the upper decks and rigging, firing the guns from time to time to keep them from freezing solid. Between decks, moisture would run down the side plating and bulkheads in rivulets to make a damp misery of the mess-decks.

In time to come a process of 'Arcticization' would be applied to all ships on the Kola Run, steam or electrical heating being led to gun mountings, torpedo tubes and depth-charge stowages and special insulation given to the ships' side plating, but at this time there were none of these refinements.

The special warm clothing available for all hands was effective enough but was heavy to wear and very tiring and when, for day after day, incessant calls to the bridge or to action stations reduced the possibility of rest to a minimum, this became an important point. What was needed was clothing that was waterproof enough to prevent it becoming saturated and thus stiff with ice, supple enough to allow easy movement in action, yet not so heavy as to be over-tiring. It was a nice problem to strike the happy mean amongst these opposing requirements. With it all, it had to be possible to wear the standard inflatable lifebelt which was, in theory at least, *de rigueur*.

Everyone developed ideas of his own in this matter and

weird and wonderful were some of the ensembles which resulted.

*　　*　　*

The sailing date came round at length. As a signal from the yard-arm of the *Scylla* came fluttering down, the wire slip-ropes of the sixteen destroyers of Bob Burnett's force splashed into the water, sterns frothed as the ships were manoeuvred to head for the harbour entrance and then, one after the other, gathered way. They were off on the Kola Run – a few newcomers, including the *Scylla* herself, but for the most part hardened veterans.

9

THE NIGHTMARE LOCUSTS

They took the familiar route through the boom 'gate' hauled open by the boom defence vessel. From her deck the little handful of men waiting to set the winch clattering to heave the gate shut behind them waved a greeting. On the warships' bridges men waved in reply and wondered what it must be like to have to endure the monotony of their lives; while the boom defence men no doubt thought of other occasions when they had watched destroyers heading out into the teeth of a gale and thanked their stars they were snugly in harbour instead of enduring the lift, plunge and shudder or the crazy corkscrew rolling of a destroyer in heavy weather.

But today it was lovely summer, the gorse and the heather making vivid patches of colour in the sunshine. On the calm surface of the sea, the puffins and guillemots scuttered in ungainly flight from under the advancing bows; out in the Pentland Firth the wide swirls made by the racing tide were clear to see.

While the *Scylla* and *Avenger* skirted round the treeless shores of the Orkneys, the destroyers scattered in a brief flurry of curling bow waves and tumbling stern wash to take up their screening positions. Soon the course was north, leading up into the Arctic which many of the crews already knew so well; which they had learnt to hate for the vindictive savagery of its weather, yet which could sometimes enchant with its pure, unearthly beauty.

Early on the morning of 9th September the topmasts of the convoy hove over the horizon and soon the great mass of forty heavily-laden merchant ships was in view, formed in its broad-fronted rectangular formation with the little ships of the through escort weaving back and forth in their stations round it.

With the arrival of the Admiral to assume control, there was a bustling of escorts to their screening positions and signal lamps winked excitedly. Gradually the flurry died away as the last ship reached her station. The *Scylla* had taken up a position in the convoy leading the column next to the Commodore's, while the *Avenger* tagged on astern of a column whence she could readily turn into wind to fly her aircraft on and off.

So quiet settled down as the convoy drove on at a steady nine knots through blue summer skies. But it was an ominous quiet to those who saw the wireless signals warning that the enemy had located the convoy as early as the 8th when still north of Iceland. It could easily be surmised, as was indeed the fact, that a dozen or more U-boats were even then speeding on the surface across the empty Arctic Ocean to take up patrol positions where they could lie in wait.

But the *Avenger's* Swordfish planes were aloft, patrolling round the horizon and any approaching U-boat would be forced to submerge and would not find it easy to get within range of the convoy.

On the 10th, more evidence arrived of the enemy's intentions. The *Scheer, Hipper* and *Köln* had been sighted by all four of the British submarines patrolling the Norwegian coast, as they sped northward from Narvik to Altenfiord. It began to look as though the fighting destroyer escort was to be given a try-out. The torpedo tubes' crews went about their work of maintenance and preparation of torpedoes with an increased air of purpose as the news filtered down to them.

But there had been no further sign of enemy activity when, on the 11th, Bob Burnett signalled the 3rd Flotilla to join him as he swung away in the *Scylla* bound for Spitzbergen, to top up fuel tanks, leaving the other half of Force 'B' to fuel from the tankers in the convoy.

So far, the Kola Run had provided little excitement, which was as well, as it gave the large escort force time to settle down. In the fine, clear weather, the perpetual daylight and the crisp cold were showing their more attractive side. There had been no cause yet to curse the absence of any darkness during which there would be some respite from the threat of air attack; nor had it been weather to bring the freezing spray laying a skin of ice on to everything, the whirling snowstorms and the icy breath coming out of the north. The Arctic was proving thoroughly invigorating, in fact.

The fabulous coastline of Spitzbergen loomed up the next evening and soon the destroyers were following the *Scylla* through the narrow entrance of the Sound. The bleak, barren, snow-covered landscape, unearthly in its apparent total lack of life, yet had its own jewel-like beauty. The dark mass of a glacier on one side glistened where slabs of ice had broken off to drift away as icebergs. Everywhere snow and ice glittered like a myriad diamonds where the sunshine fell on it or lay, deep purple, in the shadows.

The brittle quiet of the frosty atmosphere was now broken by the soft hiss of bow waves, the low whine of turbines and the roar of forced-draught fans. The hoarse cries of the bosuns' mates piping the hands on deck to secure the ships alongside the oilers awaiting them sounded an uncouth disturbance of the immaculate peace.

Through the weird twilight of the Arctic night, the ships lay alongside the tankers while the heavy oil, heated to make it flow easily, gushed into their fuel tanks. By early morning they were full again. The last massive, brass-bound hose was disconnected and hauled back, to clang on the oiler's decks. The signal ran up to the yard-arms of the destroyers, 'Ready to Proceed'; was briefly acknowledged by the flagship and soon the little force was making its way to sea again, ready to meet the challenge which must lie ahead.

It was not long before it was seen that the enemy was indeed deploying his forces. First a black speck hovering above the horizon was identified as a Ju. 88 shadowing and, no doubt, following the force back to the convoy. It was lost to sight as a typical Arctic transformation of the weather brought low cloud and drifting, smoky patches of fog. Suddenly there was a growing roar of aero engines off the starboard bow of the *Milne*. Guns' crews swung their weapons in that direction and peered up at the overcast. The black shape of a Heinkel III came momentarily into sight as it passed across a gap in the cloud layer. The Oerlikons and pom-pom hammered briefly, spewing a stream of tracers skywards. Then it was over. The roar of engines faded away into the distance as the German pilot, undoubtedly rudely surprised, and, it was to be hoped, frightened, put a safe distance between himself and the destroyers.

That afternoon, 13th September, Force 'B' rejoined the convoy. Force 'A' had joined earlier so now the escort would be at full strength. And an impressive armada it made – twenty destroyers and eleven smaller warships ringing the central mass of the convoy in which three anti-aircraft ships and a carrier were waiting to show their teeth if any aircraft penetrated the screen.

But that other insidious enemy, the U-boat, had already clashed with the convoy in the absence of Force 'A'. During the 12th, the patrolling Swordfish had sighted the wolves closing in but had managed to keep most of them at bay. Some, however, had reached a position directly ahead of the convoy where they could wait, submerged, for their target to come to them. The first of these, *U88*, had lain patiently waiting, each observation through the periscope showing the ships looming larger, the roar in the hydrophones of their propellers getting louder. A little before 9 p.m. the U-boat captain took his last look before going deep to let the escort screen pass over him. It was to be his last sight of the world above for, at that moment, the questing sound beam of the asdic in the *Faulknor* pinged against his hull and sent back the echo which told of a submarine in its path. Soon the depth charges were sinking remorselessly down to erupt around the U-boat and send it to its lonely grave on the bottom of the Arctic Ocean.

It was first blood to the British. But *U88* was only one wolf of a pack which had gathered and which was snarling round the outskirts seeking a way in. Time and again during the 13th the *Avenger*'s Swordfish detected others on the surface, trying to gain bearing so as to come in to the attack from ahead. Each time they were forced to dive their speed became limited to a crawl and the convoy drew ahead. But persistence on the part of the U-boats brought its reward eventually when one at last got through the screen and torpedoed the *Stalingrad* and the *Oliver Elsworth* in the starboard wing column.

The ominous gap in the line of ships was there to see and to whet the escorts' vigilance as the destroyers dispersed to their screening stations. But they had barely reached them when the air battle for P.Q. 18 opened. Above the almost continuous layer of cloud, its base at about 4000 feet, could be heard the throbbing roar of a formation of Ju. 88s seeking gaps in the cloud through which they could dive to drop their bombs. On the *Avenger*'s flight deck, there was bustle and activity as Hurricanes were manned and their engines started with a cough and a roar. The carrier turned into wind and five fighters took the air and climbed away to seek the enemy above the clouds.

A confused mêlée ensued as the Hurricanes chased fleeting targets in and out of the clouds while the guns of the escorts banged away at briefly sighted bombers emerging momentarily to drop their bombs. Neither side achieved any results. Bombs burst harmlessly between the ships; no bombers were hit.

But, whether it was the enemy's intention or no, he had for the time being drawn the sting of the carrier. This was the first time that a carrier had been used to provide fighter defence for a convoy. The technique was yet to be developed. Commander Colthurst of the *Avenger*, galled by the immunity enjoyed by the shadowing aircraft droning impertinently round the horizon, had sent sections of two Hurricanes each away to deal with them, only to find that his obsolescent Mark I fighters, armed with light machine-guns, could make no impression on the armoured Blohm and Voss 138 reconnaissance aircraft or the Ju. 88s which worked in groups of as many as nine planes at times.

While some of his Hurricanes were thus employed, the bombing attack had developed and his remaining fighters were sent up. Thus, when the really dangerous attack developed thirty minutes later, as more than forty He. IIIs and Ju. 88s each carrying two torpedoes, swept in low from the starboard side of the convoy, not one fighter was available to meet it. Those which were still airborne had used up all their ammunition on the armoured Ju. 88 bombers. Now they did what they could by making feint attacks on the oncoming Heinkels, but to little effect.

Watchers in the ships gazed with undisguised awe on the approaching swarm, spread clear across the southern horizon in line abreast, thirty to forty feet above the water, looking, as Commodore Bodham-Whetham so vividly described them, 'like a huge flight of nightmare locusts'.

With a roar the guns of the escorts opened up a barrage to be followed, as the enemy came closer, by the mad clatter of Oerlikons and the staccato bark of pom-poms. The *Scylla*, at full speed, had drawn away ahead of the merchantmen to get a free arc of fire for her guns, her quick-firing 4·5-inch guns spitting viciously.

But it was all of little avail against the serried array of planes, their pilots, urged on by the memory of exhortations for a 'special effort' against this convoy, keeping perfect station, grimly determined to get through the screen and into the mass of merchant ships. A few, smashing headlong into a destroyer's shell or a stream of machine-gun fire, staggered, burst into flame and plunged into the sea. But the majority survived the barrage, zoomed over the escorts and pressed on for the convoy.

In the Commodore's flagship, a flag signal ran up the halliards and a plume of white steam appeared as her siren bellowed to draw attention to it. It was the signal for an emergency turn of forty-five degrees by each ship of the convoy simultaneously to starboard, that is to say in the direction from which the attack was coming. Such a turn would make it easier for any ship seeing a torpedo approaching from the starboard side to swing parallel to its track and so greatly reduce its chance of hitting.

But by now, bedlam reigned in and around the convoy as the guns of every ship came into action. The masters of the ships of the two starboard columns, attention riveted on the oncoming aircraft even now dipping down to loose their torpedoes, saw nothing of the Commodore's signal, or, if they did, were too stupefied to take any action. Like oxen to the slaughter, they ploughed straight ahead as the great swarm of torpedoes sped straight for their vitals.

Of the seven ships remaining in the two starboard columns, six were hit, one vanishing in a terrifying detonation. In the middle of the convoy, also, torpedoes found their mark in two more ships. The convoy steamed on, eight ships fewer. The smaller escorts and the rescue ships were already picking up survivors while the enemy were still attacking. Gradually the firing died away. The 'nightmare locusts' could be seen growing smaller and smaller as they retreated towards the southern horizon.

The torpedo attack had been a startling and woeful experience. Though there had been little chance from the escorts on the screen to see much of what was going on in the convoy while the wild mêlée continued and the ships lurched and trembled at the shock and recoil of the guns coughing out their barrage and the pom-poms and Oerlikons blazed away as targets came fleetingly within range, the eight new gaps in the ranks were now plain to see. Even the thought-deadening hammer of the guns had been unable to conceal from anyone the awful fate of the exploding merchantman.

But there was no time to ponder on it just yet for more torpedo-bombers had come in sight, three approaching from ahead and six from astern. However, this was not of the same calibre at all as the earlier attack and, as the guns roared into action, the pilots made haste to drop their torpedoes at long range and get away, though not before two of them had been shot down. The torpedoes were of no danger to the convoy, but for a time the water round the ships screening ahead was alive with tracks, which were only narrowly avoided by the *Scylla* and some of the destroyers.

At last quiet settled down again and stock could be taken. There was no doubt that the enemy had scored a notable success with his mass attack. At a cost of five aircraft, he had eliminated nearly a quarter of the convoy. It was a rate of exchange which simply could not go on. The convoy had six more days to go before it could reach harbour. Furthermore, ammunition had been used up at a tremendous rate during the attack. In the 'M' class destroyers, for instance, from each of the three twin turrets, 4·7-inch shells could be fired at the rate of between twelve and fifteen rounds per minute. Thus, in barrage fire, when the rate of fire was not slowed down through the need to lay the guns accurately on to a target, ammunition was being used up at about a ton a minute. It would not last long at that rate and Captain

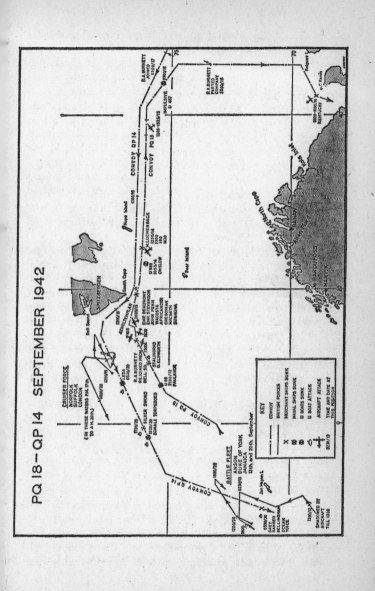

PQ 18 – QP 14   SEPTEMBER 1942

Campbell gave orders to his ships to limit the duration of barrages.

But, in fact, that first attack on 13th September marked the high water of enemy air effort against the Arctic convoys. Never again would they get together such a number of torpedo-planes for a massed assault. At the same time, some lessons learnt by the defence were being studied. In the *Avenger*, the disadvantage at which she had been caught owing to the premature launching of her very limited force of fighters was bemoaned and vows made not to be caught that way again. Instead of launching the Hurricanes piecemeal against small and unimportant attacks, they would be held on deck until the enemy was committed to his mass torpedo-bomber assault and then they would be operated in a continuous cycle so that some sections were always airborne while others were being re-armed and re-fuelled.

In the anti-aircraft ship, *Ulster Queen*, too, Captain Adam had fretted at the orders which kept his handy little ship tied to a station in the convoy where his guns could not be brought into action against approaching low-flying aircraft. Admiral Burnett's orders had been framed with the prospect of high-level bombing in view when, no doubt, the *Ulster Queen* would perform better as a steady gun platform in the middle of the convoy. But after the experience of the 13th Adam decided that he would take advantage of his ship's good manoeuvring powers and move out of the convoy to bring his guns to bear if a further torpedo attack impended.

So, in the various escorts the situation was examined and plans laid to beat off the enemy's next effort. But thoughts turned from time to time to the crews of the merchantmen. Everyone wondered how they were taking the ceaseless suspense and foreboding. Knowing little of the tactical or strategical situation or the relative strength of the opposing forces, unable to do anything to defend themselves, but forced to stand and wait for whatever fate might be in store for them – an instant launch into eternity as had happened to the crew of the ship which had blown up, or a hasty leap from their sinking ship into icy Arctic seas – it must have been an experience of long-drawn terror for them. Many, indeed, collapsed and lay helpless in extremities of fear; but others displayed qualities of cool courage and heroism that have rarely been equalled.

All of them must have felt what Rear-Admiral Bodham-Whetham described later to Bob Burnett as 'a funny feeling to realize one is sitting on top of 2000 tons of T.N.T., but we nearly all carry between that and 4000 tons. I don't think the bigger amount would make more than some tiny fraction of a second's difference to the time one entered the next world.' As far back as May, Admiral Bonham-Carter had said, 'It is beginning to be too much to ask of the merchant seamen.' P.Q. 17 and P.Q. 18 showed how right he had been.

Survivors from the sunken ships swarmed in embarrassing numbers in the minesweepers which had joined in the rescue work. In the lull which lasted through the dog watches, they were taken one by one alongside the *Scylla* which had more space to accommodate the unfortunates.

Even in the escorts it was with no light-hearted insouciance that the prospect of the next few days was faced; but at least they were free to manoeuvre clear from the path of torpedoes if they could see them in time; they could hit back hard, too, and while doing so there was no time for anyone to be frightened. It was sheer fatigue that weighed most heavily on the warships' crews, with no moment throughout the twenty-four when vigilance could be relaxed against the double menace of the U-boat and the bomber.

At 8.30 that evening, the 13th, came another effort by some dozen torpedo-carrying Heinkels. Attacking in small numbers, they failed to penetrate to the convoy, however, and dropped their torpedoes ineffectively at long range. For the rest of the night, U-boat alarms were incessant. Bearings obtained by ships fitted with radio direction finders betrayed the fact that at least five of the sinister craft were hovering around. Asdic operators were keyed up to the highest pitch of alertness.

But in spite of this, at 3.30 in the morning of the 14th, a torpedo struck home in the *Atheltemplar*, one of the tankers on whom the escorts were relying for fuel. The blow was not a mortal one, but with other U-boats in the vicinity, there was nothing for it but for an escort to take off her crew and sink her.

Another fine ship gone! With so large an escort, it was galling that U-boats should be able to get through the screen; but it was known that the water conditions in the Arctic, especially in the summer, reduced the efficiency of the asdic and gave the submarine a big advantage.

As the sun reappeared from just below the horizon that morning, Bob Burnett could not look back with much satisfaction on the results of the first day of the battle for P.Q. 18. If the Germans could keep up the same weight of attack, prospects for the future did not seem bright. But the various elements of his force, many of them new to this form of warfare, had absorbed the lessons of the previous day and were ready for the second round. A dogged defence on the one side and a failure on the other to follow up the first assault with the same vigour as before was now to turn the tide of fortune.

10

A FIVE-DAY BATTLE

The first to fall a victim to the increasing efficiency of P.Q. 18's combined air and surface escort was one of Doenitz's U-boats – U589. Surfacing safely out of sight of the convoy, as her captain thought, she was sighted by one of the *Avenger*'s Swordfish soon after 9.30 on the morning of the 14th and forced to dive.

Reporting the position to the flagship, the pilot marked it with a smoke float and waited near it for the destroyer he felt sure would be sent out to co-operate. And, indeed, the Admiral had at once despatched the *Onslow*, whose captain, 'Beaky' Armstrong, was an old hand at submarine hunting, with an experienced anti-submarine team under him.

But even at thirty knots it would be nearly an hour before she could be on the scene. While the 'Stringbag' waited impatiently, German eyes from the cockpit of a reconnaissance plane fell on the slowly circling biplane. The much faster Ju. 88 came swooping down. Almost defenceless against its much more powerful opponent, the Swordfish turned to run for the shelter of the convoy's protection, using its ability to turn in tight circles and to fly at a slow speed, impossible to the high-performance monoplane, to evade its attacks.

It escaped unharmed, but the U-boat captain, searching the sky with his periscope, saw that he was again free to surface to continue the charging of his batteries and to keep touch with the convoy. Thus, when the *Onslow* came dashing out, Armstrong saw the low silhouette against the horizon and could mark the U-boat's position on his plot. So when the submarine dived again at a range of six miles, it was a fairly limited sea area that had to be searched by the destroyer's asdic.

Even so, asdic search was a slow process. A cast in the wrong direction could give the submarine time to get well away, every minute undetected greatly improving its chances of escape. But luck and skill were now combining on P.Q. 18's behalf. From the long ping-g-g . . . of the *Onslow*'s asdic suddenly came back the sharp pip of an echo and the hunt was on. For three hours, as the U-boat twisted and turned, accelerated and stopped, plunged deeper and deeper to evade the deadly patterns of depth charges, the asdic team held contact. At length, after many accurate attacks, the answering echo faded and died.

Not daring to hope that this spelt success at last, 'Beaky' cast this way and that to pick it up again should the U-boat have, in fact, managed to sneak away. But then, returning to the scene of his last attack, Armstrong came upon the evidence he needed. In the midst of a widening pool of oil on the surface, great bubbles were bursting and wooden debris was floating. *U 589* would haunt the convoy routes no more!

But, while the hunt was still in progress, P.Q. 18 had been demonstrating the new ability to defend itself which it had gained from the experience of the previous day. At the warning of a strong formation of more than twenty torpedo-bombers approaching, besides the familiar sight of the *Scylla* streaking out ahead to gain a free arc of fire for her guns, the convoy saw the *Avenger* disengaging and manoeuvring inside the screen, with the *Ulster Queen* in support. Six Hurricanes were all ready ranged on deck, their propellers turning.

As the enemy aircraft in two groups neared the outer screen, the destroyer barrage opened up. One group chose the screen and *Scylla* as targets, but they soon regretted it. As the leaders met the barrage they smashed headlong into the sea. The remainder hastily dropped their torpedoes at long range and swerved away.

The larger group had evidently had orders to concentrate on the carrier, but the *Avenger*, attended by her two destroyers and the *Ulster Queen*, sent her brood of fighters streaming into the air while her escorts blazed away with every gun they had. The Heinkels made a desperate effort to get her, chasing persistently after her as she circled the convoy. No less than seventeen torpedoes were launched at the *Avenger*; but, with Hurricanes tearing into them from behind and a seemingly impenetrable barrier of shell bursts and tracers ahead, the pilots' aim was understandably poor and *Avenger* avoided them all. When the enemy at last drew off they left eleven of their number destroyed and not a single ship hit.

A feeling of immense exhilaration spread through the escorts at this success. Bob Burnett called it 'a most gratifying action'. Commander Colthurst signalled light-heartedly to claim the 'honour of being the sole object of the attack'.

But there was little time for self-congratulations. There had been barely time to clear away the litter of cartridge cases around the guns and to pass a hurried action of soup and sandwiches to the men at their quarters when the next alarm came crackling over the radio telephone. Bombers, coming in high above the overcast, had appeared on the radar screens and soon the throbbing drone of them could be heard.

Avenger was not going to be lured into sending her fighters after them – indeed they were still being hastily re-fuelled and re-armed. So it was left to the guns to engage the Ju. 88s which came momentarily out of the clouds, one by one, over the next hour to drop their bombs and climb back into safety. It was nerve-racking to have to wait passively under the continuous rumble of aircraft, listening for the rising change of note that heralded one of them going into a dive, while the gunners tried to forecast where it would appear and everyone wondered if his ship was to be the selected target.

Fortunately, it was not a very effective form of attack and, though many ships, including the *Avenger*, had narrow escapes, none were hit and one aircraft was shot down. But as the Ju. 88s expended their last bomb, Colthurst's wisdom in holding on to his fighters was seen. Another swarm of more than twenty-five torpedo-bombers came swooping in.

Once again they made the carrier their principal target as she manoeuvred on the starboard quarter of the convoy. Ten Hurricanes had been launched and soon the air was full of a mad whirl of aircraft, shell bursts and tracers as the Heinkels came boldly in to close range to drop their torpedoes and the *Avenger*'s fighters followed them, disregarding the storm of shell through which they were flying. Aircraft were plunging into the sea in every direction, including three of our Hurricanes, whose pilots were picked up safely, however. Miraculously the carrier avoided every torpedo aimed at her.

But in the midst of this fantastic circus of whirling wings, roaring engines and the thought-deadening bedlam of gunfire, there came a cataclysmic thunderclap as the *Mary Luckenbach* in the ill-fated starboard column blew up. As the last shattered morsels of debris from her fell back into the sea, nothing remained but a tremendous cloud of smoke reaching up and flattening itself against the overcast.

For a moment the gunfire died away as guns' crews contemplated in awe the frightful happening. Then it burst out again. But the fight was nearly over and the survivors of the enemy formation, leaving nine crashed behind them, were streaming for home.

The convoy's new-found confidence was temporarily shaken by the manner of the *Mary Luckenbach*'s passing and the thought of the appalling loss of life. But there was still cause for grim satisfaction at the outcome of this latest effort by the enemy. They were losing aircraft and highly-trained crews fast. At a cost of twenty-one of them they had succeeded in depleting the convoy of one more ship only.

However, to temper any false confidence there now came a reminder of that other threat to the safe passage of the convoy, the huge *Tirpitz* and her smaller but still powerful consorts lying in wait on the flank of the route to Russia. Reconnaissance of the Narvik area on this day, the 14th, had disclosed that the *Tirpitz* had left harbour and had not since been located.

She might be out, therefore, making for a rendezvous with *Scheer*, *Hipper* and *Köln* off the advanced base in Altenfiord to bring against the convoy that overwhelming force which was the constant pre-occupation of the Admiralty and the Commander-in-Chief. The bad luck which seemed to dog the Royal Air Force reconnaissance in the North at crucial moments now caused a hiatus in their scouting operations. As a stop-gap the squadron of Hampden torpedo-bombers was itself sent out to search and to attack if the enemy were found at sea.

As it turned out, the enemy surface ships had not left harbour and the Hampdens found nothing. But until they were re-located there were too many threats looming for any easy confidence amongst the escorts. Indeed, as the naval staff had pointed out before, if the German resources were boldly and skilfully handled they ought to be able to prevent any ships getting through to North Russia.

For the rest of the afternoon of 14th September, some Ju. 88s harried the convoy, dropping their bombs through holes in the cloud layer or occasionally making surprise shallow-dive attacks. But few would face the volume of fire which the strong escort could put up and none of their bombs did any damage. How quietly reassuring it sounds, writing of it thus so long afterwards. But at the time nerves were kept at full stretch for hour after hour in escort and merchant ship alike.

Any one of the attacks might be the exception to the rule and be boldly and skilfully carried through, sending a bomb crashing into a ship's hull in spite of all that the guns could throw at the aircraft. Eyes grew tired and sore from ceaseless search of the sky. Unable to relax, bodies became deadly weary. Food, hastily snatched at odd intervals, lay heavy in stomachs gripped by a sensation reluctantly acknowledged as fear. Running through it all, in the escorts, was the leitmotiv of the never-ceasing, twenty-four hours a day 'ping . . . ping . . .' of the asdic. The sub-conscious mind listened unceasingly for an echo to it. The slightest variation in it brought an immediate, anxious attention.

The closing down of night, or more accurately twilight, brought some relief as the enemy airmen seemed unwilling to venture on the long sea passage to the convoy then. But it was now that the U-boats liked to close to the attack, their periscopes less visible in the gloom. So, for the escort captain night brought little real rest. The little box-like sea cabin under the bridge was there with a bunk for him to rest in, but he was never out of hearing of the ping – nor did he want to be – and in the difficult water conditions common in the Arctic, repeated false alarms kept him continually dashing up and down, which in heavy cold-weather-clothing was very wearying.

So captains rarely left the bridge except to eat, wash or perform the natural functions. In most destroyers, there was fitted a stout wooden chair beside the binnacle, with an alternative position in the sheltered fore end of the bridge. In it they spent most of their time when attack threatened, dozing when things were quiet, instantly awake at the slightest change in the even tempo of the bridge routine.

No doubt, as they steadily ran more into debt to sleep, efficiency seeped gradually out of them, but at the time it was not apparent. It is, however, noticeable that in reports on Arctic convoy operations, comment was sometimes made that calamities had occurred towards the end of a long period of tension when the escorts were perhaps no longer at their best. But, short of neglecting their responsibilities in command, responsibilities which can never be shared, there was no remedy for the captains of ships.

The night of the 14th passed quietly. During the forenoon of the next day, too, some relaxation was possible for, with the convoy now well into the Barents Sea, 400 miles lay between it and the German Air Force base at Banak. Taking off at dawn, the enemy aircraft were not to be expected before mid-day.

Sure enough at 12.45, after radar warnings, there came the growl of aircraft engines above the clouds. With the overcast at 4000 feet, the enemy obviously feared to face the gunfire to press home their attacks with accuracy. In groups of three, they came briefly out of the cloud base to attack. Greeted by a great volume of fire, they lingered only long enough to take a browning shot at the convoy before retiring to safety again. Such methods relied largely upon luck to achieve anything and the luck had now turned against the Germans.

From the *Avenger*, sections of Hurricanes were sent off to harry the bombers and, for nearly three hours the enemy airmen were chivvied above the clouds by the fighters and shot at whenever they appeared below, doing which they lost three of their number.

Thoroughly disgruntled at this churlish reception, the enemy took to circling hopefully inside the clouds, waiting for the convoy to pass into a clear area to give them a chance. Appreciating this, Admiral Burnett was just considering diverting the convoy for a time to keep it under cloud when the German leader was heard ordering his flock to return to base and jettison bombs, being at the end of their fuel endurance.

It had not been a very high-spirited effort and one wonders what the German high command thought of it after their frenzied appeals for a 'special effort' against P.Q. 18!

Meanwhile the U-boats were doing no better. Never less than three were always in contact during all this time but none could bring themselves to face the very powerful screen.

The bombers were still playing hide-and-seek in the clouds above, when that other hazard, the enemy surface ships was brought to mind. From one of the wing escorts came a report of two columns of smoke on the southern horizon.

We could not know it at the time – the *Tirpitz* was still un-located, *Scheer, Hipper* and *Köln* were still poised for a sortie from Altenfiord – but there was, in fact, no question of the German surface forces coming out at that period. Hitler's infatuation with the idea that an invasion of Norway was planned by the Allies effectively tied the hands of the German naval command in the matter. On no account were any risks to be run which might imperil their availability to counter such a move by the Allies. With such instructions, it is not surprising that Admiral Raeder vetoed the plan of the German Command, North, to sail the three ships at Altenfiord. The temporary disappearance of *Tirpitz* was later found to be owing simply to her being engaged in exercises in the Vestfiord.

In any case, there now came the reassuring report from the *Opportune*, sent out to investigate, that the smoke was simply the exhaust, much magnified by mirage, from two U-boats on the surface, away beyond the horizon. They dived on sighting *Opportune*. There were no dividends to be had from hunting U-boats so far from the convoy, so they were left to their own devices – to stay where they were, harmless, or to engage the escort on its own terms in the vicinity of the convoy.

It may have been one of them which did the latter in the early hours of the next day. At 3 o'clock in the morning, the asdic operators in the *Impulsive*, in her screening position ahead of the convoy, gained a contact. There was an experienced and well-drilled team in the *Impulsive*. Her captain, Lieutenant-Commander E. G. Roper, had just time to make one quick attack before the advancing convoy ran over his target. He was then forced to wait, chafing impotently, until the lines of merchant ships had made their stately way past before he could return to the attack. But when the time came, there was no need for further depth charges. A growing circle of wreckage and oil told their tale. Later it was established that it was *U457* which had ventured once too often within range of a convoy escort.

The score was levelling up in the record of P.Q. 18. It was nearly further evened later that forenoon when *Opportune* and *Offa*, sighting another submarine on the surface, gained contact with it after it had dived and attacked it heavily. But they could not claim a kill.

That morning came the first sign that the most dangerous part of the convoy's voyage was nearing its end, when the first Catalina arrived from the squadron based in North Russia to take over the duties of anti-submarine patrol from the devoted, tireless Swordfish of the *Avenger*. The homeward Q.P. 14 would be passing soon, and Bob Burnett's force would have to transfer to it, to give it the same cover that P.Q. 18 had enjoyed. In theory, cover from Russian fighters would be available for P.Q. 18 from now on and, though experience had not bred any confidence that any such thing would be provided, priority of task for Burnett's squadron obviously lay with Q.P. 14 from this point.

So, during the 16th, in three separate groups so as not to make it too obvious to the enemy, *Scylla*, the destroyers, *Avenger*, the two fleet oilers, the *Alynbank* and the two submarines parted company. We will join them later, but for the moment let us follow the fortunes of P.Q. 18 to the end.

Early on the 17th came further signs which, like the dove from Noah's ark or the signs of land which restored Columbus' confidence, told of friendly territory not far ahead. For two Russian destroyers now joined, and it was known that they never ventured far from their own coasts! However, these, with their fine armament of four dual-purpose 5-inch guns each, and two more smaller Russian destroyers which arrived early on the 18th were a very welcome addition to an escort which looked alarmingly sparse to Archie Russell when the last of Burnett's force left.

The Russians were to have plenty of opportunity to show their skill – and indeed they did put up a splendid performance when put to it – for the German Air Force was being urged on by Reichsmarschall Goering, furious at the impending escape of so much of the convoy, to persist in their attacks right to the very entrance to Archangel harbour.

As the convoy passed Cape Kanin at the entrance to the White Sea early on the 18th, radar warnings came from the *Ulster Queen*, which had fortunately been retained as part of the escort, that aircraft were again gathering for the attack. With full daylight they arrived – twelve torpedo-bombers spread in line abreast and coming in low over the water from astern.

In the absence of the strong outer screen from which they had shrunk before, the airmen were able to get their torpedoes well into the convoy. But, running almost parallel to the ships' tracks, they were all avoided by individual alterations of course – all but one, which hit and damaged the *Kentucky*, which dropped astern immobilized. At the same time there arrived the Ju. 88 bombers. But they lacked the nerve of the torpedo-bomber pilots. Attacking intermittently through gaps in the clouds, they failed to score any hits until they decided to take the easy target of the stationary *Kentucky*, whose destruction they completed.

At this stage Archie Russell decided that the moment had come to release the Hurricane which throughout the voyage had sat on its catapult in the *Empire Morn*. Available for just one flight only, it was always most difficult to know when to throw the solitary trump card on the table. But now Flying Officer A. H. Barr, the Hurricane's pilot, made the most of his opportunity. Tearing into the enemy formation, he shot down one torpedo-bomber and then, by the bare threat of his empty guns, repeatedly drove off others. Finally, with just enough petrol remaining, he left to seek an airfield near Archangel, 240 miles away, which he succeeded in doing with just four gallons splashing in the bottom of his tank when he landed.

A second torpedo attack an hour later than the first failed to score any success whatsoever and three of the enemy fell to the guns of the escort – two to those of the *Ulster Queen*. It is impossible not to speculate on the astonishing lack of success of the German airmen against the Arctic convoys with the exception of rare occasions such as the first torpedo attack on P.Q. 18. At much the same period, in the Mediterranean, Italian and German airmen were playing havoc with the convoys being fought through to the relief of Malta under very heavy escort.

It is tempting to ascribe the difference to the employment of lower grade, less well-trained pilots in the Arctic theatre, but this does not, from German records appear to be so. In September there were no great climatic difficulties of maintenance or operation either. Yet even after the withdrawal of the carrier and its fighters and a huge reduction in the fire power of the escort force, egged on by a frantic Goering, the German airmen could account for but one merchantman in their repeated attacks.

One is forced to the conclusion that the long sea passage between target and base, with the prospect of a 'ditching' resulting from even minor damage during the attack, took the guts out of airmen of a land-trained air force. In the Mediterranean, a flight of fifty to 100 miles brought them to their objective; a warm sea waited for them if they were forced down. In the Arctic there were hundreds of miles of icy water and a poor chance of survival. It may be that here is the one crucial reason why the Arctic convoys got through against all that the enemy air force could bring against them.

We have seen how Hitler's famous 'intuition' was inhibiting any surface attack. As for the U-boats, it was in the Arctic that the solution to the problem of their defeat was first demonstrated in the employment of a combined sea and air escort throughout the convoy's voyage.

But to follow P.Q. 18 to the end, the attacks on 18th September might have been expected to have been the end of their ordeal, for on the next morning the convoy arrived off the Dvina Bar. But the long, weary voyage, already seventeen days in length, with six of them under incessant enemy attack, was to be cruelly prolonged. A gale descended to hold the ships at sea; and while they tried to find shelter from the elements, Ju. 88s made yet another effort to retrieve their lost reputation. But even with the convoy so handicapped, the enemy utterly failed to achieve any success.

The gale, indeed, was more to be feared than the foe, for three merchantmen of the convoy were stranded for a time. Even then, with targets stationary, though guarded by the faithful *Ulster Queen*, two bombers which attacked during the afternoon of the 21st failed to achieve a hit.

So ends the story of P.Q. 18. At a heavy cost, techniques had been learnt which would have their application elsewhere in the war. Q.P. 14, to which we must now return, was to point another lesson, again, unfortunately, at a grievous cost.

11

THE U-BOATS SCORE

The company which formed the convoy Q.P. 14 was one composed mostly of the much-tried survivors of P.Q. 17. For two weary months they had suffered the monotony of life at Archangel where amenities were almost non-existent, the flat, barren countryside making a backdrop of unutterable dreariness to the scene. Now at last, under the leadership again of Commodore Dowding, his flag in the *Ocean Voice*, they were heading thankfully for home. Admiral Burnett's force joined it on 17th September.

The names of the ships of the close escort as well as those of the convoy will be familiar to those who have read the misadventures of P.Q. 17. In command of it was Captain Crombie in the minesweeper *Bramble*. Under him were the two anti-aircraft ships *Palomares* and *Pozarica*, the destroyers *Blankney* and *Middleton*, corvettes *Lotus, Poppy, Dian'ella* and *La Malouine*, the minesweepers *Leda* and *Seagull* and those veterans of the Kola Run, the trawlers *Lord Middleton, Lord Austin, Ayrshire* and *Northern Gem*.

With the convoy of fifteen ships were the rescue ships *Zamalek* and *Rathlin*. Sailing, rather ominously to the superstitious, on 13th September, they had made good progress for the first four days and, though the enemy undoubtedly knew their position, they had been left alone, partly owing to welcome thick weather and partly because the Luftwaffe was concentrating all its effort on P.Q. 18.

We have seen how the German naval command's intention to

send *Scheer*, *Hipper* and *Köln* to attack Q.P. 14 had been hamstrung through Hitler's misunderstanding of the strategical situation. It is profitless but nevertheless fascinating to speculate what might have happened if the German Navy had been given a free hand. It is difficult to see how disaster to the convoy could have been avoided, though perhaps the R.A.F. squadron of Hampden torpedo-bombers might have made the enemy pay heavily for any successes.

However, the fact remained that when Burnett's force joined the convoy far up in the Barents Sea, its passage had been entirely peaceful. Now, in intermittent fog and snow it was heading westwards to pass close south of Spitzbergen. Though the enemy shadowing aircraft had lost touch in these conditions, they had seen enough to direct U-boats to the scene, and by the 18th reports by escorting Catalinas and Swordfish revealed that some were in touch and prowling round.

It was bitterly cold far up into the Arctic. The convoy was not far from the ice barrier as the appearance of that curious phenomenon 'ice-blink' told, a dazzling, eye-hurting light caused by the reflection off the ice. In sight passed what must be one of the loneliest, dreariest islands in the world, named for some unexplained reason Hope Island. From time to time the motionless, dead, yet menacing bulk of great icebergs loomed by, seeming but to stress the lifeless desolation of the Arctic.

While the sea remained calm, the destroyers went in turn alongside the two tankers to replenish their fuel tanks; but long before their thirst was satisfied the available stocks in the oilers were exhausted. So the Admiral sent away two destroyers to fetch one of the tankers lying in Lowe Sound to join him, which she did on the following evening.

By the morning of the 19th, the South Cape of Spitzbergen was abeam and now the Admiral put into execution a plan designed partly to keep as great a distance as possible between the convoy and the German air bases and partly to try to shake off the trailing U-boats. Sending two Swordfish up to ensure that no U-boats were on the surface to watch and a screen of destroyers and minesweepers out to the southward to keep the submarines down, he altered the convoy's course north-west up the coast of

Spitzbergen, intending to keep on that course for the rest of the day before turning again south-westward for home.

Though U-boats were sighted by the Swordfish and duly forced to dive, Bob Burnett's plan came to naught so far as deceiving the enemy went, for at the very moment of altering course a shadowing aircraft arrived to note and report it. However, whether the Admiral's stratagem was the reason or not, it was a fact that Q.P. 14 was not attacked from the air at all during its passage. Only U-boats were to harry it.

A considerable pack of these had gathered round by the evening of the 19th, and for the next three days they were handled with skill and unusual boldness which brought them a rich reward. It began with the sinking of the minesweeper *Leda*, torpedoed in her screening position astern of the convoy in the last hour before dawn of the next day. Eighty-six of her crew were rescued but the submarine responsible, *U435*, escaped.

In spite of repeated sightings and persistent hunting and attacks by aircraft and destroyers, none of the wolf pack was accounted for, though one had a narrow escape when one of the two British submarines sent to patrol astern of the convoy sighted *U408*. In and out of snow squalls, *P614* stalked its surfaced and unsuspecting quarry. But the fleeting glimpses of it through the periscope were too infrequent to allow an accurate attack. The torpedoes went wide, the startled enemy hurriedly diving when he saw their tracks in the calm sea.

On the evening of that day Q.P. 14's very strong screen suffered the humiliation of seeing one of the convoy torpedoed. A U-boat had got through in spite of all their vigilance. But at that time it was not altogether appreciated to what an extent water conditions in the Arctic often stultified the use of the asdic, the only means available of detecting a submerged submarine.

Particularly in the summer, varying layers of temperature played queer tricks with a sound beam and might deflect it above or below its target so that a submarine could pass closely by, undetected. It was fortunate that the enemy did not understand this either, so that it was only the occasional U-boat, more boldly handled than usual, which reaped the benefit without realizing why.

The best defence for a convoy under these conditions was provided by continuous air patrols preventing U-boats from surfacing to run at high speed to positions ahead of the convoy whence they could make their approach submerged. This the *Avenger*'s three Swordfish had been doing with considerable success on behalf of P.Q. 18 as well as Q.P. 14. But now these aircraft and their crews were showing signs of strain after so many days of almost continuous operation. Commander Colthurst decided they must be given overhaul and rest.

Learning of this, the Admiral, appreciating that air attack was by now most unlikely, decided to detach both the *Scylla* and the *Avenger* to return to base. He himself would shift his flag to the *Milne*. Accordingly shortly before dusk on the 20th, the *Milne* was taken alongside the *Scylla* and as the two ships steamed along together at fourteen knots Bob Burnett, enthroned on a modern, steel version of a bosun's chair, was hoisted by the cruiser's boat-crane and delivered to the deck of the *Milne*. He was received, in spite of this novel form of embarkation, with due formality and twittering of bosuns' pipes. At the masthead his Rear-Admiral's flag was broken out.

The *Scylla* was undoubtedly best away out of it. To keep her tied to the slow-moving convoy, a constant encouragement to any U-boat commander anxious to earn his Knight's Cross, would certainly have been wrong now that the danger of air attack was past. But the absence of *Avenger*'s splendid old 'String-bags' circling on the horizon to keep the U-boats down was a different matter. The Admiral had asked for and confidently expected air escort to be provided by Coastal Command of the Royal Air Force; so that when Commander Colthurst reported that his three hard-worked Swordfish and their pilots had reached the end of their endurance and must be given refit and rest, the valuable carrier was but a hostage to fortune if she remained in the convoy. It seemed as well to send her off also.

But Coastal Command was still far from being able to meet all the requirements of the war at sea. A convoy battle in the North Atlantic now absorbed all its resources, leaving nothing for Q.P. 14. Though one Catalina did arrive on the 21st, it was early damaged in an attack on a submarine and forced to alight near the convoy which was left from then on with no air escort. It was to cost it dearly.

Already at the time of the *Avenger*'s departure the absence of air patrols during the day had allowed a U-boat to reach ahead of the convoy and lie in wait. Hardly had the carrier gone than calamity struck. The large 'Tribal' class destroyer, *Somali*, port wing ship of the convoy screen, was torpedoed. Brought to a standstill, she showed no signs of sinking and was taken in tow by Richard Onslow's ship *Ashanti*. Her subsequent adventures will be given in some detail later as being a tale of gallant endeavour besides bringing home from the personal experiences of her captain something of what it was like to be cast into the grasp of the Arctic sea, even at that time of the year a circumstance likely to be quickly fatal.

Bob Burnett decided that *Somali* was worth a big effort to get home and sent *Eskimo, Intrepid* and *Opportune* as well as the trawler *Lord Middleton* to escort her and the *Ashanti*. It was a big bite out of the convoy's available escort but it still left twelve destroyers and nine smaller craft which should have been ample to guard fifteen ships. When the Catalina arrived the next day it seemed to make the convoy doubly safe; but alas this was the aircraft which crashed after a few hours and was the only one to arrive.

The absence of the *Avenger*'s Swordfish was now to be sorely felt. With asdics almost useless in a sea which had been calm for a period unusual in those latitudes and cooled on the surface by freezing polar air and the melting of innumerable icebergs there was every chance of a U-boat which had got ahead of the convoy penetrating the screen submerged and undetected. With no aircraft there was no way of preventing them from running at high speed on the surface beyond the horizon to gain such a position.

When the *Milne*, returning from taking the Admiral to see how *Somali* and *Ashanti* were getting on, sighted a U-boat which dived when only four miles away, her asdic team failed to get even a breath of a contact. *Bramble* and *Worcester* had a similar experience with another one.

Had the U-boat commanders appreciated the fact, they could have done what they liked. But for a day and a night the convoy steamed on unmolested and at daylight on the 22nd Burnett decided that there was no further need for so senior an officer with the convoy. Turning over command of the escort to Captain Scott-Moncrieff in the *Faulknor*, he left in the *Milne* for Seidisfiord in Iceland to transfer back to the *Scylla*.

One less destroyer in the still large escort can have been of little significance. But an hour after *Milne* had left, a submarine, slipping submerged between escorts, got amongst the convoy. Within five minutes of each other, *Ocean Voice, Bellingham,* and the fleet tanker *Grey Ranger* had been sunk. Poor Commodore Dowding was once again adrift in the Arctic Ocean. Fortunately it was not for long as the rescue ships were quickly on the scene, scooping up the crews of the torpedoed ships; but one's heart must go out to the luckless Commodore.

Fortunately this U-boat was the only one to try breaking through the screen and by the next day, with Iceland and its guardian minefields drawing near, the submarines abandoned their efforts and withdrew.

Now came a northerly gale with blinding snowstorms to harry the convoy as it shaped course to pass down between Iceland's rock-bound east coast and the minefield to seaward of it. It was tough on the acting-Commodore, Captain Walker of the *Ocean Freedom*, who was responsible for the navigation of the gathering of unwieldy merchantmen in ballast, riding high out of the water and often barely manageable in such conditions.

It was hard on the escorts too. They had been by now fifteen days at sea under attack or threat of imminent attack and the commanding officers were near the end of their tether when at last, two days later, the local escort arrived to relieve them off Cape Wrath. The convoy gladly headed for the shelter of the Minches and Loch Ewe. The destroyers turned for the meagre comforts of Scapa Flow.

* * *

Meanwhile, far to the north, the drama of the damaged *Somali* had been played out. It will be remembered that we had left her in tow of the *Ashanti* somewhere near Jan Mayen Island.

The torpedoing of the *Somali* was a typical example of the kind of sudden calamity which threatened night and day, the thought of which kept Commanding Officers restlessly haunting the bridge, tensed and ready for emergency. Lieutenant-Commander Colin Maud, commanding *Somali*, was actually a 'stand-in' for her regular captain who had fallen ill. His own ship, the *Icarus*, which he had commanded since the beginning of the war, had become due for a refit. Never happy away from destroyers, Maud had volunteered for *Somali*, a display of zeal he was to regret!

On that evening of 20th September, he had been all day on the alert. The loss of the *Leda* and the *Silver Sword* had sounded the warning that U-boats were getting in undetected. Conditions for the asdic were obviously poor but operators had been adjured to pay special attention to listening for the sound of approaching torpedoes which might well be the only warning of a U-boat's presence.

The B.B.C. news was about to come on the air and Colin Maud, with a last search of the surface of the leaden sea through his binoculars, told the Officer of the Watch where he was going and turned stiffly to clatter awkwardly down the ladder to his sea cabin, his heavy winter clothing embarrassing him.

The headlines of the news had hardly finished when that inexplicable malaise which often warns the experienced destroyer captain in war that all is not well sent Maud on his way back to the bridge. As he stepped out from the ladder canopy, there was a hoarse, excited shout from the asdic operator, 'Torpedo approaching port side!'

A single leap took Maud to the voice pipe to the wheel house. Automatic reflex action drew the shout from him, 'Full ahead. Hard-a-port!', to swing the ship parallel to the track of the racing torpedo. But it was too late. With a concussion which shook the ship, causing her to leap in the water and whip madly fore and aft, the torpedo hit square in the engine room.

As the sea rushed in, the ship came to a shuddering stop, heeled over and lay with a heavy list, the roar of escaping steam drowning all other sounds. But *Somali* was a credit to her builders. With the engine room, one boiler-room and the gearing compartment flooded, she yet showed no inclination to sink. The well-trained ship's company was quickly at work, shoring up bulkheads and plugging leaks. On the forecastle preparations went ahead for being taken in tow; for as soon as it was clear that *Somali* would remain afloat, Richard Onslow had decided that he 'was damned if he would let her go without an effort'.

By great good fortune casualties had been few – five killed and four wounded. Now surplus hands not required to work the ship in her crippled condition were taken off by the trawler *Lord Middleton* to the number of about sixty. While the tow was being passed, the heavy steel hawser, 4 inches in circumference being hauled aboard the *Ashanti* and secured, chain cable from *Somali* backing it at its other end, *Eskimo, Intrepid* and *Opportune* circled the two ships to discourage the U-boat from completing its work.

At last all was ready. *Ashanti* went gingerly ahead. The tow rope rose, dripping from the water and was suddenly bar taut and trembling with the strain. The *Somali*, lying deep and with a heavy list, gave a lurch. Sluggishly she moved forward and the rope slackened for a moment to come again taut and pluck the unwilling ship on to a faster pace. At last, after several of these anxious moments, each one bringing a threat of a parted hawser, the two ships were slipping along, one behind the other at something over five knots in the mercifully calm sea.

But *Somali* was an awkward tow with hundreds of tons of flood water weighing her down. The flooding spread during the night to further compartments and by the morning she was yawing clumsily from side to side, bringing fears of a parted tow. But then engineers who had been frantically working on it, got a diesel dynamo to cough into life, providing power to work an electric submersible pump. This and reduction of top weight by transferring a quantity of stores and heavy gear to the *Lord Middleton* made a great improvement. So much so that it was decided to strip the *Somali* further. *Ashanti*'s motor cutter was lowered and in the calm conditions still prevailing, took working parties to *Somali* to assist.

Everything movable on the upper deck was ruthlessly torn from its stowage and thrown overboard, an operation which gave the sailors a curiously hilarious pleasure and kept their minds off the insecurity of their position which was clearly indicated by the ominous noises coming from the damaged section amidships from time to time.

When the diesel engine seized up the following evening, Richard Onslow called for all ships to contribute their quota of electric cable which joined together just reached from *Ashanti* to *Somali*. A devoted party of men under Lieutenant Lewin of the *Ashanti*, working for four hours in a temperature well below freezing point with arms continuously immersed in the icy water, succeeded in hitching this cable along the tow rope and bringing power once again to the *Somali*'s electric pumps.

So for the next two days, while the sea lay quiet, the two ships made slow but steady progress westwards towards Iceland. A shortage of fuel in *Ashanti* was almost miraculously taken care of by the appearance of the tanker from Spitzbergen on her way back to Scapa. Still towing *Somali*, Onslow manoeuvred his ship with consummate skill astern of the *Blue Ranger* and was soon refilling his nearly empty tanks.

As time dragged by and the sea maintained its unnatural calm, it really began to look as though *Somali* might reach the safety of harbour. But then on the third evening there came the uneasy swell, the vicious little gusts, familiar forerunners of the long-anticipated Atlantic gale. On the *Somali*'s bridge, Maud anxiously watched the tow rope whipping out of the water and throwing off a shower of spray as it pulled momentarily taut, then dipping to the water again as the *Somali* sluggishly answered the sudden haul. Each time it came up and quivered with the strain it seemed as though it might be the last.

As the swell met the dead weight of the hull, lifted the bow and ran on under the ship towards the stern, alarming creaks and snarls came from the tortured metal amidships where only the upper deck and the keel were holding the bow and stern together on the port side. The crippled ship could not stand much of such motion without breaking her back. But the falling barometer, the lowering sky with its scudding black clouds told an unmistakable story.

Looking over the side at the already surging water, Maud remembered that it was not much above freezing point and shuddered at the thought of launching himself into it if the ship sank. There was nothing more he could do for the ship or her company. Though the boats had been destroyed in the explosion, there were rafts enough for the eighty hands remaining on board as well as 'flotanets', rope nets with cork floats attached to which a large number of men could cling and be kept afloat.

Over the telephone line which, bent on to the tow rope, ran between the ships, Onslow's voice had come asking if he was all right. 'All right for the moment,' he had replied, 'but if the weather gets up any more, it's anyone's guess what will happen,' he had added ruefully. And steadily the wind was rising, the sea increasing. The poor *Somali* was labouring and protesting.

As the night wore on, Maud, who had been taking his turn of watches with the two officers he had retained on board, could no longer leave the bridge. The end might come at any time, he felt. All hands were warned to stay on the upper deck, getting what shelter they could.

Peering over the front of the bridge, Maud suffered the endlessly repeated crisis as the menacing white smother of the breaking crest of each successive wave charged remorselessly towards him, frothing up the ship's side and curling on to the deck before the bows reluctantly heaved upwards, hung poised as the wave passed on and plunged into the trough with a sickening swoop. The savage tugs of the tow rope became more frequent and more violent. The end came with dramatic suddenness.

Over the roar of the wind streaming past his ears there came a terrifying, rending screech as the plates and beams holding the two ends of the ship together at last gave up the struggle and broke. Still floating, the two halves drifted apart. The tow rope had parted at the same time.

In the forepart, on the bridge and on the signal platforms around it, the little group of officers and men clung desperately to any handholds they could find while their feet sought a firmer grip on the steeply canting deck. All looked to their captain for a decision as to what to do.

Maud was deeply reluctant to give the order that would send his men over the side into the icy waves. He knew that in that temperature they could only survive a short while unless quickly picked up. But then, from under his feet, he felt the ominous thuds of bursting bulkheads which told him the end was near.

Carley rafts and flotanets were quickly hove over the side and then Maud gave the order which every seaman dreads to hear. 'Abandon Ship!'

As the order was obeyed and the last man went over the side, the forepart of *Somali* slid beneath the waves and Maud launched himself into the water. The appalling cold cut through his clothing to the skin. He started to gasp, 'Christ, the cold!' but the words froze in his throat. It was as much as he could do to breathe as he struck out for a flotanet to which he could see his men clinging as he rose on the crest of a wave.

A brief, frenzied struggle took him to the net and thankfully he clutched it with already numb hands. Glad of its support, Maud and his men clung miserably to it as the bitter cold working its way into their very vitals sapped their strength and power to survive. In the black darkness they lost count of time as the interminable minutes dragged by and the savage waves struck vindictively at them in ceaseless succession. Hope of rescue sank lower. Despair was not far off when to their numbed brains suddenly came the realization that towering above them was the bulk of one of the escorting destroyers.

A line came snaking through the air. Clumsy, frozen hands secured it to the net. Aboard the destroyer the line was hove in to haul the net alongside. But as it gathered way through the water, its edges were torn from the feeble grasp of lifeless fingers. One after the other, men lost their hold and drifted away, including Maud who cursed his weakness and the over-enthusiasm of his would-be rescuers.

But at least he had been brought alongside the destroyer and was drifting down her side when he saw a Jacob's ladder thrown over her quarter.

With a frantic effort he forced his numb and almost powerless body to obey him and managed to get a feeble grasp of the lowest rung. His last remaining strength he put into a despairing demand that the sailor at the top of the ladder should come down and give him a hand. But, alas, the man was fully occupied in holding the ladder which he had not had time to secure at the top.

At that moment a Carley raft, bumping and twirling down the destroyer's side, struck him. It was but a light nudge but it was enough in his frozen state. His hand slipped from the ladder and once more he was adrift, borne up by his lifebelt.

Then, as despair threatened to descend on him, there came a shout from the stern of the destroyer. 'Here you are, sir. It's your last chance' and, with it, a heaving-line fell in a coil around his bobbing head, only to tighten round his neck as he drifted away down wind. Instinctively Maud struggled to free himself from the throttling grip of the line but, as he succeeded in doing so, weakness and the turmoil of the tossing water combined to make him lose his feeble grip. His fast-freezing body gave up the struggle at last and, with an inward shrug of despair, he lapsed into unconsciousness.

* * *

Colin Maud knew that he was dead. At least he was quite sure he must be in Hell, so presumably he must be dead. Excruciating pains racked his body as devils stabbed him unmercifully with pitchforks. Fearfully he opened one eye to see before him as he lay the red glow of a fire. 'My God, it really is Hell!' he thought crazily and hastily shut his eye again.

A voice spoke to him and he opened his other eye. Glaring down at him was a face with thin black moustaches and a pointed black beard. 'The devil himself,' he thought with mounting horror. With a groan of pain and dismay he again shut his eye. But returning consciousness brought an element of doubt to his mind.

'I must get a better look at this place,' he vaguely told himself. 'I'm lying on my back. If overhead it is black, then this is really Hell. If it's white, I'm all right.' With a tremendous effort he opened both eyes and looked upwards. A relief which only later seemed ludicrous flooded through him. Above were the white paint, steel beams and the maze of electric leads of the overhead of a destroyer's cabin where he had been taken to thaw out, an electric fire glowing red beside him.

At that moment he saw Mephistopheles again and saw that he was wearing a naval officer's uniform with the red cloth of a surgeon between his lieutenant's stripes. It was the ship's doctor.

His mind at rest, strength and warmth poured into his body

and within a few hours there was little wrong with him that a stiff whisky could not put right. By something like a miracle, his unconscious form had been sighted from the *Ashanti* as Richard Onslow searched the wild welter of sea for survivors. Skilful seamanship had brought the ship alongside him, willing hands had done the rest.

* * *

Colin Maud's story has been given in some detail as it may serve to typify the experience of so many from merchantmen and escorts alike who had to submit themselves to the meagre mercy of the Arctic sea. In a book of this nature it would become tiresomely repetitive to try to describe such experiences on each occasion. Let Maud's story tell it for all of them. Alas, in nine cases out of ten, death came so swiftly from cold and exposure that unless rescue came within a minute or two it was too late. A tough constitution saved Maud from that.

Yet from Maud's story comes also a message of comfort. Writing to the next-of-kin of the forty-five men from *Somali* who lost their lives when she finally sank, he was able to tell them from his own knowledge that death came with gentle hands, without pain and preceded by blissful unconsciousness.

12

CHRISTMAS CONVOY

The passage of P.Q. 18 had been a close-run thing. Bob Burnett in his report stressed this and pointed out how fortunate he had been with regard to several aspects of the operation, any one of which going wrong could have spelt tragic disaster. The whole plan hinged on the ability of the 'fighting destroyer escort' to refuel at sea. If the weather had prevented this or if the precious tankers had been amongst the victims of the first devastating torpedo attack, the convoy must have either turned back or gone on with a much depleted escort and suffered heavy losses from aircraft and U-boat.

If the enemy had been able to mount a simultaneous air and surface attack, losses in the convoy must have again been heavy. Finally, the immunity of Q.P. 14 from air attack was most fortunate as ammunition in the escorts was running low and would have had to be carefully husbanded had any attacks developed.

It is only of academic interest, however, to speculate on what might have been the outcome if a further trial of strength had been staged in the following month. For Germany's best chance to inflict a serious naval reverse on the Royal Navy had, in fact, gone, never to return in quite such favourable circumstances.

Allied political pressure on British naval authorities which had caused them repeatedly to present the enemy with the opportunity to deal a grievous blow to British naval power and prestige had been up to now always counterbalanced by a similar misunderstanding of naval matters by Hitler. Now, even had Hitler woken up to the possibilities, it was too late for him to deliver the co-ordinated blow against which there was no real answer.

For after three years of trial and tribulation, the Allies were at last turning from the defensive to the offensive. Now instead of the Allies having to make do everywhere with inadequate forces, it was Germany who was to be forced to transfer forces from one place to another as she tried to stop the leaks in her wide-spread frontiers. So far as the naval war in the north was concerned the immediate effect of this was the withdrawal of the majority of the Luftwaffe from northern Norway, in particular all the torpedo-bombers. Events in North Africa and the Mediterranean required their urgent presence in that theatre.

However, these same events were in any case to bring the Arctic convoys to a temporary halt. For every ship which could be spared from the Home Fleet was wanted to take part in Operation 'Torch', the great Anglo-American landing in North Africa.

It was therefore not until winter had again clamped down on the Arctic that the Kola Run was re-opened. Yet it was a re-opening which lacked nothing in drama compared to the daylight passage of P.Q. 18 and Q.P. 14.

The new series of convoys to Russia were planned on different lines from those during the summer. The almost total absence of real daylight as well as the transfer of the Luftwaffe squadrons from northern Norway made provision of strong anti-aircraft defence unnecessary. U-boats, however, were coming to sea in ever-greater numbers as Germany's submarine effort was reaching its peak. Air escort could do little to help until daylight returned in which the carriers could operate. It was not until a later stage of the war that operation of aircraft from the decks of auxiliary aircraft carriers by night became possible.

Defence therefore lay with the destroyers and corvettes of the close escort with a force of cruisers in the offing ready to intervene should a surface attack be launched by the enemy. The Admiralty's plan for the first convoy was for one of thirty ships with a destroyer escort comparable to that of P.Q. 18. But experience with a winter convoy of that size which had been run in November to bring back empty ships from Archangel caused the Commander-in-Chief Home Fleet to propose instead that two eastbound convoys of fifteen ships each should be sailed a week apart.

The November convoy, Q.P. 15, had been caught in a succession of heavy gales by which it was so scattered that it soon lost all semblance of order. Small groups of ships were spread over a large area with no knowledge of each other's whereabouts. Destroyers sent to reinforce the close escort of minesweepers failed to find any of them. However, the weather was so foul that the enemy air reconnaissance also failed to detect them, while the German Naval Command North, which had rightly guessed that the escort would be a light one while the North African landings were in progress, was forced to abandon a plan to send the *Hipper* and destroyers out. The German destroyers could not even put to sea in such conditions and even the *Hipper* would have been unable to make efficient use of her guns.

Thus, though U-boats did find and sink two of the merchant ships, the remainder arrived safely, storm-battered and weary, at their destinations. Admiral Tovey felt that large convoys were more liable than small ones to be split up in this way, making for confusion and uncertainty in the covering force should an attack develop. In the winter snow and darkness, reliance would be entirely on radar for making contact and the defending force would have no way of deciding which group of ships was under attack or knowing which radar contacts were friendly or enemy.

The Commander-in-Chief's views gained the day and plans were made for fifteen ships to sail from Loch Ewe on 15th December and a further convoy of fourteen on the 22nd.

The nomenclature of this new series of convoys was changed, the eastbound being known as JW convoys, the homeward as RA. The first JW having been thus split, the two halves were numbered J.W. 51.A and J.W. 51.B, while the first homeward convoy would be R.A. 51.

J.W. 51.A duly sailed from Loch Ewe on 15th December and made a quiet and uneventful passage, arriving safely in the Kola Inlet on Christmas Day. The covering force of cruisers under Bob Burnett with his flag in the *Sheffield* and accompanied by the *Jamaica* carried on to Kola Inlet to wait there until it was time to sail to provide cover for R.A. 51 and J.W. 51.B.

Meanwhile on the morning of 22nd December there had come

together a company of men, unassuming in manner, inconspicuous in appearance. They all wore the dark blue uniform of seamen all over the world and an air of solid self-reliance. Their meeting place was a long Nissen hut round which the winter wind moaned and rattled. The convoy conference for J.W. 51.B was assembling ashore at Loch Ewe.

The majority of those present was formed of the masters of the fourteen ships about to set out on the Kola Run. A few shook hands, old acquaintances of the seven seas, before taking their places round the long table to start sorting through the bundle of documents in front of them – the convoy list, the order of sailing, the convoy formation, the sealed envelope containing the route. But most of them were strangers to one another, brought fortuitously together to form a convoy.

The seat at the head of the table was taken by the man who had organized the convoy, the Naval Control of Shipping Officer, or N.C.S.O. For weeks he had been preparing for this moment, as he did for every convoy which sailed from Loch Ewe, gathering information about the various ships so as to ensure they could fulfil the minimum conditions required, listing their cargoes and destinations, planning the convoy formation and obtaining the orders for the route. A hundred and one details had to be checked before a ship could be ticked off as suitable for a particular convoy. Now, with the list complete and the ships assembled he was here to see that every master had his written instructions and to answer any questions.

Next to him was a grizzled officer wearing the broad stripe of a Commodore R.N.R., the convoy commodore. Though he was probably personally a stranger to most of the masters, the chances were that he was known by reputation to them – a reputation perhaps as a fusser who must always be making unnecessary signals; perhaps as a disciplinarian who would stand no nonsense from bad station-keepers or masters who could not impress their engineers with the importance of making no smoke; or perhaps he received the supreme mark of confidence by being known as one who got things done efficiently with the minimum of signalling and the maximum of understanding of a master's problems. But whatever his reputation the masters knew that the responsibility for the safe navigation and the internal discipline of the convoy was his.

On the other side of the N.C.S.O. was a naval officer with the four stripes of Captain's rank – the senior officer of the escort. He was almost certainly a stranger to the assembly on this occasion for he was Captain Sherbrooke who had only recently taken over command of the *Onslow* and 17th Flotilla from 'Beaky' Armstrong. He was no stranger to northern waters or to battle, however, for he had commanded the destroyer *Cossack* at the second battle of Narvik.

Now, after the N.C.S.O. and the Commodore had addressed the assembled masters and answered their questions, Sherbrooke rose to introduce himself as the senior officer of the escort. He would have with him, besides the *Onslow*, the destroyers *Oribi*, *Obedient*, *Orwell*, *Obdurate* and *Achates*, the corvettes *Rhododendron* and *Hyderabad*, the minesweeper *Bramble* and the trawlers *Vizalma* and *Ocean Gem*.

He dwelt briefly on his tactics in case of U-boat or air attack, explaining that there was little that the ships in convoy could be expected to do under those circumstances except to stick together in rigid formation whatever happened. He then went on to discuss the possibility of attack by German surface warships, and here definite tactics were required of the convoy.

At the first alarm, the destroyers of the escort would concentrate on the threatened flank and would then steer to meet the enemy. While the remaining escorts gathered in a close screen and laid smoke, the convoy itself would be turned away from the enemy, each ship dropping smoke floats at intervals. Meanwhile, he assured them, the cruisers of the covering force would be hurrying to the scene to take over the defence.

They were simple and indeed the obvious tactics. What Sherbrooke could not enlarge upon, though it was no doubt clear to the audience of experienced master mariners, was the element of doubt as to how soon the cruiser force, hovering out of sight and perhaps uncertain of the position of the convoy, could come into action through the dim Arctic twilight and the fog or snow of the northern seas. All that Sherbrooke could assure his listeners, by implication rather than in words, was that the enemy would have to destroy every one of the British destroyers before he could with impunity proceed to attack the convoy.

The conference came to an end with the scrape of chairs on the concrete floor of the Nissen hut. The masters shrugged themselves into their heavy coats against the winter wind outside and, with a last jocular comment on the fate that had chosen them for the Kola Run, they left to catch the drifter which would take them to their various ships. Within an hour or two the last ship had cleared the boom defences to join the local escort waiting for them outside and the voyage had begun.

Sherbrooke in the *Onslow* had hurried away to join his destroyers at Seidisfiord where they were topping up with fuel prior to joining the convoy as it passed Iceland. The few extra days in harbour were expected to give the crews rest and to send them out fresh to take over their duties after which sleep and rest would be hard to come by for many a long day. But there was little repose to be had in those waters in mid-winter.

Punching their way through a screaming gale to Iceland, the destroyers had been hove-to for a time, unable to make headway against the heavy seas. When at last they reached the anchorage, the vicious squalls which came hissing down between the steep sides of the fiord denied all relaxation.

In the engine-rooms, watchkeepers stood by the manoeuvring valves ready instantly to set the turbines turning at a clang on the engine-room telegraph; on the forecastles cable parties huddled out of the biting wind in their duffle coats watching the jerking, straining cable, waiting for the order yet again to weigh anchor so that their ships could shift berth away from the threatening, rocky lee shore; on the bridges, officers of the watch crouched over the compass binnacles checking and rechecking the bearing of objects on shore by which they could gauge how much the anchors had been dragged; captains hovered behind them or sat restlessly in their sea-cabins making up their minds whether they should for the tenth time turn out the watch to get the ship under way and shift berth.

It was indeed a relief when the time came at last on Christmas Eve to follow *Onslow* out of harbour to the rendezvous with the convoy and on to the long haul up into the Arctic.

13

BATTLE IN THE BARENTS SEA

For the next six days J.W. 51.B steered north and then north-east in fair weather. Up through the Minches and the east coast of Iceland where the destroyers of the escort joined them. Then veering north-east to leave Jan Mayen far to port and on towards Bear Island and the Barents Sea. Half-way between Jan Mayen and Bear Island on 28th December, the unseasonable calm weather broke and a furious gale with snow and low visibility took its place.

During the black winter night two escorts, *Oribi* and *Vizalma*, and five merchant ships lost touch. *Oribi* and one of the merchantmen never succeeded in regaining contact in the brief daylight hours and they eventually arrived at Kola independently. Three of the freighters rejoined during the 29th. The *Vizalma* and one merchant ship followed a route well to the northward of the convoy and would be on their own until New Year's Day.

By the 30th the gale had died away. The fresh breeze from the north-west which took its place brought an icy breath from the polar ice cap. Sixteen degrees of frost in the air laid a hard skin of ice over everything on the upper decks, constantly thickened as spray which fell on deck instantly froze.

So far there had been 'no enemy but winter and rough weather'. No knowledge of the progress of the convoy had reached German naval headquarters. But now, on the forenoon of the 30th, came a U-boat alarm. From the *Obdurate* a conning-tower was sighted some distance away. Streaking after it, the destroyer forced the U-boat to dive, preventing it from getting in to attacking distance. But the convoy's position was now known to the enemy. Surfacing as soon as he could, the U-boat captain sent his message, 'Convoy bound for North Russia, south of Bear Island. Lightly escorted.'

This was the news for which Admiral Schniewind had been impatiently waiting since it became known that the convoy had sailed. The *Hipper*, flagship of Vice-Admiral Kummetz, the *Lutzow* and six destroyers, already at short notice for sea in Altenfiord, were at once ordered out to the attack. Heading north, they steered to intercept the convoy on the early morning of the next day so that they would have the whole of the few hours of twilight in which to hammer it before night again came down.

Unknown to Kummetz, Admiral Burnett's two cruisers had sailed from Kola on the 27th and were ranging to and fro in the area between Altenfiord and the convoy's route. However, in ignorance of the convoy's true position and thinking it to be further north and east than it was, Burnett swung north-westward on the evening of the 30th, intending to be only a few miles north and some forty miles astern of it on the next morning. Then, should an attack develop, he would be able to come into action with all the advantages of the feeble daylight on his side. Due to the position error, he was in fact to find himself about thirty miles due north of the convoy at that time, but the advantage of light would still be with him.

So through the night of 30th December the convoy plugged steadily on through the clear frosty darkness, fading from time to time into the grey obscurity of snow squalls. Escorting the twelve ships still in company were now five destroyers, two corvettes and a trawler. Some forty-five miles to the north were the *Vizalma* and one merchantman. Somewhere in the vicinity was another straggler and the minesweeper *Bramble* searching for her.

Steering across the convoy's route ahead of it were *Sheffield* and *Jamaica*, hoping to pick up radar contact with it but actually passing too far ahead to do so. None of these scattered British forces knew even approximately where the others were, for strict wireless silence had been enforced for many days to avoid detection through the enemy's radio direction finders.

Finally, coming up from the south, all unknown to the British,

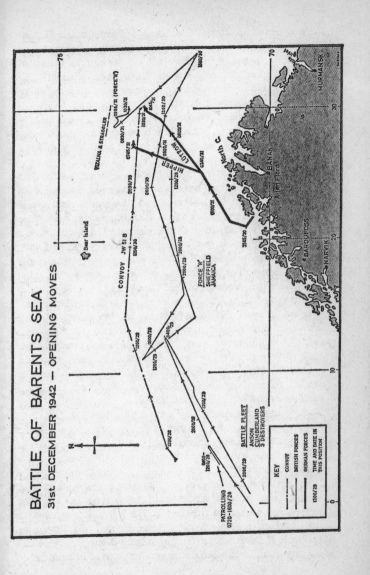

BATTLE OF BARENTS SEA
31st DECEMBER 1942 – OPENING MOVES

CONVOY JW 51 B

VIZALMA & STRAGGLER (FORCE 'R')

Bear Island

FORCE 'R'
SHEFFIELD
JAMAICA

LÜTZOW

HIPPER

North Cape

MURMANSK

BANAK
Alten Fiord
BARDUFOSS
NARVIK

BATTLE FLEET
ANSON
CUMBERLAND
3 DESTROYERS

PATROLLING
0720–1600/28

KEY
CONVOY
BRITISH FORCES
GERMAN FORCES
1200/29 TIME AND DATE IN
THIS POSITION

was the German squadron. Vice-Admiral Kummetz had evolved a plan whereby the *Hipper* and the *Lutzow*, each accompanied by three destroyers, would fall separately on the convoy from two directions. Ruling out any idea of night action which he felt would give the destroyer escorts a dangerous ability to bring off unseen torpedo attacks, Kummetz planned to bring *Hipper* in from the port quarter of the convoy at first light. This, he rightly judged would draw off the escorts in his direction while the convoy would veer away from him to the south-east – into the arms of the *Lutzow* and her destroyers.

The plan was a good one; but the best-laid plan of battle must go awry if the will to carry it out with courage and determination is lacking. Kummetz was labouring under the same disadvantage that had hamstrung previous sorties of German surface warships – Hitler's hysterical insistence that no risks must be taken and that he must avoid action with equal or superior enemy forces. Furthermore, even against the destroyers of the convoy escort one of his heavy ships, the *Lutzow*, was expected to avoid taking any injury. For on completion of the operation she was under orders to make for the Atlantic on a commerce-raiding expedition. It was vital that she should be fully fighting-fit for such a task.

However, serious opposition was not expected, for Kummetz was unaware of the presence of Burnett's ships, and at 2.40 on the morning of the 31st the German force divided in accordance with Kummetz's plan. With *Hipper* went the destroyers *Friedrich Eckholdt, Richard Beitzen* and *Z.29*, while the *Z.30, Z.31* and the *Theodore Reidel* accompanied *Lutzow*.

As the dim, grey Arctic day was coming unwillingly to life, the stage was thus set for the sort of disastrous encounter which the Admiralty had always feared must one day befall the convoys to North Russia and against which it was so difficult to provide an adequate defence.

The curtain rose at 8.20 on the morning of New Year's Eve, the scene disclosed being the bridge of the corvette *Hyderabad* on the starboard quarter of the convoy. Her captain, searching the murky horizon as feeble daylight grew, sighted two dim shapes identifiable as destroyers, steering north across the convoy's wake. Knowing that two Russian destroyers were due to join the escort, he gave a grunt of satisfaction at this unusually punctual arrival, which he took it to be, and took no further action.

But ten minutes later, from the *Obdurate*, the same ships were sighted. Her captain, Lieutenant-Commander Sclater, was not so easily satisfied. A signal was at once on its way to the *Onslow* – 'Two unidentified destroyers bearing west, course north." Already *Obdurate* had swung round and was nosing after the strangers when Sherbrooke's reply came back – 'Investigate.'

Sherbrooke had little doubt as to what the *Obdurate*'s report signified. He piped his ship's company to breakfast and to shift into clean underclothes, a traditional though rather alarming prelude to naval battle, a precaution against infected splinter wounds, an order rarely given since the passing of the era of predictable pitched battles at sea.

It was some time before confirmation of his belief came, however. Chasing after the German destroyers, which were soon seen to be three in number, Sclater could get no clear view of them against a background of black snow clouds. By 9.30 the range had closed to a mere four miles but there was still not enough light by which to identify them. But then all doubt was set at rest as a ripple of flashes from the German guns was seen and the tall water-spouts of shell splashes rose from the sea near-by. Sending off an immediate enemy report, Sclater swung his ship round to fall back on the support of his flotilla-mates.

The Germans, too, turned away. They had been detached by Admiral Kummetz to search eastwards along the convoy's track and had been about to comply when this sighting of the *Obdurate* made further search unnecessary. Now, with singular lack of enterprise, they veered north-eastward to rejoin the *Hipper* where first contact with the convoy escort was also about to be made.

Before *Obdurate*'s alarm signal had reached the bridge of the *Onslow*, Sherbrooke was already steering his ship for the gun-flashes and calling for *Orwell*, *Obedient* and *Obdurate* to join him. Thus his plan which he had outlined at the convoy conference was at once put into operation and the remainder of the escort force knew just what they had to do. *Achates*, which was on the convoy's port quarter and so between the enemy and the convoy, began to belch out a cloud of black, oily smoke from her funnels and white smoke from smoke floats on her quarter deck and to steam up and down laying an impenetrable screen which drifted slowly on the wind after the merchant ships.

But now Sherbrooke obtained some idea of what he was up against as, at 9.39, out of the hazy gloom to the north-west the massive top hamper of a large ship loomed, heading straight for him. As he peered at the dim outline, trying to identify it, he saw it swing away to port, disclosing its silhouette, unmistakably the *Hipper*. A definite enemy report could now be radioed to the cruiser force. Here was an opponent which would need more than a flotilla of destroyers to combat. Five minutes later Bob Burnett, who had been decoyed away to the north by the need to investigate a radar contact of the *Vizalma* and her straggler, was reading the message which at once resolved his doubts as to what he should do. He had already seen the gunflashes far to the south at 9.30 but until more definite news had come in he had not been able to neglect the contact to the northward which might have been that of the enemy's main force. Piling on speed until the two cruisers were racing along at thirty-one knots, he turned to the support of the convoy and its escort.

Meanwhile, the *Hipper*'s turn to port had been made with the object of bringing all her guns to bear on the little *Achates*, standing out stark against the black background of smoke. *Achates* was hit but not seriously damaged before the *Hipper* shifted her fire to the *Onslow*, now accompanied by the *Orwell*, as they came into view. At a range of five and a half miles, *Hipper* and the two British destroyers exchanged desultory fire as both sides ran in and out of smoke patches and snow squalls, the British firing by radar.

It was at once clear to Sherbrooke that his opponent was far from willing to 'mix it' with him, probably fearing to run into torpedoes fired, unseen, from the British ships. With their camouflaged hulls merging with the grey background of sea and sky, *Onslow* and *Orwell* were difficult targets and hard to see. Rather than close and smash them with his much heavier armament, Kummetz kept the *Hipper* away, hiding in smoke whenever possible and edging his way to the north-east.

He could, indeed, well afford to; for now the convoy was

behaving as he had forecast, turning away behind the smoke screen to the south-east where Kummetz knew the *Lutzow* must be waiting to spring on it. Sherbrooke had no knowledge of this second threat but instinctively he refused to be lured away by his slippery opponent. He was concerned as to what the three destroyers originally sighted might be up to – they had, in fact, been ordered to rejoin *Hipper*. As the *Obedient* and *Obdurate* came streaking up to join him, he ordered them to turn back to guard the convoy against them. Meanwhile he decided that he himself with the *Orwell* would keep *Hipper* in sight and withhold his torpedo fire, keeping it as a constant threat. He rightly judged that so long as the enemy remained unwilling to face this threat, the *Hipper* would be unable to break through to the convoy.

Nevertheless the situation was one of the utmost peril for the British force. Five destroyers could not indefinitely hold off a heavy cruiser and three larger destroyers boldly handled. Sherbrooke believed Burnett to be a long way off and that it might be many hours before he could come to his aid. But now came a signal from the *Sheffield* which altered the whole situation. It told Sherbrooke that she and *Jamaica* were approaching on a southerly course at thirty-one knots. As the glad tidings filtered down to the guns' crews and on to the supply parties in the magazines, the stokers in the boiler rooms and the engine-room crews, cheering broke out in all the ships.

At this moment the *Hipper* was seen to haul away to the north and break off the action. She had up to now made a very poor showing. Unable to get a clear view of the camouflaged British destroyers as they slipped in and out of the smoke clouds and snow squalls, her gunlayers seemed to shoot in a most aimless and erratic fashion. The gunnery of the British destroyers was similarly handicapped as well as by the constant icing-up of gun barrels and of the ammunition at their unsheltered gun mountings. No hits on the enemy had been obtained.

Kummetz's turn to the north had been made with the object of drawing the British destroyers after him. But when they failed to follow him Kummetz suddenly turned back again and for the first time the *Hipper* brought accurate fire to bear. What had always been inevitable in the long run but had been so fortunately long delayed, now occurred. At 10.20 a salvo of heavy shells fell square around the *Onslow*. Four hits in rapid succession wreaked fearful destruction. Both the destroyer's forward guns were knocked out, fierce fires raged in her fore superstructure and on her mess decks. A hole was torn in her side abreast the engine room.

Across the bridge, splinters had flown from a shell which had burst against the funnel. One had hit Sherbrooke, inflicting a dangerous and horribly painful wound in the face, partly blinding him. In spite of pain and shock, Sherbrooke held to his post on his shattered bridge, giving orders to *Onslow* and *Orwell* to turn away under cover of smoke before *Hipper*'s new found aggressiveness could do further damage.

Meanwhile a signal had gone to Lieutenant-Commander Kinloch of the *Obedient*, the next senior officer present, ordering him to take over control of operations. But not until confirmation came that the signal had been received in the *Obedient* would Sherbrooke allow himself to be led away to have his wounds treated, wounds which the doctor thought at first must be fatal.

Fortunately at this perilous moment a heavy snowstorm swept across the scene bringing a lull in the action. As the damaged *Onslow*, unable further to play an active role, limped away to join the convoy, *Obedient*, *Obdurate* and *Orwell* also turned south, refusing to be lured too far from their charges. And now Kummetz, all unaware that twelve miles to the north-west, in radar contact and tearing along towards him, were the *Sheffield* and *Jamaica*, had his attention distracted by a fresh target. Out of a snow squall to the eastward of him emerged the little *Bramble*, which since the previous day had been wandering solitarily in search of the two missing stragglers from the convoy.

It is doubtful if her two 4-inch guns even came into action before she was overwhelmed by a blast of fire from her huge opponent and was reduced to a smoking wreck. Leaving the destroyer *Eckholdt* to give the *Bramble* her quietus, Kummetz swung southwards again at 10.47 to find the British destroyers as soon as the snowstorm in that direction should have passed on.

Behind him, still out of sight, were coming the two British

cruisers, curling bow-waves mounting white up their forecastle sides, their hulls trembling as the high-pressure steam from the boilers forced the screaming turbines round at maximum revolutions. Their ensigns stood out stiff and crackling in the wind of their wild progress. Halliards slatted impatiently against the masts as though to whip the ships on to greater speed.

On their bridges, huddled figures peered through the murk and snowfall ahead for the first sight of the enemy being fast overhauled.

Meanwhile the denouement for which Kummetz had planned was taking place to the southward. While the *Achates* still prowled back and forth across the rear of the convoy laying smoke to shield it from the *Hipper*, and *Obedient* and her companions were still to the north of the convoy for the same reason, from the corvette *Rhododendron* came a report of smoke to the south-west, amplified ten minutes later into news of a large warship steering across ahead of the convoy. The *Lutzow* had arrived punctually on the scene, an almost defenceless prey presented to her and her three destroyers.

At this moment Providence cast in her lot with the British. For the same thick screen of snowfall which had saved *Onslow* and *Orwell* overtook and blanketed the convoy. Captain Stange of the *Lutzow*, mindful of his instructions to risk nothing, decided to stand off to the eastward until the weather should clear. With him he retained his three destroyers which could, with a brief cannonade, have sent most of the twelve merchant ships to the bottom before any aid could have reached them.

Kinloch, his hands already uncomfortably full with the difficult situation to the control of which he had succeeded, was unwilling to believe that a second enemy heavy ship could be on the scene. When no signal came from the *Hyderabad* which must have been even closer to the reported ship, he decided that *Rhododendron* must have been mistaken.

There was, indeed, little that he could do about it in any case, with the *Hipper* hovering menacingly to the north. He therefore kept his force where it was, between *Hipper* and the convoy which, as things turned out, left him well placed to fend off the *Lutzow* also when the time came. In the meanwhile he contented himself with ordering the *Achates* to reinforce the crippled *Onslow* at the head of the convoy.

So for a few minutes silence settled down over the scene with all ships shrouded in the softly falling snow. On a score of ships' bridges, warships and merchantmen alike, captains and masters waited and wondered what would be the situation to meet their eyes when the weather cleared.

At 11 o'clock it suddenly did so. From the *Obedient*'s bridge Kinloch sighted an enemy capital ship and two destroyers to the north-east and realized that *Rhododendron*'s report had been all too true. It was the *Lutzow*, steering south-east to head off the convoy. Kinloch at once led off towards her and then turned parallel to her course, laying smoke between the enemy and the convoy. As both forces ran to the south-eastwards thus, gun-flashes from beyond the *Lutzow* suddenly appeared. The *Hipper* coming south at full speed after the convoy had sighted the *Achates* as she cleared her own smoke screen, obeying the order to make for the head of the convoy.

Almost at once the *Achates* received a devastating hit which crippled her, reducing her speed to a painful twelve knots with a heavy list. Amidst a shambles in which more than forty men had been killed, her captain, Lieutenant-Commander A. H. T. Johns, lay dead. Her second in command, Lieutenant Peyton-Jones, assuming command at this critical moment, realized that in her broken state the ship could do little good by trying to overtake the convoy. With superb disregard of danger he decided therefore to continue for as long as possible to interpose his smoke screen between his assailant and the convoy.

Turning at once to meet this more urgent threat, Kinloch had led his three ships round on to a north-westerly course and now, mercifully, the *Hipper*'s fire was shifted from *Achates* to *Obedient* which, with her companions, had opened fire on the *Hipper* at 11.20. In a brief, fierce exchange of shots, *Obedient* was closely straddled, the near misses putting her wireless equipment out of action. But once again fear of the British destroyers' still unexpended torpedoes induced Kummetz to turn away to the north-ward. Well satisfied, Kinloch swung back towards the convoy to await the next attack.

Now came the crowning moment of this long-drawn, confused drama, played out amidst the drifting banks of smoke, the sweeping snowstorms, against a back-drop of grey sea and grey sky pricked with the intermittent flicker of gunflashes. As the *Hipper* turned north-west at 11.25 to bring her guns to bear on the *Obedient*, her dim shape, which could at last be made out from the bridge of the approaching *Sheffield*, was seen in silhouette and identified. At a range of six and a half miles, the British cruiser's guns opened on the unsuspecting German. Four times salvos fell closely round her, scoring one damaging hit, before the *Hipper*'s crew recovered from their surprise and brought their own guns into action.

Making smoke to screen herself, the *Hipper* swung round in a full circle before steadying on an escape course to the south-westward, but not before two more hits from *Sheffield*'s 6-inch guns had smashed home. Kummetz lost not a moment in calling off his whole force. Already he had done what he had been so strictly enjoined not to do – allowed one of Hitler's precious ships to be damaged in action. A signal went out ordering all German forces to break off action and retire to the westward.

Now from the *Sheffield*, with *Jamaica* in line astern of her, were sighted two German destroyers emerging from the gloom some 4000 yards ahead and well placed to deliver a dangerous torpedo attack. They were the *Eckholdt*, returning from sinking the *Bramble*, and the *Beitzen*. The former had mistaken the British cruisers for *Hipper* and *Lutzow* whom she was trying to rejoin. Before the error was realized, the range was down to point blank. Every gun in the *Sheffield* from 6-inch down to pom-poms opened up on her a devastating hurricane of fire reducing her almost at once to a sinking, shattered wreck, dire vengeance for the little *Bramble*'s traceless doom.

The *Beitzen*, turning away at once under fire from the *Jamaica*, escaped unharmed. The brief action had, however, taken the British cruisers round on to a northerly course causing them to lose touch for the time being with the *Hipper*, retiring at her best speed to the westward.

Meanwhile, the convoy, shying away from the more immediate threat of the *Lutzow*, had altered course to south and later to south-west. Captain Stange, maintaining his incredibly timid behaviour, thereupon turned back to the north-west to keep in touch with the *Hipper*. As he did so, however, some ships of the convoy came into sight clear of the smoke, and at 11.41 the *Lutzow* opened fire on them. At once Kinloch's destroyers, where a feeling of great elation had swept through everyone at the welcome sight of the flashes of Bob Burnett's guns, turned to renew the covering of smoke and to engage as best they could the barely visible pocket-battleship.

For about five minutes the *Lutzow*'s cannonade continued during which one merchant ship was damaged. But then the destroyers' smoke once again drew a protective veil and firing ceased. But now once again to the north, *Hipper* and her two remaining destroyers came in sight steering to the south-west and therefore offering again an apparent threat to the convoy. The indomitable British destroyers turned with undiminished vigour to oppose them, their very appearance out of the murk causing the enemy to veer hastily away to the west.

But the *Lutzow*, now intent only on rejoining the *Hipper*, an order which the irresolute Captain Stange had gladly accepted, had not yet been shaken off. Opening fire on the *Obdurate*, which was then leading the line of destroyers, she soon found the range and a near miss caused some damage. However, with all the enemy ships steering away again, the escorts' task was for the moment fulfilled and they could turn back to the convoy and out of range.

Their task was indeed fulfilled for Kummetz had already repeated his order for all German forces to withdraw to the west. The convoy was saved. One further short and inconclusive encounter there was between *Sheffield* and *Jamaica* and the German heavy ships but by 12.36 the enemy had fled far to the west and Bob Burnett, unwilling to get too far from the convoy, gave up the unnatural chase of two heavy ships and five destroyers by two light cruisers.

The short hours of daylight were already drawing to a close. As darkness fell, the escorts gathered once again round the convoy and course was resumed for Kola.

But one more heroic tragedy of that day was still being played out. Throughout all this time the *Achates*, though mortally wounded, had continued to steam slowly up and down screening the convoy with smoke. Gradually her bows had sunk deeper in the water, her list had steadily increased. Peyton-Jones had scorned to call for assistance while every ship was fully occupied driving off the enemy. He had, however, asked the trawler *Ocean Gem* to stand by. When the list had increased to sixty degrees at 1 o'clock in the afternoon and it was no longer possible to keep steam, the end was obviously near and Peyton-Jones called the trawler alongside to take off the eighty-one surviving members of the crew. This had hardly been done when at 1.15 the gallant little *Achates* suddenly capsized, lingered thus for a while and then sank.

It was the end of a story worthy of the honoured name she bore. Twenty-six years before, the previous *Achates* had distinguished herself at the battle of Jutland where another and better-fought *Lutzow* had been an opponent and, flying his flag in her had been the Kaiser's battle-cruiser admiral, the gallant Hipper.

Captain Sherbrooke was awarded the Victoria Cross for his leadership and gallantry in this action. It was a well-deserved honour, but no one will wish to dispute that there were others on that memorable day who shared in that supreme award which Sherbrooke received as leader of them all. It was fitting, too, that Kinloch's name, at the very time he was leading his destroyers so skilfully and bravely into action, appeared in the naval half-yearly list of promotions to Commander.

The convoy sailed on, arriving at its destination without further adventures, while the west-bound convoy R.A. 51, benefiting by the enemy's preoccupation, reached Loch Ewe in safety, undetected and unassailed. The battle had been an insignificant action in its scope and in the record of damage inflicted on either side. But its effect on morale was supremely heartening from the British point of view, while in the field of grand strategy and the higher direction of the war, its results were to be crucial.

'That an enemy force of one pocket battleship, one heavy cruiser and six destroyers, with all the advantages of surprise and concentration, should be held off for five hours by five destroyers and driven from the area by two 6-inch gun cruisers is most creditable and satisfactory,' said Admiral Tovey, with customary economy of praise. A wave of increased confidence went through the Royal Navy, at last emerging from the bitter years of defensive warfare with inadequate and insufficient weapons in its hands, a confidence which was to play its part in the decisive battle with the U-boats which was nearing its climax in the Atlantic.

The Germans had relearnt the old lesson that the personnel of a fleet kept mewed in harbour can never meet on equal terms a fleet used to keeping the seas constantly in all weathers; that a service with a tradition of attack regardless of loss, in defence of merchant convoys, will not be defeated by even a greatly superior force which is timorously handled. From Admiral Kummetz himself down to the destroyer commanders, irresolution, ineptitude and an astonishing lack of confidence were shown.

That the big ships should have held back was perhaps understandable in the light of Hitler's prohibition against taking any risks. But that the fast, well-armed destroyers should have rejected their opportunities to pounce on the convoy and its remaining close escort of two badly damaged destroyers and two corvettes is incomprehensible in spite of Kummetz's lame explanation, 'To make a destroyer attack was out of the question owing to possible confusion with the enemy. As the action developed I should no longer have been able to assemble our own destroyers round *Hipper* before darkness and would thus have left her without destroyer protection at a difficult period.'

Has ever a weaker excuse for pusillanimity been made? Only an admiral commanding a squadron seriously lacking in tactical experience at sea could speak in such terms. Only a fleet devoid of morale and self-confidence could behave in so poor-spirited a fashion. From the Germans themselves comes a lament at the sorry outcome of the action. In the War Diary of the *Lutzow*, written as she made for Altenfiord, her foray into the Atlantic abandoned, is found the sad comment, 'As we withdrew from the scene of action the unsatisfactory feeling reigned that, in spite of the general position which was apparently favourable at first, we had not succeeded in getting at the convoy or scoring any successes at all.'

The German navy and, through it, the German people as a

whole, were to pay heavily for this shameful display. Hearing the news first from the B.B.C., Hitler gave way to paroxysms of rage at his navy's craven behaviour, ignoring the fact that his own restrictions on their acceptance of risks were largely to blame. Summoning Grand Admiral Raeder to his headquarters, for an hour and a half he stormed and raged at his unfortunate Commander-in-Chief, expressing his belief that the big ships of the German Navy were nothing but a waste of men and material. Raeder was to produce a detailed plan for the paying-off and laying up of all of them. Palace politics took a hand as Goering gleefully seized the opportunity to point out how many Luftwaffe squadrons were tied up guarding the capital ships as they swung uselessly and endlessly round their anchors in harbour.

Raeder's pleas for a reprieve for the navy in the creation of which he had played the leading part could not shake Hitler's 'firm and unalterable resolve' to pay off the big ships. Rather than stay to supervise such an emasculation of the fleet, Raeder handed in his resignation and passed into retirement. In his place reigned the ambitious Doenitz, with his faith in the ability of his U-boats to win the naval war on their own.

So a minor naval engagement far up in the Arctic Ocean brought consequences which were to alter the basic German strategy. It is arguable that the changes were fatal to Germany's hope of winning the war.

14

BLUFFING THE U-BOAT

The news of Captain Sherbrooke's fight in defence of J.W. 51.B made a splendid start to 1943, a start which was to set the tone for the rest of that year. The Royal Navy had again disclosed that the German Colossus had feet of clay and that it only needed the confident hammer blows now becoming possible to a re-armed alliance to bring the whole daunting edifice down in ruins.

1943 was to see the Battle of the Atlantic decisively won by the Allies and the Mediterranean re-opened. Before it ended it was to see Hitler's surface fleet finally eliminated.

While winter held, the Kola Run was no longer the gamble that it had been. For the New Year's Eve battle had shown that Hitler's capital ships were not for the moment to be seriously feared. The long hours of darkness reduced the threat from the scanty force of aircraft in northern Norway to manageable proportions. U-boats, however, were still to be reckoned with.

The next pair of convoys, J.W. and R.A. 52, made successful passages with a comparatively small escort under the command of Commander W. H. Selby of the *Onslaught*. The skilful use which he made of the High Frequency Direction Finding equipment, familiarly known as 'Huff-Duff', now being fitted in more and more escorts was the principal reason for the discomfiture of the submarines. For this apparatus to be used successfully it was important that a number of ships should be equipped so that the various frequencies known to be used by the U-boats for their signals could be listened to. Then, whatever frequency was chosen by the U-boat's wireless operator on which to make his sighting

164

or other report, there would always be one escort ready to take a bearing of it. Smart 'drill' amongst the Huff-Duff operators of the various ships might even get several sets tuned to the frequency before the U-boat ceased signalling. Then cross-bearings would give an approximate position of the enemy craft.

With this information a judicious alteration of course by the convoy soon after dark could be selected which would throw the shadowing U-boats off the scent. The submarines would toil through the night at top speed to get round ahead of the convoy only to find at daybreak a blank and empty ocean.

Thus Selby played successful hide-and-seek to leave the U-boats frustrated and empty-handed while the convoy with a south-westerly gale under its tail made a fast passage. Not until it had reached the Barents Sea did the naval aircraft, unwieldy Heinkel 115 torpedo seaplanes, find it on the 24th January. Only four could be mustered for an attack. Only two got home safely to base after failing to do any damage to the convoy.

Two days taken up mostly with fuelling gave little opportunity to make up for lost sleep before Selby's force was on its way back with R.A. 52. This time his defence was penetrated on one occasion and a ship in the convoy lost. But there was no loss of life, and when the escort left to return to Scapa on 8th February, Selby could reasonably congratulate himself on a successful conclusion to his round trip.

As spring approached, however, conditions were once again changing. By the middle of February, when J.W. 53 was to set out, the period of perpetual night would have passed and there would be nearly as much daylight as darkness. Furthermore at this time of the year the ice-barrier forced the convoy route southwards until it was only 250 miles from Altenfiord and the German air base at Banak. In spite of Hitler's 'firm and unalterable resolve' to pay off the heavy ships of the German surface fleet, *Tirpitz*, *Lutzow* and *Nurnberg* were still based in northern Norway.

Both air and surface attack would thus be possible for the enemy, so a much stronger destroyer escort was to be provided, a fighting destroyer escort, as for P.Q. 18. For brevity this became known as the 'ocean' escort, additional to the 'through' escort of small destroyers, minesweepers, corvettes and trawlers.

This 'ocean' escort, which was to join the convoy at a rendez-vous to the north-east of Iceland, was to consist of the anti-aircraft cruiser *Scylla*, the auxiliary carrier *Dasher* and twelve destroyers – *Milne* in which Captain Campbell would be senior officer of the anti-submarine screen, *Faulknor* where Captain Scott-Moncrieff would be second-in-command, *Boadicea*, *Ingle-field*, *Fury*, *Intrepid*, *Impulsive*, *Eclipse*, *Orkan* (Polish), nearly all veterans of the Kola Run, as well as the victors of the New Year's Eve battle, *Orwell*, *Opportune*, *Obedient* and *Obdurate*.

Once again Bob Burnett was to provide the cruiser cover flying his flag in the *Belfast* and accompanied by *Sheffield* and *Cumberland*. All would assemble at Seidisfiord where fuel tanks would be filled before sailing for the rendezvous.

The through escort, commanded by Commander Lewis of the minesweeper *Jason*, would bring the merchant ships there from Loch Ewe and then join up with the ocean escort for the re-mainder of the voyage. With the *Jason* would be three small 'Hunt' class destroyers, *Pytchley*, *Middleton* and *Meynell*, the minesweeper *Halcyon*, the corvettes, *Dianella*, *Poppy* and *Berga-mot* and those habitués of the Kola Run, the trawlers *Lord Middleton* and *Lord Austin*.

But like all plans for operations at sea, these were at the mercy of the weather, which was in unforgiving February mood. The *Milne*, in which Campbell had gone to Loch Ewe for the convoy conference, was the first to suffer. Even in the comparatively sheltered waters of the Loch, the wind that hissed across the anchorage streaking the surface with foam and raising a vicious little lop left no doubts as to the reception which might be ex-pected outside. The bottom seemed to have fallen out of the barometer and as she nosed her way out past the boom defences the blast swooped on her with a vindictive howl.

But it was not until she lost the shelter of the Hebrides on rounding the Butt of Lewis that she felt the full strength of the gale and knew that the Atlantic was 'pulling out all the stops' for her benefit. Rolling crazily she headed for Seidisfiord where on reaching the narrow entrance to the fiord it was hoped that shelter might be found inside. But it was not to be.

Gusts of gale force came leaping at her from every direction, sometimes whistling down the length of the fiord, at others rebounding from the sheer cliffs that flanked it, driving her bodily sideways as she made her way anxiously up to the oiler moored in the middle. Twice Campbell got *Milne* alongside only to have all berthing wires snap like string before she could be hove in snugly to the tanker's side. At last she was firmly secured with the wind no longer able to funnel down between the destroyer and the tanker and she could start to take in fuel.

Campbell realized then why Scott-Moncrieff with the remainder of the destroyers and Macintyre of the *Scylla* had preferred to go on round to Akureyri on the north coast rather than try the doubtful amenities of Seidisfiord. The gale was indeed causing havoc to the convoy and its escorts. Commander Lewis of the *Jason* had a full-scale problem on his hands trying to keep his storm-tossed convoy together. His escort force of little ships, barely manoeuvrable in the huge seas, could do little to help as merchant ship after merchant ship reported weather damage or shifted cargoes.

When it is remembered that these cargoes were often huge Sherman tanks stowed in the holds or railway trains complete with locomotives lashed on deck, it is not surprising that six of the freighters were forced to return to harbour for repairs.

Among the escorts, the *Dasher* and the *Sheffield* each were badly damaged and had to drop out. The latter, being continually swept by green seas, had trained her turrets round on to the beam to prevent the blast screens, where the guns passed through the front plate, from being smashed in. Instead, a huge sea, heaping itself up against the steel side of the fore turret, bent it inwards and squeezed the turret roof clean off. The great sheet of steel sailed away over the side, fortunately falling clear into the sea without hitting anything in its flight.

On the 19th, four days after the convoy had sailed, the storm began to abate and the ocean escort was able to assemble at Seidisfiord to sail on the following day to join the convoy being painfully herded together again to the north-east of Iceland.

By the time they joined the convoy its twenty-two remaining ships had been reformed and were on the course for Bear Island and beyond.

As usual, it was not until well past Jan Mayen Island that the enemy began to bother it. Then, on the 23rd, one of the long-range reconnaissance aircraft which the Germans sent out daily sighted the convoy. If the *Dasher* had been present it might have been possible to shoot down this first snooper and gain immunity for a little longer. But with no fighters available the escorts were condemned to watch it and its successors fly endlessly round the horizon day after day sending out, as they guessed, homing signals to bring U-boats or bombers to the scene.

The U-boats were the first to arrive on the 24th, for it was still a long flight from Banak. The very strong escort must have been discouraging to the German submarine captains hovering beyond the horizon by day and hoping to get in to bring off an attack by night. But the Huff-Duff fitted in a few of the escorts, though not in *Milne* as yet, was Campbell's greatest aid in keeping them at a distance.

What a boon it was that the system on which Doenitz operated his U-boats required them to chatter on their radio to such an extent all unaware that the direction of high-frequency radio transmission could be determined so accurately. They had no inhibitions and would report on sighting a convoy, would follow up with details of its size, course, strength of escort and speed and would finally announce their intention to attack or inability to do so. Thus by keeping a plot of the bearings on which all these transmissions were heard, a fair idea of the positions of all U-boats in contact could be obtained. Campbell relied on this occasion upon Scott-Moncrieff to keep such a plot as the *Faulknor* was equipped with Huff-Duff; and most successfully he did so.

From it, though never so much as a conning tower was sighted, Campbell was able to send pairs of escorts out from time to time to harass and unnerve the enemy. Starshell would blossom in the sky in the direction in which a U-boat was known to be, sending the submarine hastily below the surface in fear of being detected; or depth charges would boom in the U-boats' hydrophones, making their crews wonder which of their comrades was being attacked.

It was an intriguing game of bluff very necessary in those

waters where the asdic was unreliable and no air escort was available to keep the U-boats at a distance. It sank no U-boats, it is true, but it ensured what was always the main objective – 'the safe and timely arrival of the convoy' – and no U-boats got near enough to attack.

But the continuous strain that the defence of a convoy imposed on the escort force commanders at such times can be seen if we transport ourselves in spirit to the chart room of one of them at such a time.

We should find it bathed in a dim red glow, for red or orange lights keep the eyes dark-adapted and without them anyone stepping out on to the bridge at night would be quite blind for several minutes. By the plotting table would be grouped the escort force commander, who is also captain of the ship, a bulky figure in his heavy Arctic clothing, ready to go up to the bridge at any emergency, and his navigating officer stooped over the plotting chart drawing on it the latest bearing from the Huff-Duff operators. On the plot, too, the convoy would be marked in and the ships of the escort in their stations around it.

If the ship was fitted with a surface radar – and at this time a great many ships of the Home Fleet were not – a plotting rating would from time to time adjust this picture from bearings and ranges passed down from the radar operator.

The latest Huff-Duff bearing might give a fix of a U-boat which was getting unhealthily close. His signal had perhaps been a short one – reporting that he was going in to the attack. Very well, an escort must be sent out to scare him off. Which is the most suitably placed? The nearest is a minesweeper with not enough speed to get out and back again quickly. But there is a destroyer in the next station. Right! Pass to 'X', 'Investigate position so and so with star shell and fire a series of single depth charges.'

That should put him down. But nothing has been heard for some time of another on the other side of the convoy. He is probably making at high speed on the surface to get to a good position for a submerged attack at dawn. 'Y' on that side is suitably placed for a sortie but she is pretty low in fuel and it may not be possible to top up from the tanker tomorrow. High speed running is extravagant of fuel. However it will have to be risked. Send her off!

Quiet settles down for a while as the two escorts are going out on their missions. The air in the chart house is frowsty with tobacco smoke. Thick mugs with a drain of the hot cocoa they had contained stand wedged where the roll of the ship will not dislodge them. The captain gives a cavernous yawn and thinks of his bunk. But he will not see it this night or for several more probably.

'Going up top for a look round, pilot,' he says, tightly buttoning up his Arctic clothing and pulling on his sheepskin gloves. 'Ought to be able to see something if the Northern Lights are still putting on their show,' and he turns to stump up the ladder.

The bitter, frosty air slaps his face as he steps out on to the open bridge. With a hiss of indrawn breath he makes for the shelter of the windscreen at the fore end. Turning he sees a lumpy, bulbous silhouette which looks odd at first. But it is only the hooded shape of the Officer of the Watch hunched over the compass binnacle, his life belt, partly inflated in accordance with the orders, bulging under his duffle coat. He is watching the card of the gyrocompass repeater jig round as the ship turns on its endlessly repeated zigzag course to and fro about its screening station.

The ping ... ping ... of the asdic is louder up here and for a moment the captain stands by the indicator watching the pointer sweep round the compass card in steps. Then he moves to the side of the bridge and brings his binoculars up for a long scrutiny of the horizon rising and falling in the direction of the convoy. Against the shimmering, iridescent curtain of the Aurora the merchant ships loom their black bulks.

Shifting to the other side of the bridge, he finds it dark black to the southward, and it is with difficulty he picks out the dim shape of the next escort for a moment.

'All seems quiet enough, Sub,' he says to the Officer of the Watch as he climbs up to the wooden chair clamped to the compass platform and lowers himself stiffly into it with a sigh.

'Yes, sir. Convoy seems to be keeping good station. The wind's got up a bit in the last hour.'

'Hm, but the glass is steady. I don't think it will get much worse. Hope not. We've got a big fuelling programme for the morning.'

Silence falls between them as the Sub-Lieutenant cons the ship round on to another leg of its zigzag. As she comes on to her new course and the Sub orders 'Steady on 125', a look-out suddenly shouts, 'Flare, Green 50.'

'Ah! good. That's "X" doing her stuff.'

More of 'X's' starshells burst and hang their lights in the sky.

'Underwater explosion heard,' comes a cry up the voice-pipe from the asdic cabinet.

'Tell them that's probably "X" firing a depth charge, Sub. Tell them to keep their ears open, too. Quite a few of Doenitz's boys prowling about tonight.'

Presently a buzzer by a voice-pipe gives a brief hoot. The Leading Signalman of the watch steps over to it and answers 'Bridge!'

'Navigator here. Tell the captain another Huff-Duff just come in.'

'Aye, aye, sir.'

The captain heaves himself out of his chair and with a muttered 'I'll be in the chart house, Sub,' makes for the ladder.

So it goes on night and day. When the convoy gets within reach of the enemy airfields, there are air alarms and action stations as well, perhaps damaged ships to be taken care of or survivors to be picked up. By the time Bear Island is past, sleep has become the most desirable thing on earth.

*　　*　　*

Not until the 25th, when J.W. 53 was well into the Barents Sea, did the bombers put in an appearance. Then fourteen Ju. 88s arrived to deliver shallow-dive bombing attacks. The *Scylla*'s radar had given warning of their approach and to many it brought back memories of P.Q. 18 to see Macintyre take his ship out ahead at high speed, stern tucked down and leaping bow-wave curling, heeling under helm as she zigzagged to and fro, every gun of the 'Toothless Terror' stabbing upwards. With the escorts joining in, it was a daunting reception for the Luftwaffe pilots who no doubt thought with little relish of the icy waters waiting to welcome them if they were hit.

Then as they swept closer every ship of the convoy let fly with its close-range weapons, a mad storm of tracer shells criss-crossing in the air. It was too much for the airmen. They dropped their sticks of four 250-lb. bombs or two 500-lb. hastily and ineffectively and fled. How many failed to reach base was never known, but when they returned the next day, the Germans could only muster eleven, and they were eleven very nervous airmen; for their leader could be heard exhorting them to fly higher and get their bombs away as quickly as possible. No doubt they had a better story to tell to their superiors when they got home but, in fact, once again they caused no damage and judging by the landing wheel which barely missed the *Faulknor* as it fell their numbers were again diminished.

It was their last effort and on 27th February the force entered Kola Inlet with fifteen ships of the convoy having detached the remaining seven for the White Sea and Archangel.

So they reached the haven where they would be, as the Psalmist has it. But it could not surely have been such a place as that desolate inlet in the barren, snow-covered Murman coast that he had in mind. One look at the place and even the aching, weary crews of the escorts had only one wish – to be on their way out again.

15

DESTINATION DREADFUL

This book has been given the title *The Kola Run* and is chiefly concerned with the long-drawn running fights to get the convoys through to Russia. But it would be incomplete if it did not give some idea of the conditions which greeted the men of the merchant ships and escorts at the far end of the run.

The Kola Inlet consists of a long stretch of water with the port and railhead of Murmansk at its head. Further to seaward, on the eastern shore of the inlet, is the bay of Vaenga where the oiler lay and which was the normal anchorage for escorts, the water too deep and the holding ground for the anchors too poor to make it comfortable. At Vaenga itself there was the hutted camp in which survivors were housed, and there was also a pier there where two destroyers could berth. Later in the war a small Royal Naval Auxiliary Hospital was set up there also.

When there was a heavy re-fuelling programme, escorts could also go to a tumbledown fuelling jetty at Rosta between Vaenga and Murmansk; but as it was in the stretch of water from Vaenga to Rosta that merchantmen moored while waiting their turn to go to the inadequate wharves of Murmansk and the enemy bombers regularly visited them there, it was not a popular berth.

On the western shore, near the entrance, was the Russian naval base of Polyarnoe. There in secure shelter warships could lie alongside the jetties; but it was not until later in the war that our inhospitable allies could be persuaded to allow our ships to do so. Polyarnoe was indeed a very snug harbour, the sides of its narrow entrance so overlapping that it was almost indistinguishable from outside.

In dismal surroundings the crews of the merchantmen and of the minesweepers berthed amongst them to give some anti-aircraft protection endured, sometimes for months on end, a dreary, cold monotony which tried the stoutest hearts, almost perpetual darkness in mid-winter with incessant gales and storms; in the summer endless daylight and daily air attacks.

To give an idea of the atmosphere which enfolded Murmansk, here is a description of it by Rear-Admiral M. W. S. Boucher, who made several journeys on the Kola Run as Commodore of convoy. 'Murmansk was a bombed city filled with black ghosts moving in twilight over the snow in deathly silence broken only by tinny music broadcast at regular intervals by the State.'

Time and again in descriptions of life in Murmansk one reads of the strange effect of the silence, the dull lifelessness of the few inhabitants as they shuffled miserably about, bringing an air of weird unreality to life.

The repeated bombing which the city suffered had much to do with this dismal effect. The greater part of it having originally been built of wood, incendiary raids had burnt it out very thoroughly leaving desolate brick chimneys sticking up through the snow to mark where houses had been. When the snow melted in summer the charred rubble and iron bedsteads disclosed were even more depressing and the smells were indescribable. All that was left were the big new concrete blocks of offices, flats and warehouses, every window boarded up, all glass having long ago vanished.

Built towards the end of the 1914–18 war simply as a railhead at the only ice-free port in the north, Murmansk can never have had any but the barest amenities. Now it was entirely utilitarian, its population composed exclusively of officials, soldiers and gangs of male and female slave labour.

But if life was dismal and depressing for sailors from the ships in harbour with time on their hands and longing only to be homeward bound, it was sheer misery for survivors and wounded from merchantmen and escorts who experienced the cold comfort of Russian hospitals and camps. The report of Captain

Faulkner of the *Edinburgh* on the treatment of survivors from that ship paints a grim picture.

On arrival at Polyarnoe the *Gossamer* and *Harrier* went alongside to land all surviving hands. It was one o'clock in the morning, very cold, and some of the men had come straight up from the engine room or boiler rooms and had very little with which to cover themselves. No one had time to save anything from the old ship and we were huddled about draped in sacks, blankets and so forth.

Apart from a few who could be taken in at Polyarnoe, the bulk of the ship's company had to be accommodated in barracks at Vaenga. This meant a slow and tedious journey by water. On arrival these exhausted men had to walk nearly four miles through the snow and they were in a low state to view the ramshackle huts, no hammocks or beds, just benches to sleep upon. However, there were plenty of blankets and centrally situated wood-burning stoves soon got some heat going. The barracks had been erected in some haste of green timber which had shrunk and into the gaps had been stuffed felting or fibre, out from which issued vermin of all sorts attracted by the warmth and the prospect of visitors so succulent. . . .

I inspected the lavatories and cook-house which were primitive and filthy. A rough sort of hygiene was observed in the cook-house and each man had to wear a special coat and to wash his hands. The food was largely boiled barley and dried fish and when I asked for something better got smoked salmon and caviare!

On my next visit I found the men in a very discontented state because, with the very poorest conditions of life, there was literally nothing for them to do. So we organized a daily morning parade and a guard armed with wooden rifles. A sports programme was arranged, training started and skis were borrowed. A concert party got going and collections were made for the dependants of those who had lost their lives.

I and some of the officers would go ski-ing on the hills near the Petsamo frontier, but it was disconcerting to find ourselves potted at by guards and patrols. They probably had not a clue as to who we were.

The Russians gave me a Captain's uniform to replace my own tattered apparel. We were waited upon by Russian girls who were wont to show their regard for an officer by pathetic little gifts such as an orange preserved in syrup or some other delicacy. If the Commissar bowled out such personal attentions, the girls were sent packing and never seen again.

Our wounded and the few with frost-bite were taken off to the Russian hospital at Murmansk which already had its quota of previous convoy casualties and Russian soldiery. Our men were worried and dismayed to hear that operations were normally carried out without anaesthetics unless it was judged that the shock would prove fatal. So one of the *Edinburgh*'s doctors was ordered to be at the hospital night and day with instructions to accompany every patient to the operating theatre and to see that they were not operated on unless properly put under. This worked, although less fortunate Russians had no such alleviation. It was said that one of them suffered a leg amputation with only a couple of aspirins.

Conditions in the hospitals at Polyarnoe, Murmansk and Archangel, on which depended the care of our sick and wounded, were indeed parlous. When the Petsamo front was active or when there had been heavy convoy sinkings, the hard, uncomfortable beds with their frowzy bedclothes of dubious cleanliness were packed close in the wards. The staff wore dirty overalls and scorned to make use of gloves.

In the airless, squalid wards, boards nailed over the windows as a black-out were a permanent fixture leaving little outlet for the varied smells. From seven in the morning till eleven at night loud-speakers blared unceasingly in Russian. Drugs were short and pain regarded with Oriental indifference by surgeons and physicians.

Dull, monotonous food did nothing to comfort men lying in fear and pain, unable to make their simplest needs or symptoms known. British surgeons did what they could but, owing to professional jealousy, were permitted only to visit the patients and attend operations as laymen. They were neither consulted nor allowed to advise.

It was not until 1944 that the Royal Navy was allowed to establish a small auxiliary hospital at Vaenga with three surgeons, a small sick-bay at Polyarnoe with two doctors and one other doctor in a sick-bay at Archangel.

With conditions such as these existing for their sick and wounded shipmates, it was not easy to keep up the sailors' enthusiasm for fighting the convoys through. It became almost impossible when they saw how the material they had brought at such heavy cost was treated by the recipients.

At both of the commercial ports of Archangel and Murmansk where the cargoes were unloaded, a state existed of such gross incompetence combined with a brutal contempt for human life and dignity that must have filled the hearts of the masters and seamen and the members of the allied missions with disgust, anger and pity in about equal portions.

The muddle and inefficiency at the wharves had to be seen to be believed. It made Admiral Boucher grim with rage to see how the material brought by his convoy was treated. Crates marked 'Delicate Instruments With Care' were thrown about and dumped higgledy-piggledy about the jetties. Under the layer of snow could be read 'Keep Dry'.

The crates were normally handled by the convict gangs. These – pathetic relics of humanity, starving and wrapped in frowzy, ragged odds and ends of clothing – did all the manual labour including the handling of cargoes. Weak and emaciated, numbers of them were necessary to do jobs that would take one or two normally strong men. If they collapsed or were hurt, as often happened, they were shot out of hand by their guards.

When the Russians did use machines, they betrayed an almost imbecile lack of understanding of the simplest principles of mechanics. One incident which Boucher watched was fairly typical. A particularly recalcitrant crate had defeated the labours of the convict gang. So a train with a crane was brought along. The wire whip from the crane was led over a considerable distance to the crate and the crane set in motion. Hauling thus horizontally instead of lifting as it was designed to do, it was not surprising that the net result was that the crane promptly capsized.

Captain Morton, who was head of the naval section of our Mission at Murmansk, has a wealth of stories illustrating the moronic incompetence of Russian methods of which the following are typical. The railway trains brought as deck cargo in the freighters in the convoys have been mentioned before. The procedure for unloading the locomotives was to hoist out the chassis first on to the rails running along the wharf. The boiler would follow and be bolted on and then the tender would be lowered and hooked on to the engine. The whole would then be towed away to make room for more rolling stock.

In the winter, however, the chassis were not unnaturally a solid block of ice from wheels to running boards, and quite immovable after being hoisted out. Watching the operation, Captain Morton assumed that the next move would be to get the freighter to provide a steam hose with which to thaw the locomotive out. But the Russian method was simpler. A seven-ton caterpillar tractor arrived to tow it; the engine shrugged slightly as the maximum strain was applied and no more. So a second tractor was called up to boost from behind. A little ice fell off from the point of impact but the locomotive remained quite unmoved.

As a third tractor was being connected up in tandem with the first, Morton foresaw disaster and took himself aboard where he could watch in safety and at the same time arrange for a steam hose to be prepared. As he climbed the gangway he heard the roar of engines from the tractors and turned in time to see the tow wire from the first tractor part, whipping an astonished driver from his perch as it coiled viciously back. Even the obstinate Russian mind was now convinced and, when Morton moved on, he left the stevedores happily hosing off great chunks of ice with the steam.

But at least the Russians had used mechanical aid in this case. Normally they preferred to use their slave labour. A gang of these poor wretches would be set to push. If their feeble efforts failed, more would be called away from other work and then more. Impatiently watching this method of trying to get an empty goods wagon moving on one occasion, Morton quietly arranged for a wire whip to be run from one of the ship's derricks and connected to the front of the truck. A gentle 'yank' and the wagon moved off. There were relieved and grateful looks from the convicts and a considerable speeding up in the work of discharge; but the overseer's expression made it clear that he thought it a needless interference with his job.

To the inefficiency entailed in using these poor creatures was added bestial barbarity in the way they were treated. Even draught-animals would presumably have been fed sufficiently to get the maximum work out of them. But the convicts were obviously given barely enough to keep them alive. If they fell by the wayside they were given short shrift.

A gang of them was re-laying some of the broken planks on one of the quays with a small shunting engine and some flat cars carrying the planks. Captain Morton passed them during a visit to the docks to see how the unloading of some stores was proceeding. Coming across a convict lying on his back in the snow, he went over to see if he could help him. Through the man's forehead was a bullet hole.

The Leading Seaman in charge of the stores now came to Captain Morton and told how the poor wretch had not heard the flat cars coming up behind him as he worked. He had been knocked over and a wheel had gone over his leg. The guard had thereupon poked him with the muzzle of his rifle, decided that he was of no further use to the state and calmly shot him.

From time to time the muddle and congestion caused by the Russian methods got so bad that convoys were held up and the whole smooth running of the convoy cycle endangered. Then it was necessary for threats and ultimatums by the Ministry of War Transport representatives on the Mission that no more convoys would be sailed until something was done about it. This would be the signal for the arrival from Moscow of a sort of super commissar who would descend on the port like a whirlwind, put the fear of Stalin into the local officials, inject them for a time with a feverish energy and bring order out of chaos. But with his departure the bad old ways would gradually return until another crisis had to be dealt with in the same way.

One of the strangest aspects of the Murmansk scene considering the desperate insistence by Moscow for more and larger convoys to be run, was the absence of cranes capable of lifting such heavy loads as tanks and locomotives. None of the fixed or mobile cranes on the wharves could lift a greater load than 11 tons. To meet the deficiency the British arranged for special crane-ships to be stationed at Murmansk with 80-ton, 50-ton and 30-ton cranes.

Even these led to the sort of controversy in which the members of our mission were constantly involved. The Russian port official insisted that a certain 90-ton load could and must be hoisted out by one of the 80-ton cranes. Arguments failing to get them their own way, the Russians resorted to their usual method of persuasion, the mounting of a 'Bolshoi Praznik' or grand banquet – in effect a drinking orgy. Only when the British officials had survived this and remained adamant in their refusal to use an 80-ton crane to lift a 90-ton load did the Russians accept defeat.

That gratitude for or even appreciation of all that their allies were doing to help them should have been entirely lacking was certainly irritating but understandable when the Russians themselves were fighting with their backs to the wall and accepting terrible losses. That the members of our Mission should have been treated with continuous mistrust and suspicion was perhaps inevitable in a country where the inhabitants moved in a similar atmosphere themselves. But it was frustrating to find, as did Captain Morton, that of the host of authorities with whom he had to deal, only three dared to visit him 'unchaperoned' or let him call to see them. These were the Diplomatic Representative, who was there to report direct to the Kremlin on everyone and everything; the Convoy Captain, who saw to the berthing and sailing of convoys; and a Russian liaison officer who was also A.D.C. to the Russian Admiral.

Co-operation as between Russian and Allied officials was a word which had very little meaning though continually heard on Russian lips. Guile and stratagem had often to be resorted to by our Mission to get anything done. An example of this occurred when some 146 tons of urgently required stores for the British and Allied Missions in Moscow arrived divided between three ships of a convoy. In spite of repeated promises by the Russian port authorities, when the three ships were unloaded the stores for Moscow remained on board and the freighters returned to a berth down the Inlet to join the next homeward convoy.

Daily appeals by Captain Morton and daily promises by the Russians brought no change in the situation. With the sailing date approaching, sterner measures were necessary. Calling on the masters of the crane-ships, Morton arranged that if necessary they would engineer a break-down of their winches at an appropriate moment.

Thus armed, and knowing that there were a number of locomotives arriving in a day or two in the next convoy, Morton and his interpreter, Lieutenant Cheshire, called upon the Director of Foreign Trade.

'Comrade Director,' began Cheshire, 'Captain Morton instructs me to tell you that the spirit of prophecy has descended on him.'

'Prophecy?' replied the astonished Director. 'I do not understand prophecy.'

'Well, it works this way,' went on Cheshire. 'Captain Morton has foreseen that unless the three ships with stores for the Allied Missions are brought alongside and the promised railway trucks provided, a most unfortunate breakdown is likely to happen to the winches in the crane ships.'

'Ah! The Captain jokes,' smiled the Russian. 'In any case your ships will be soon unloaded, you will see.'

But more days went by with no action taken. The day before the arrival of the incoming convoy the Director was informed by a panic-stricken deputy, who had been touring the port to see that all was in readiness, that none of the big cranes were in working order. The telephone in Morton's office was at once ringing furiously and a frantic Director, facing liquidation if the unloading of the convoy was held up, was demanding to know how long repairs would take.

With justifiable glee, Cheshire reminded him of his Captain's remarkable prophecy.

'Blackmail!' came a bellow from the telephone, which could be heard clear across the office.

'No, no, Comrade Director,' purred Cheshire. 'Just a little "squeeze".'

Within eight hours the three ships had been unloaded and the rail trucks were on their way to Moscow. Only in dire straits were such methods used, of course, and in any case from that time onwards a mere mention of prophetic powers was all that was necessary to bring some very dirty looks but instant compliance.

A great deal more could be written about the strange and horrible conditions existing in North Russia; but the above is probably sufficient to convey the general atmosphere of gloom and grime, barbarity and incompetence, suspicion and mistrust. Perhaps it was best summed up by the Jamaican coloured boy assigned to Commodore Boucher as his steward when he flew his flag in the American freighter *Will Rogers*. Asked by the Commodore for his impressions, he slowly shook his head and said with fervour, 'I'd sho' like to go any place else – jes' any place 'tall.'

16

SUMMER RECESS

The Jamaican boy's views of Murmansk were no different from those of the crews of the escorts for R.A. 53. So, in spite of their brief stay in harbour being taken up with oiling and ammunitioning, the consequent shifting from pillar to post leaving little time for rest, it was with few regrets that they sailed again on 1st March with the convoy of thirty ships. U-boats on patrol in the Barents Sea were almost at once in touch but once again Scott-Moncrieff's excellent Huff-Duff organization provided the means to keep them at bay. It was bitterly cold with a wind off the ice barrier not far to the north bringing more than twenty degrees of frost. The ice-sheathed ships moved along through fields of pancake ice which may have helped to make things difficult for the U-boats with their fragile periscopes.

During the night of 4th March a deathly cold from the starboard side which seemed almost tangible brought warning that the ice-barrier was getting uncomfortably close, and finally the van escorts to the north sighted it palely gleaming through the darkness. Getting through to the Commodore, Macintyre of the *Scylla* asked for an immediate emergency turn to port. This, a turn of forty-five degrees by all ships together, was not a comfortable manoeuvre to undertake at night with a large convoy. As its name implied, it was meant to be done with the least possible delay or warning. The signal initiating it was of the simplest nature – a hoist of three coloured lights repeated by all. At a blast of the Commodore's syren and the dousing of the lights, all ships would swing together through forty-five degrees, thereafter steaming in echelon until they were either altered back to the original course or through another forty-five degrees.

Fortunately the manoeuvre was ably executed and, after side-stepping thus for a time, the convoy could resume its course. In truth, clear nights in the Arctic such as that was, were rarely very dark. Even if the Aurora Borealis was not shaking its shimmering, rustling, purple, red and yellow curtain in the sky, there was always a band of lighter sky above the northern horizon against which ships stood out in black silhouette. But when a south-westerly gale brought rain, snow or hail and low-scudding clouds, then indeed the Arctic took on the darkness of the tomb, and one could barely see the hand in front of one's face.

So far, in spite of fair weather, the Luftwaffe had kept aloof. Aggressive tactics and bluff based on the Huff-Duff plot had scared the U-boats off and a feeling was growing that all was going very well. But these tactics depended for success on un-wearying vigilance on the part of the Huff-Duff operators. Other-wise a vital enemy signal might be missed and a U-boat left free to make its way, unharried, into the convoy.

The escorts had all been at sea almost without rest for seventeen days by now and no doubt the first keen edge had gone from their watchful skill. Either a Huff-Duff operator had momen-tarily lapsed or the plotters, brains numbed for want of sleep, had misapplied the information given them, or the best tactics were not employed.

Whatever it was, the first knowledge of a U-boat on the morning of the 5th came from the sight of torpedo tracks in the convoy. Almost simultaneously two ships, the *Richard Bland* and the *Executive*, were torpedoed. The former, hit right forward in her forefoot, was not seriously damaged and was able to keep going. But the *Executive* with a cargo of chloride burst into flames which were quickly out of control. There was nothing for it but to order two trawlers of the close escort to take off the crew, after which the *Faulknor* sank her with gunfire and depth charges set to burst shallow under her.

It was a keen disappointment after such a long run of immunity and dismaying to find that U-boats could get through the very strong screen, though the ineffectiveness of the asdic in those

184

waters was largely to blame. However, the sharp repulse of an attack by fourteen Ju. 88s that afternoon, the *Scylla* putting up her usual impressive performance, did much to restore confidence. The convoy was making good progress, would soon be under shore-based air cover and the U-boats did not as a rule follow the convoys far to the west.

But on the 6th came the reminder that the weather was still the greatest arbiter of fortune at sea. As the glass dropped alarmingly, the wind backed round to the south-west. A heavy, menacing swell brought warning of what was in store, and soon the ships were plunging into the teeth of a thunderous gale on the wings of which came snow. The ballasted ships could soon barely make headway. Their bows too high out of the water, they had difficulty even in keeping on their course and soon the convoy began to split into small scattered groups.

By the escort commander there was little that could be done to gather them together until the weather should relent. The corvettes and trawlers were better able, with their short length and stout construction, to manoeuvre amongst the long, angry rollers. But a destroyer, long and slim, could take fearful punishment if carelessly handled. Heading into the seas, her bow would soar upwards as it met each successive wave. As the crest passed on under the hull, she would hang momentarily poised, her keel clear out of the water for a third of its length, and then swoop sickeningly into the trough, perhaps to land with a shock felt right through the ship, followed by a crazy fore and aft whipping that would set the mast and funnel swaying and rattling.

Such treatment could buckle the hull and split bulkheads. It also worked havoc with the multiplicity of delicate instruments, the gyro-compass, the radar valves and wireless aerials. On the other hand a following sea could be equally dangerous if too much speed were attempted. At the same speed as the following rollers, the rudder ceased to have any effect. The wave might then heap up on one quarter or the other and the ship would 'broach to', swinging uncontrollably round through ninety degrees, heeling crazily over, gunwales under and even putting boats and superstructure wings under water. Tremendous damage could be caused by such a happening and men swept overboard. A destroyer low in fuel and ammunition and so lacking in ballast might capsize.

So at the height of such a storm it was necessary to stick to a course and speed which would let the ship ride as easily as possible while keeping steerage way. Chasing, sheepdog fashion, after the scattered groups of merchant ships had to be left until the seas went down somewhat.

A different problem altogether was Campbell's chief worry. Few of the destroyers had been able to take their mid-ocean drink of fuel from the tanker before the gale had descended. Now it was impossible. At the slow crawl which was all the convoy was capable of in the gale, there was a long journey still ahead and fuel tanks were getting dangerously low.

Something had to be done at once if the convoy was not to be bereft of the whole of its destroyer escort very soon. Campbell therefore sent Scott-Moncrieff away with the four destroyers lowest in fuel to make for Seidisfiord and then to return to take over from the remainder who would be down to danger level by the time they could get back. At the same time he signalled for the local escort to be sailed early to meet the convoy.

Meanwhile the merchantmen were taking a sorry battering. One Liberty ship, the *J. L. M. Curry*, had suffered a disaster not uncommon in her class of ship when a welded seam split. She struggled on for some time until the watchers in the trawler standing by saw her suddenly break in half and founder. The crew were all saved but another valuable ship had gone. As night was falling on the wild scene on the 7th, Campbell learnt from a Liberator aircraft that the convoy was scattered in groups fifty miles apart, but husbanding his precious fuel he could but wait for a break in the weather to bring relief.

The next day some of the savagery had gone out of the wind and slowly the Commodore and escorts managed to gather in some of the outlying groups until there were twenty-one ships in company. But as the weather moderated the enemy threat returned. The Focke-Wulf shadowing aircraft was back on the prowl and U-boats were about. Campbell thought anxiously of the seven stragglers sailing somewhere all unprotected.

But when Scott-Moncrieff got back on the 9th, after a fearful pounding on his way to Seidisfiord where he had found barely enough fuel in the tanker for his needs, there had been no further attacks. The local escort having also arrived, Campbell was free to leave with the remainder of the destroyers to look for fuel.

But they had hardly gone when an S.O.S. from the *Porto Rican* revealed that a U-boat had found a victim. The U-boats, told by the shadowing aircraft of the stragglers, were slinking like the sea-wolves they were and coming further west than usual after such easy victims. Almost in sight of Iceland they found the *Richard Bland*, which had struggled so gamely through the gale in spite of her torpedo damage. Now a second torpedo put an end to her.

One other ship now chose the moment to break down when the Iceland minefield was close under her lee and began to drift towards it. In the nick of time the trawler *St. Elstan* got a tow line aboard her and held her clear until the *Opportune* arrived to tow her into Seidisfiord.

Meanwhile Campbell's search for fuel had taken him to Akureyri on the north coast and with the *Orwell* and *Orkan* he had felt his way in through a blinding snowstorm. With tanks refilled the three ships sailed again to search for stragglers and for any survivors, though it was daunting to think of any poor devils adrift in that bitter weather. Yet when they arrived the next morning in the position where the *Richard Bland* had sunk they found the *Eclipse* and *Impulsive* on the spot and rescuing a great many of the crew.

During the day as they continued their search with *Eclipse* and *Impulsive* in company, one of the stragglers, the *Yorkman*, passed and from her Campbell learnt that her master had, with wise initiative, kept to the north and inside the edge of the ice packs since losing the convoy during the storm.

Hopes of finding any further survivors were running low by the evening of 12th March, but one last sweep of the area had just begun when, from the *Impulsive*, wreckage was sighted. Eyes searching pitifully through the pathetic jumble of flotsam, suddenly fell on a small raft bobbing in the middle of it, two figures lying motionless on it. When the raft was brought along-side it was seen to everyone's amazement that one of the men was still alive though the other was dead. For three days that one man of all the crew of the *Porto Rican* had clung grimly to life in that freezing weather, constantly soaked in sea water and lashed by the cutting wind. The imagination boggles at what he must have gone through.

So the voyage of R.A. 53 came to its end. Four ships had been lost but three of them could be counted as the victims more of the weather than of the enemy, though all but one had been sent to the bottom by torpedoes.

It was a weary and battered force of escorts which reached harbour at last, sorrowing for the losses sustained but yet by no means discouraged. As their captains shrugged off the damp, unappetizing clothes which had not left their backs for many days to revel in the joys of a bath, a few rounds of drinks and gossip in a wardroom no longer crazily heaving, a hot meal which need not be guarded from slithering to the deck, and at last a night of undisturbed sleep, they could feel they had little with which to reproach themselves.

For once again fifty-eight ships in all had been convoyed right past the enemy's doorstep and an immense quantity of vital war material delivered to our churlish and utterly unappreciative allies. Four ships and a proportion of their crews was a low cost in the brutal accountancy of war.

*   *   *

The light losses of these two convoys in February 1943 and the evident paucity of enemy air strength in Norway led once again to proposals to continue the Arctic Convoys through the summer. From Moscow the pressure for more and more supplies to be sent never ceased. Had Hitler's 'irrevocable decision' to lay up the German surface fleet not been abandoned, convoys might well have been run in March. But Doenitz, once he had settled in Raeder's chair, had seen the wisdom of his predecessor's insistence on the maintenance of a balanced fleet. Being high in the Fuehrer's favour, he had been able to make such views prevail.

On 11th March, the *Tirpitz* was sighted leaving Trondheim and it was not long before air reconnaissance revealed that not only she, but the battle-cruiser *Scharnhorst* and the *Lutzow* were all in Altenfiord. Admiral Tovey at once told the Admiralty that under these circumstances he did not consider the continuance of Arctic convoys justifiable. Only by taking his battle fleet into the Barents Sea, which he had never considered a worth-while risk for the comparatively minor object of covering a convoy, could he give protection against such a formidable force.

The Commander-in-Chief's objections gained support from an unexpected direction. The Russians chose this moment when they were pressing with unabated vigour for a continuation of the convoys, to make it more difficult for us by obstructive tactics. Two British wireless stations in the Murmansk area were ordered to close down and the entry of Royal Air Force ground staff for the squadrons to be based there was forbidden.

It was not difficult therefore for the Admiralty to persuade the Government, when the Battle of the Atlantic reached a critical stage in March, that all possible escort craft and destroyers would be better thrown into that decisive struggle than dissipated on operations of doubtful wisdom to fight Arctic convoys through.

Not all Home Fleet destroyers could be spared to reinforce the Western Approaches Command, of course. The Home Fleet still had to bar the way to the Atlantic against any sortie by the German surface fleet and a certain number of flotillas had to be retained. But none could be spared for Arctic convoys. So while decisive defeat was being inflicted on Doenitz's U-boats by the Western Approaches Command aided by the Home Fleet flotillas, the Kola Run came to a halt.

Then as the summer wore on and the newly-won immunity of the trans-Atlantic convoys made the reinforcement of the Western Approaches no longer necessary, the Home Fleet flotillas began to return to Scapa and the berths in Gutta Sound were once again filled. By the beginning of the autumn sufficient destroyers had assembled to resume the Kola Run. But the new Commander-in-Chief, Sir Bruce Fraser, who had relieved Admiral Tovey in May, was no more inclined than his predecessor to expose the Arctic convoys to the threat of the three German capital ships still lying in Altenfiord.

Then at the end of September the whole picture changed. An attack of infinite daring by British midget submarines had seriously damaged the *Tirpitz*, putting her out of action for many months to come. Victoria Crosses, awarded to Lieutenants D. Cameron, R.N.R., and B. C. G. Plaice, R.N., for their valour in this operation, had been added to those already won in Arctic waters. The *Lutzow* had already returned to Germany for refit; so now only *Scharnhorst* and six destroyers were left effective in the north. The Admiralty decided at once to resume the Arctic Convoys.

The first and most urgent need was to fetch back the empty ships, the unfortunate crews of which had been lying idle in North Russia since the spring. A force of eight fleet destroyers, one Western Approaches destroyer-escort, two minesweepers and a corvette was assembled to form their escort under the command of Captain Ian Campbell of the *Milne*.

It was decided to take advantage of this force to convoy five Russian minesweepers and six Russian motor submarine chasers which were on their way to Polyarnoe, the fleet destroyers to act as a covering force, the remainder under the command of Captain Jay of the *Harrier* to be their close escort.

All arrived safely at Kola on 28th October and for the first time the escorts were berthed alongside the jetties in Polyarnoe naval base, Admiral Archer, head of our naval Mission, having at last persuaded the Russians to offer this small hospitality. Encouraged by this, Campbell made a brave effort to establish normal friendly relations with their fleet.

Besides the usual official calls, visits were exchanged between his ships and the Russians. The Commander-in-Chief, Admiral Golovko and Campbell exchanged dinners and presents. But it was uphill work. The language difficulty could have been overcome with good will, but all gaiety and light-hearted talk was smothered by the attitude of the dour, unsmiling political commissars who attended every occasion, their mean, suspicious eyes flickering like those of cornered animals.

The return convoy of thirteen ships suffered no interference from the enemy. Indeed it would have been something of a miracle if the Germans had found it at all in the combination of fog, snow and winter gales through which it made its blind, storm-tossed way. The only moment of interest in the voyage was the sighting in a brief clearance of the weather on 6th November of the legendary Bear Island, so often referred to but so very seldom seen by travellers on the Kola Run.

Pale winter sunshine, almost the last it would see for two months, lighting up the hump of land solidly encased in virgin snow gave it a forlorn beauty of its own. But it did not invite closer acquaintance, though a wag amongst the escort captains made a signal to the escort commander, 'Request permission to land libertymen'!

Bear Island was one of those sinister, solitary outcrops of land in the ocean which the seaman views with a shiver of distaste. Another is Haalsbakur or the Whale's Back off the coast of Iceland, a smooth expanse of glistening grey rock lying awash and quite unmarked. In calm weather a long uneasy swell laps it, spreads smoothly over to smother it with barely a hint of warning foam so that it seems to lie waiting in malevolent ambush for the unwary mariner.

The Kola Run had become a very different affair now that Doenitz had accepted the unwisdom of pitting his wolf-packs against well-escorted convoys. Through November and early December of 1943 they ran unmolested.

In his flagship *Duke of York*, the Commander-in-Chief, Admiral Fraser, pondered this strange immunity. For he knew that the powerful battle-cruiser *Scharnhorst* and her attendant destroyers were still lying in brooding menace in Altenfiord, whence a short run would bring them to the convoy route. He could only conclude that the Germans had not woken up to what was going on. So that when convoy J.W. 55.A, which had left Loch Ewe on 12th December was sighted and shadowed by an aircraft, he felt sure it would rouse the German fleet to some activity.

He therefore decided that the time had come to give close battleship cover to the convoys even inside the Barents Sea. While J.W. 55.A was making its passage therefore he took the *Duke of York* through to Kola and berthed her in Vaenga Bay for a few days.

The Commander-in-Chief was quite right in his belief but for the wrong reason. The German Naval War Staff had known at once when the Arctic convoys were resumed. But to do something about it was quite another matter. Doenitz was unwilling to accept the losses in U-boats which attack on convoys now entailed. Improved, fast, Type XXI boats and others fitted with the schnorkel, the breathing tube which enabled them to stay submerged indefinitely, would be coming to sea soon, but until then the convoys were to be left alone.

On the other hand Doenitz's staff and the Group Command, North, had been greatly impressed by the evidence that had accumulated on the British radar equipment – radar using the centimetric wave band which gave greatly improved surface warning performance. The German ships had nothing like it. To risk the *Scharnhorst*, the last of Germany's big ships fit for battle, in the winter darkness and snow under such a handicap would be foolish. Such was the view of the German Naval High Command.

But Doenitz, who had achieved his Grand Admiral's baton by his assurance to Hitler that victory at sea could be won by his U-boats on their own, was now forced to eat his words or admit himself impotent to interfere with allied sea traffic a bare 200 miles from German-held territory. Thus he found himself seeking Hitler's permission to send *Scharnhorst* out against the next convoy.

The Fuehrer's intuition was as unreliable in naval matters as ever. Now, when the opportunity to strike at the Arctic convoys with impunity had gone with the steady attrition his fleet had suffered, Hitler took courage to give Doenitz his head.

Two Arctic convoys were at sea in the latter half of December. J.W. 55.B, with a big escort under the command of Captain James McCoy in the *Onslow*, had left Loch Ewe on the 20th. A homeward convoy R.A. 55.A left two days later from Kola, its escort under Captain Campbell in the *Milne*. This latter convoy slipped out of harbour and away into the dark and fog to the north undetected and by Christmas Day had passed Bear Island in safety.

J.W. 55.B, however, was located as early as 22nd December. At once preparations were put in hand in Altenfiord. Minesweepers were set to sweep the exit channel and *Scharnhorst* and her five destroyers were prepared for sea. They they lay, ready to pounce as soon as air reconnaissance or U-boats reported the convoy well into the Barents Sea.

17

BATTLE OF GIANTS

As Christmas approached that year of 1943, it was the crews of the German ships who were best able to enjoy the traditional celebrations up there in the bleak northern latitudes. Snug in harbour they sang their nostalgic Christmas songs; the strains of 'Heilige Nacht' echoed from the steep sides of the fiord. Only a bustling of staff officers round the Admiral's cabin in the *Scharnhorst*, a coming and going of signalmen, an increase in the frequency of gun drills gave an indication that the interminable wait, the ships moored securely inside anti-torpedo nets, was about to come to an end.

But for the allied ships of the two convoys and the British and Canadian ships of their escorts there was nothing but the date to tell them that it was Christmas. In wild, tempestuous weather they were rolling and plunging their way. There was no turkey or plum pudding for them – more likely a sandwich and a mug of cocoa from a swamped galley.

In the British fleet there was a strong feeling, based on no real evidence, that great events were impending. Both James McCoy, commanding J.W. 55.B's escort, and Bruce Fraser, one an Irishman, the other a Highlander, had strong premonitions. The latter so much so that as early as the 24th, when *Scharnhorst* was still mewed up in harbour, he gave orders for J.W. 55.B to reverse its course for three hours, calculating that this would prevent the enemy from making contact with it before dark on that day, though in fact German surface forces had never operated so far west.

By Christmas Day the homeward convoy, R.A. 55.A, was past

Bear Island and reasonably safe, while J.W. 55.B was approaching the danger area. Still convinced that something was up, the Commander-in-Chief, at sea in the *Duke of York* with the cruiser *Jamaica* and four destroyers, ordered Captain Campbell, escorting R.A. 55.A, to send four of his destroyers to reinforce James McCoy. Accordingly Commander Fisher of the *Musketeer* was sent with *Matchless, Opportune* and *Virago*.

Meanwhile in Altenfiord, the *Scharnhorst* and five destroyers were raising steam. A Rear-Admiral's flag flew at the battle-cruiser's masthead, for Vice-Admiral Kummetz was on leave. In his place was Rear-Admiral Bey, a destroyer man through and through, senior surviving officer of the destroyer squadron annihilated in the battles of Narvik and lately Commodore of destroyers.

Since the 22nd, when J.W. 55.B was first located, his staff had watched the situation developing. The Luftwaffe was entrusted with the duty of maintaining contact and of reconnoitring the whole area for 300 miles round the convoy to bring warning of any covering force. For Bey's orders were precise that though there were to be no half measures in taking *Scharnhorst* in to smash the convoy with her big guns if contact were made, on no account was he to stand and fight if heavy units were met.

The German airmen kept contact with the convoy for the next two days but failed to locate either the *Duke of York* and her squadron to the west or Vice-Admiral Burnett's force of cruisers, *Belfast, Norfolk* and *Sheffield*, to the eastward. As darkness fell on Christmas Eve the weather was deteriorating and by the following day was too bad for air reconnaissance. U-boats were in touch, however, and continued to keep Bey informed as to the position and progress of the convoy.

By the evening of Christmas Day it was calculated that by daylight the next morning the convoy would be nicely placed for an attack on it. As dark was falling, Rear-Admiral Bey led his force to sea. The plan which he had communicated to his destroyer captains was for interception to be made shortly before dawn, when three of the destroyers would shadow until there was sufficient light for the battle-cruiser to bring her big guns into play. Then *Scharnhorst* would move in and, with point blank, devastating salvos, annihilate the convoy. If any heavy ships should appear the action was to be broken off immediately by the *Scharnhorst* while the destroyers would fight a delaying action to cover her retreat.

The plan entirely ignored the greatly superior radar in the British ships or assumed that the escorts would stand idly by while the Germans waited for daylight to begin the action. In any case the Germans would have had to show a great deal more daring than in the past to carry it out in face of the torpedo threat from the British and Canadian destroyers of the escort. But it was never to be put to the test.

Hardly had the German squadron put to sea than Bey began to have doubts. In the heavy seas running, the fighting efficiency of the German destroyers would be much reduced. The heavy guns with which they were armed made them bad sea-boats compared to their British counterparts. Bey asked the shore command for instructions whether the operation should proceed.

The matter was referred to Doenitz himself. There can be little doubt that by now the politician in him was overriding the seaman. His reputation with the Fuehrer was at stake. In spite of his sea commander's obvious misgivings, he ordered the operation to proceed. What is more, Bey was told that the *Scharnhorst* might carry on alone at his discretion.

So the die was cast. The great ship rolled on northwards through the rough cold night. Bey's signal picked up by Allied direction-finding stations told the Admiralty that the *Scharnhorst* was out. When the Commander-in-Chief Home Fleet received this news early on the 26th, he knew the time was past for finesse. All that mattered now was to draw the *Scharnhorst* as far north as possible and to get Burnett's force in the convoy's vicinity where they could hold the battle-cruiser in play long enough for the *Duke of York* to come pounding eastward to gain a position between *Scharnhorst* and her base.

To do this, the exact positions of the various units must be known to each other. Wireless silence was broken to order McCoy to divert his course to the north-east to delay the enemy's interception and lure him northward, to order McCoy and Admiral Burnett to report their positions and the latter to close the convoy.

By 7.30 that morning these moves were in train. While the German squadron held to its northerly course, closing it rapidly from the eastward were Burnett's cruisers. Then at 8 o'clock a signal reached Bey from one of the U-boats which made it appear that he had crossed ahead of the convoy and was now too far to the north. He at once swung round to a south-westerly course and, reducing to 12 knots, spread his destroyers five miles apart across his front to search.

The British wireless signals if intercepted by direction-finding stations would have given the enemy a rough picture of the disposition of the forces they were liable to meet. But for some reason no advantage seems to have been taken by the Germans of the information thus handed to them, and Bey knew nothing of the near presence of Burnett's squadron nor of the more distant force under the Commander-in-Chief.

Similarly in the British cruisers there was as yet no sure knowledge of the enemy's position. But it was known that *Scharnhorst* was somewhere at sea and Burnett was following sound principles in heading north-west to join the convoy, the prize which must surely lure the *Scharnhorst* to it also. He was thus closing the *Scharnhorst* on a course roughly at right angles to the enemy's when at 8.40 a.m. radar in the *Belfast* reported a contact at seventeen and a half miles range, west-north-west.

The range decreased rapidly but it was still night, clear and cold but rough and very dark, so that it was not until nearly 9.30 that, from the *Sheffield*, the dim bulk of the great battle-cruiser could be made out. At the same moment the *Belfast* opened fire with starshells.

In the *Scharnhorst*, in spite of two presumably serviceable radar sets, there was no forewarning. The first thing that her commander, Captain Hintze, knew was the sudden blossoming overhead of the brilliant yellow flare of a starshell, lighting up the whole length of the ship and exposing her to a hidden enemy. Immediately afterwards the first tall columns from the splash of eight-inch shells rose out of the water alongside.

Surprise was complete and became consternation as an 8-inch shell from the *Norfolk* burst against the *Scharnhorst*'s fore-top, causing many casualties and wrecking her forward radar set.

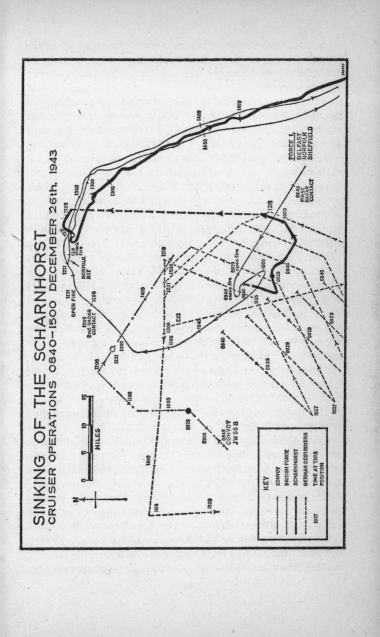

SINKING OF THE SCHARNHORST
CRUISER OPERATIONS 0840–1500 DECEMBER 26th. 1943

A second shell burst on her forecastle immediately afterwards.

Unable to see the enemy who had taken him thus unawares, Hintze called for full speed and swung his ship round to the south and then south-east. Shells continued to fall around her but there were no further hits and, as speed worked up, her smaller opponents were shaken off. Burnett's cruisers were unable to match the *Scharnhorst*'s thirty knots in the heavy seas that were running, but they struggled along in chase for a time.

As the ranges coming down from the radar steadily increased, Burnett appreciated that he was unable to hold contact with his speedier enemy. All would be thrown into doubt again as the *Scharnhorst* ran out of radar range. But before this took place the British admiral realized that the enemy was edging gradually round to a course of east and then north-east, circling round the cruisers for a new thrust at the convoy. By turning back to his north-westerly course, Burnett could again get between the *Scharnhorst* and the convoy. This he did, confident that it would bring about the further contact which was so vital.

But in the *Duke of York*, still nearly 200 miles away to the westward and pressing forward at her best speed with the south-westerly gale behind her to get between *Scharnhorst* and her base, Sir Bruce Fraser could not be so sanguine. If Bey had turned at once for home, the *Duke of York* would be too late and the *Scharnhorst* would have slipped out of the net. Meanwhile contact had been lost and all was agonized guesswork.

But it was not only on the British side that the brief action had brought uncertainty and anxiety. Communications between the German admiral and his destroyers had been disrupted and while the *Scharnhorst* swerved away to the north-eastward, the flotilla continued on their south-westerly search all unaware that the battle-cruiser had been in action.

By 10 o'clock communications were restored and when Bey found that his destroyers were still searching in the wrong direction he ordered them to turn back to the north-east at high speed. But they were by then too far separated and, as we shall see, were never in fact able to rejoin their flagship.

So for the next two hours, while the Arctic winter daylight

grew towards a twilit noon, the two German units and three British went on their separate ways. The convoy was steering away to the north-eastwards on orders from the Commander-in-Chief, who had also told McCoy to send four of his destroyers to join Admiral Burnett. Accordingly Commander Fisher's division of four ships was despatched and shortly before eleven joined the cruisers. Burnett now disposed his ships to await the thrust at the convoy he was sure the *Scharnhorst* would make. While his cruisers zigzagged across the convoy's front and ten miles ahead of it, *Musketeer*'s division was thrown forward four miles as a screen.

Meanwhile a German reconnaissance aircraft had at last located Admiral Fraser's force and had reported its position as 150 miles to the westward of *Scharnhorst* and coming east. The signal as it reached Bey omitted to say, however, that amongst the force was a battleship. Confident in the strength of his splendid ship, designed to withstand as many as fourteen torpedo hits, and urged on by a signal from Doenitz exhorting him to 'strike a blow for the gallant troops on the eastern front by destroying the convoy', the Rear-Admiral had discounted this new threat and pressed on for the convoy.

As time wore on without further development, McCoy had decided to resume the convoy's course to the south-east as he had been given discretion to do. The resultant protracted manoeuvre by the unwieldy convoy was still in progress when, at five minutes past twelve, the *Belfast*'s radar picked up the *Scharnhorst* approaching from the east and Burnett knew that his hunch had been right. Fifteen minutes later she hove in sight.

The cruisers' guns at once roared out and Fisher's destroyers were ordered to attack with torpedoes. But Bey, exasperated to find his late antagonists still barring his way to the convoy, at once turned away to the south-east. Though Fisher took his destroyers in chase and added the fire of his guns to that of the cruisers, there was no possibility of getting into torpedo-firing position.

With daylight, *Scharnhorst* gave a better account of herself in this second action. Revenge was taken on the *Norfolk* who was twice hit. One 11-inch shell plunged through the barbette of a turret putting it out of action. Another hit amidships did much damage and started a serious fire. One officer and six ratings were killed and five others seriously wounded. But *Norfolk* remained in the line, her speed not affected.

From the British angle, though it was thought at the time that *Scharnhorst* was again hit, she did not in fact suffer further damage then. But Bey had had enough and was now heading for home. However, shortly before this encounter he had given his flotilla the convoy's position as reported by a U-boat and had ordered them to attack it.

The U-boat's signal had been greatly delayed in reaching him and the position was too far to the westward. As the German destroyers turned to obey they were, had they but known it, a bare eight miles to the southward of the convoy. Another ten minutes on their previous course and they would have run slap against it as it steered south-east.

It is fascinating to speculate what might have occurred. The five powerful German ships would have been facing seven less well-armed British and Canadian destroyers, and three older destroyer-escorts. The British force, however, would have been caught widely scattered round the perimeter of the convoy, and before they could have concentrated individual ships might have been overwhelmed. On the other hand, the lack of seaworthiness of the German ships might have cancelled out their advantage in the heavy weather prevailing.

It is impossible to guess what might have happened, and the encounter was not to be. Running off to the westward the German destroyers passed off the scene and an hour and a quarter later were ordered to break off operations and return to harbour.

For Bey had given up all hope of carrying out his mission after his second brush with Burnett and was anxious only to get back safely to harbour himself. But *Scharnhorst*'s fate was already sealed. The time spent in chasing northwards after the convoy had, as Admiral Fraser had hoped, destroyed any chance of escaping the doom hurrying towards her. For all the while, Fraser's squadron, in spite of the heavy following seas which threatened his destroyers with the danger of broaching-to, was racing on at twenty-four knots.

As Bey now set off for home at high speed, the range opened out. The cruisers ceased fire and settled down to shadow from astern, their excellent radar keeping them informed of every move made by the battle-cruiser, the information being passed on to the Commander-in-Chief.

Burnett was well content with the situation. For, all unknown to the Germans, interception by the *Duke of York* was now certain. Already Admiral Fraser had divided his destroyer force into two sub-divisions and stationed them one on each bow whence, when the time was ripe, they would be able to press on to take the *Scharnhorst* under torpedo fire from two sides.

Time crept by with agonizing slowness in the British force as the two great ships drew near, their courses at right angles to one another, while the short Arctic day faded. Radar operators' eyes in the *Duke of York* almost left their sockets as they strained towards their 'scans' to get the first signs of a contact. Captain Guy Russell paced the bridge in feverish impatience. The Commander-in-Chief's burly form stood rigid with anticipation in his operations room as he waited for the word which would tell him that the enemy was delivered into his hands. Excitement through the ship was intense. The weary months of oft-repeated sweeps without ever catching a glimpse of the enemy were now to be rewarded.

Then, at last, at 4.15, there was a sudden stir. The 'blip' was there on the 'scan'. Contact at twenty-three miles.

Almost Bruce Fraser could feel he had the *Scharnhorst* in the hollow of his hand. But the German battle-cruiser still had the legs of any big ship in the British force. Unless her speed could be somehow reduced, she might slip out of the trap yet. How well Guy Russell had trained his ship to shoot would be the ultimate arbiter of the coming action.

For another thirty-five minutes the *Duke of York* pounded on, the range coming steadily down. At 4.50 the *Scharnhorst* was withing hitting range and once again, all unaware of her danger, she was suddenly illuminated by a starshell from the *Belfast* as Burnett delivered her into the hands of his Commander-in-Chief.

As the great silver-grey length of the *Scharnhorst* sprang into view, the 14-inch guns of the *Duke of York* erupted into action.

Out of the very first salvo, a shell hit the German on her starboard bow, abreast the foremost turret which was put out of action at once. A minute later another wreaked heavy damage on the quarter-deck. As a demonstration of accurate gunnery it was superb.

Surprise was again complete. The huge pillars of water showing that they were large shells falling round were Bey's first indication that a battleship had come on the scene. Turning to flee, Captain Hintze swung his ship round to the north. But there he found *Belfast* and *Norfolk* waiting for him. Only to the eastward was there temporary safety and, piling on his utmost speed, Hintze headed in that direction.

Running now directly away from the *Duke of York*, the *Scharnhorst*'s range began to increase again. As the battle-cruiser swerved with each salvo so as to bring all her guns to bear, the gunnery problem for the *Duke of York* became more difficult. No more hits were scored for more than an hour, while the *Scharnhorst*'s gunnery, once she had recovered from her initial surprise, steadily improved. The *Duke of York*, pressing on in chase, moved through leaping shell splashes and had both her masts shot through though the shells did not explode.

At 5.15, Fraser's two pairs of destroyers had been sent on at their best speed to try to get into position to fire torpedoes. Careering wildly along in the following sea, they were more than ever in imminent danger of broaching-to. Sweating coxswains in their wheelhouses wrestled with the wheel as each successive wave gathered under the stern and threatened to spin their ships round and over on their beam ends. Fuel was low in all of them and such a happening might have meant capsizing. But the hunt was up, the quarry in view. The destroyers' torpedoes might be the deciding factor in bringing the *Scharnhorst* to book. On they drove at full speed.

They were gaining but slowly, however. Commander Meyrick in the *Savage* was leading the *Saumarez*, aiming to get out on the enemy's port side, while Lieutenant-Commander Clouston in *Scorpion* and the Norwegian *Stord* were slanting southwards to take the enemy on her other flank. Commander Fisher's four destroyers, also sent off to the attack, were creeping forward on a course parallel to the enemy's and some miles to the northward, hoping to be in a position to synchronize their attacks with the others when the time came.

But it was only with agonizing slowness that the range in the destroyers was coming down. The *Duke of York* was dropping back, unable to match the battle-cruiser's speed. If the enemy kept on her easterly course it was likely that the *Scharnhorst* would yet escape. By 6.20 the destroyers were still six miles astern of the fleeing battle-cruiser. Then, suddenly, the whole picture changed. A shell from the *Duke of York* landed square on the *Scharnhorst* causing underwater damage. Her speed rapidly fell away from thirty knots to twenty. The exultant destroyer captains found themselves overhauling their target hand over fist.

By 6.40 the range from the *Savage* was down to 10,000 yards and rapidly decreasing. As the *Scharnhorst* turned her secondary armament on to them, the destroyers also opened fire. In the *Scharnhorst* there was great confusion in the gunnery control. Her fire was wild and ineffective and the two destroyers pressed on undamaged, while from the other side of the battle-cruiser, *Scorpion* and *Stord* were coming in unseen.

At 6.49, in the light of starshells from *Savage* and *Saumarez*, the enemy was seen to be swinging round to a southerly course, turning at bay. This put *Scorpion* and *Stord* at last in a good position for torpedo fire and they at once turned to starboard to bring their tubes to bear, each firing eight torpedoes at a range of a mile. The *Scharnhorst* swung to comb the tracks so that only *Scorpion* was able to claim one hit. At the same time the battle-cruiser's secondary armament came belatedly into action, firing wildly and without effect while the destroyers' 4·7-inch guns slammed shells into the superstructure of their huge target.

Continuing her circle round to starboard until she was on a south-westerly course, the *Scharnhorst*, continuously illuminated by starshell flares hanging like a chandelier in the sky over her, now offered herself a target for *Savage* and *Saumarez*. Turning in to the attack at 6.55, they drew heavy fire on themselves, particularly the nearer of the two, the *Saumarez*. Hit several times and her decks swept by a storm of splinters which killed one officer and ten ratings and wounded eleven more, *Saumarez* yet managed to get four torpedoes away at a range of 1800 yards while *Savage* launched her full outfit of eight from a longer range. As they withdrew to the northwards, three distinct concussions were felt as torpedoes got home.

In the *Scharnhorst* there was great confusion by this time. Bey had for some time realized that her end was in sight and had made his last signal to the shore announcing that 'they would fight to the last shell'. And now the *Duke of York* and *Jamaica*, who had ceased firing while the destroyers were so close to their target, re-engaged at a range of 10,400 yards, a killing range for their guns. The great battle-cruiser was smothered with shell hits, fires blazing up and ammunition round the guns exploding. Her main armament was partially out of action and firing only intermittently. Her speed was falling away until it was barely five knots.

At 7.15 the *Belfast* also joined in from the northward. The death struggles of the dying giant were a fearful sight. Built to be virtually unsinkable by gunfire, her end when it came was bound to be prolonged and agonizing. The Commander-in-Chief ordered the *Duke of York* to cease fire and the *Belfast* and *Jamaica* to go in and finish her off with torpedoes. Closing in with guns blazing, the cruisers each fired three torpedoes but, misjudging the speed of the *Scharnhorst*, hidden as she was in a pall of smoke, none hit.

A last wild burst of gunfire from the German's secondary armament achieved nothing. By the time the *Jamaica* had turned to fire three more torpedoes, two of which hit, the *Scharnhorst*'s guns were finally silent.

The *Belfast* was similarly manoeuvring to repeat her attack when she found the target masked by the arrival of Commander Fisher's four destroyers bent on being in at the death. *Scharnhorst*'s turn to the southward had left them toiling astern and only now had they been able to reach the scene of action. The oily wake left by the dying battle-cruiser led them to their quarry. Dividing into two sub-divisions, they came, punching into heavy seas, to the attack, *Opportune* and *Virago* from starboard, *Musketeer* and *Matchless* from port. From *Opportune* eight torpedoes sped away of which two were claimed as hits. From *Virago*, out of seven fired, two were seen to find the target. Then *Musketeer* got four torpedoes away and saw at least two of them hit. Only *Matchless*, the training gear of her torpedo tubes damaged by a heavy sea which had swept her decks, and the bridge swamped by another, was unable to fire.

But it was enough. A dense cloud of smoke, a dull glow at its heart, was all that could now be seen of *Scharnhorst's* death throes. At 7.45, after a heavy underwater explosion, the glow vanished. Nearly 2000 men and a once splendid ship had met their end. Thirteen hits by 14-inch shells and a dozen more by 8-inch, besides numerous smaller hits by the destroyers' guns, had battered the *Scharnhorst* to a wreck. But it had taken eleven torpedoes to send her to the bottom.

Nothing remained but to rescue as many survivors as possible. But out of 1903 officers and men and 40 cadets, only 36, all ratings, could be found by *Scorpion* and *Matchless* as they searched amongst the debris. The bitter cold and high seas had claimed most of those who had survived the savage hammering their ship had suffered before its end.

Now, gathering together his scattered forces, Sir Bruce Fraser, well satisfied, steered for Kola where all arrived on the next day to be followed shortly by the convoy, from which nothing of the great fight in its defence had been seen or heard.

Well might the Admiralty reply to the Commander-in-Chief's signal of success with, 'Grand. Well Done.' For the sinking of the *Scharnhorst* marked the last effort of Germany's surface fleet to challenge British seapower. Henceforth the convoys to Russia would have only Doenitz's U-boats to face and a minor threat from the demoralized Luftwaffe, to meet which the escorts were now fully equipped and trained. The Kola Run had another seventeen months of life ahead of it but never again would the convoys have to accept the heavy odds which had always been potentially there if the Germans had been prepared to use their powerful surface fleet with confidence and vigour.

18

CONVOY DEFENCE PERFECTED

With the destruction of the *Scharnhorst* and the consequent elimination of any surface threat, service on the Kola Run assumed a different complexion. Escort commanders would concentrate on the problem of beating off the U-boats. These, after their heavy defeat in the Atlantic in the spring of 1943, had had their wilting morale partially restored by the issue to them of a new weapon, the acoustic homing torpedo, designed to enable them to hit back at their hunters.

This ingenious weapon, soon dubbed The Gnat by the Allies, contained a sensitive hydrophone which picked up the noises made by a ship's propellers and steered it to the source of the sound. Its great advantage was that it need only be fired roughly in the direction of its target; its homing mechanism would do the rest. Thus a hunted submarine need not come to periscope depth and expose its periscope while its captain took aim. Nor need the future course and speed of the target be correctly forecast for a hit to be obtained as with a normal, straight-running torpedo. Everywhere the target ship went, the Gnat was sure to go.

Fortunately the Gnat had its limitations. It was not very fast and could not catch up with a ship going more than 25 knots. Furthermore it was only a propeller cavitating which made the noise which attracted it. Cavitation takes place only when the propeller is biting hard into the water as when the ship is being driven at moderate or high speed or when accelerating. So a ship jogging along at slow speed was immune. A destroyer at seven knots or less or at twenty-five knots or more was considered to be safe.

The Gnat also had an over-sensitive firing device so that it was apt to explode on meeting the disturbed water of a ship's wake. This could shake a ship badly but probably no more and on a number of occasions escorts had narrow escapes in this way.

Naturally as soon as it was known that the Germans were using such a weapon, brains were set to work to devise an antidote. This took the form of towing at a distance astern of the ship noise-makers which provided a stronger lure than the propellers. A somewhat complicated device whereby a pair of these noise-makers, one on either quarter, was towed was known as a 'Foxer'. A simpler version in which a single noise-maker was towed in the wake was called a 'Cat'. Both these remedies were effective but they made a distracting racket in the ears of the asdic operators and reduced their efficiency. So they were not popular, particularly in the Arctic where the asdic was already handicapped by difficult water conditions. It was always a problem whether it was better to risk the Gnats and keep the asdic efficient or to be free to move at any speed and accept the muffling of the asdic note.

Other devices were employed by the U-boats. To deceive the asdic operators a 'Pillenwerfer' or Bubble Target was introduced which, ejected from the submarine, effervesced and provided a target from which the asdic beam echoed strongly. The inexperienced asdic operator would accept this clear echo in preference to that from the submarine which would sneak away into safety while the pillenwerfer was soundly depth-charged.

When the efficiency of British radar came to be appreciated, the Germans produced a decoy target for that also by setting adrift on the breeze a light wire held aloft by a balloon. Neither of these tricks would deceive the experienced operator, but with the tremendous expansion of our escort forces, for every tried veteran of the U-boat war, there were a dozen green hands among both officers and men.

It was the Gnat, however, which was the Germans' best weapon in 1944. With it the U-boats tried to stage a great comeback. In the Arctic the loss of the *Scharnhorst* gave them a particular incentive and a strong effort to disrupt the convoys in the New Year was anticipated. The first convoy to sail in 1944,

J.W. 56.A, though only twenty strong, was given a strong escort and cruiser cover.

But it was still the weather rather than the enemy on which thoughts dwelt as convoys set out on the Kola Run. Even the bleak, treeless hills of Western Ross looked infinitely beguiling to the crews of the freighters and escorts as the anchors thudded home in the hawse-pipes in Loch Ewe, when it was northward up into the Arctic that their ships would be turning as they followed the Commodore out into the Minches.

As they ploughed north past the Summer Isles, mates and First Lieutenants would be seeing that heavy weather lashings were in place, that anything which the remotest stretch of imagination could picture as movable was firmly secured. For the winter gales of the black north could make normal precautions seem laughably inadequate. By the time Cape Wrath had faded to starboard it might be too late, with nothing now between the ships and the whole broad Atlantic to westward across which the savage south-westerly gales raced unchecked.

J.W. 56.A was assailed by one of these and three days after sailing was hopelessly scattered, the ships so damaged that they were forced to make for shelter at Akureyri. Five were too badly knocked about to continue but the remainder were given help by working parties from the cruiser support force and the ocean escort and set off again.

It was a small convoy with a very adequate escort so far as size went; but some of the escorts were short of experience, so that when a U-boat pack gathered round them as they were passing Bear Island, they were unable to prevent the loss of three ships. It was clear that the methods which had proved so successful in the Atlantic must be applied to the Arctic convoys.

The basis of these was 'defence in depth'. As efficient surface warning radar came to be fitted in more escorts, it became feasible to throw an outer ring round the convoy at night, perhaps six miles or more from the convoy, where they would be able to detect the surfaced U-boats as they made for their attack positions. Forcing them to submerge, these outer escorts prevented the U-boats from travelling at the high speed necessary to gain such positions.

Alternatively any surplus escorts over the close screen could be formed into support groups with a roving commission to sweep the areas around, where the U-boats would be on the surface, or to run down bearings obtained by Huff Duff.

To provide this surplus for the next convoy, the ocean escort which had delivered J.W. 56.A was brought out to meet J.W. 56.B in the danger area where it could operate as a support force. Captain Campbell in the *Milne*, commanding the escort of J.W. 56.B had been watching an ominous situation developing round his convoy since the first shadowing aircraft had made contact five days out from Loch Ewe.

Warnings had come in from the U-boat tracking organization in the Admiralty of concentrations lying in wait ahead. In spite of a diversion to the northward in the hope of circling round them, Huff Duff reports of submarines in the vicinity began to come in at ever-decreasing intervals till the air seemed heavy with threat. Sorties to put the U-boats down or scare them off, kept them away for two days, but by 29th January the volume of enemy signals was evidence that the odds were piling up. There was a danger of the defence being swamped by the sheer weight of numbers, as had happened in some convoy battles in the Atlantic.

The situation was therefore tense, to say the least of it, when to Campbell's infinite relief Captain Robson in the *Hardy* with six other destroyers arrived from Kola in support. This changed the whole aspect of things. With Robson's ships patrolling wide and able to pounce quickly on any U-boat betraying its position by its happy custom of wireless chatter, the enemy found themselves thwarted at every move.

As the convoy moved steadily on under the eerie light of the Aurora through a sea dappled with patches of drifting pack-ice, Campbell had evidence of the despairing efforts to which the enemy was reduced as a torpedo fired more or less at random exploded against an ice floe more than a mile ahead. No sound reached him, but the great column of water rising mysteriously in the air ahead could have come from no other cause.

But foiled of his primary prey, the convoy, the enemy now turned in exasperation against the destroyers. A U-boat put down by the arrival of Robson's division of four let loose a Gnat. As the *Hardy* swept by at twenty knots the torpedo homed on to her propellers and blew off the destroyer's stern. The Norwegian destroyer *Stord* was quickly in contact with the submarine and sending down a well-placed pattern of depth-charges blew it to the surface. But before another attack could finish it off, the enemy had dived again and, going down deep, was able to sneak away to safety though no doubt badly shaken and too damaged to play any further part for some time.

The heavy concentration of U-boats made it impossible to think of taking *Hardy* in tow so the *Venus* took off her ship's company and sent her to the bottom with a torpedo. It was a sad loss of such a lovely new ship, successor to the *Hardy* in which Warburton-Lee had led his flotilla to victory in the first battle of Narvik in 1940. But the object was being attained nevertheless – 'the safe and timely arrival of the convoy'.

Revenge was to be taken later that day also, when the *Meteor* and *Whitehall* of Campbell's escort force, gaining contact with a submerged U-boat, hunted it skilfully and persistently for four hours. They returned to the convoy disappointed, under the impression that their prey had escaped them; but later it became known that *U314* had been sent to its account.

The U-boats had exhausted their tricks against this convoy. Gnats and radar lures failed to help them and the merchantmen arrived safe and sound at Kola Inlet on 1st February.

Such was a typical mid-winter voyage on the Kola Run at this phase of the war. But with February and increasing daylight, the possibility of the Luftwaffe again taking a hand had to be considered. Partly for this reason and partly because it had been by now fully realized that a combined sea and air escort was the complete answer to U-boat attack, auxiliary carriers were brought in to reinforce the escort.

Improved radar in the escorts also gave greater confidence in their ability to keep their 'flock' together in thick and tempestuous weather. The convoys could be increased in size therefore. J.W. 57 which left Loch Ewe on 20th February was forty-two strong, and the auxiliary carrier *Chaser* joined the escort. In addition to the through and ocean escorts, a support group from the Western Approaches was also to accompany it as far as Bear Island.

In command of the sizeable fleet which thus finally assembled when the ocean escort joined the convoy off the Faeroes on the 22nd, was Vice-Admiral Glennie, who had relieved Bob Burnett in his post as destroyer admiral, flying his flag in the cruiser *Black Prince*. Control was divided so that the Admiral operated the support group and the carrier while Captain Campbell in the *Milne* controlled the convoy screen.

As had been demonstrated in the Atlantic, this combination of close escort, support group and air escort was too much altogether for the submarines. Their efforts were completely disorganized and not once did they penetrate to the convoy, while an escorting Catalina caught and sank one of them and the *Chaser*'s Swordfish harried them, making repeated attacks with their new rocket projectiles, which were a great improvement on the old depth charges.

But once again, thwarted of their main objective, the enemy turned his weapons on to the escort. In the black of night, with a heavy swell running and frequent blinding snow flurries, a U-boat brought off what was, to give the devil his due, a brilliantly skilful attack in putting two torpedoes into the destroyer *Mahratta*. This calamity was made doubly tragic by the fearful loss of life that resulted.

The *Impulsive* had quickly come to the *Mahratta*'s aid and found her still afloat. In touch by radio-telephone and manoeuvring round as guided by Lieutenant-Commander Drought, the *Mahratta*'s captain, to come bow to stern alongside her forecastle, Lieutenant-Commander Bekken of the *Impulsive* could see lights from the damaged ship gleaming through the falling snow. Suddenly the lights vanished, the *Mahratta* rolled steeply over to port and capsized. By the time *Impulsive* reached the spot only struggling figures, saturated and blinded by oil fuel and rapidly becoming paralysed by the cold were to be seen.

As *Impulsive* drifted down to them, scrambling nets over the side, few had the strength left to grasp them, fewer still were able to hoist themselves up the stiffly frozen rope nets. Volunteers from the *Impulsive*'s crew at the bottom of the nets, repeatedly

211

doused into the icy water as the ship rolled, did what they could to help them. But, alas, the total number saved was but seventeen out of a company of more than 200. Though forty-two fine ships loaded deep with tens of thousands of tons of vital war equipment were delivered safely into the grasping but unappreciative hands of our Russian ally, the Kola Run had again taken its toll in human lives.

The battle with the U-boats was one which never ceased, however. After a successful passage such as this, thought had to be given to what the enemy's reaction would be. Attack in mid-ocean was obviously bringing him few dividends. It was forecast by the Commander-in-Chief's staff that the enemy command would try concentrating in the approaches to Kola Inlet. There they might expect to find the inward convoy breaking formation to file through the entrance, the outward convoy still strung out before getting into its compact ocean disposition, the escorts unable to give their scattered flock adequate protection.

The return convoy, R.A. 57, was accordingly given a route which took it on a wide diversion eastward before circling round to take the westerly course for Bear Island and beyond. At the same time the Russians were induced to put up a special air patrol to keep the U-boats' heads down. It is not known whether the enemy did in fact act as the Commander-in-Chief surmised or whether this was only intelligent anticipation on the latter's part. For later in the war the approaches to Kola did become a favourite hunting ground for the U-boats. The fact remains that R.A. 57 was not located until it was two days out from Kola.

When the enemy finally made contact they found themselves up against an active and skilful defence which took a heavy toll of them. Though there was no support group this time, the aircraft of No. 816 Squadron in the *Chaser* more than made up for this lack. The outward voyage had given the Swordfish pilots the experience and practice they needed in order to take the measure of the U-boats. Of six submarines gathered round, three were caught on the surface and sent to the bottom, two by the Swordfish on their own and one in conjunction with the destroyer *Onslaught*. Though one other U-boat succeeded in getting a torpedo into one of the convoy which had to be sunk after the crew had been taken off, it was a poor return for the expenditure of three submarines and their skilled crews.

But the increasing immunity of the merchantmen in no way eased the strain on the commanding officers of the escorts. Now that the warships were becoming the favourite targets for the U-boat commanders, only too happy to be able to squirt off a Gnat from comparative safety rather than press on through the screen to get at the convoy, there was not a minute, night or day, when the utmost precautions were not necessary. Asdic operators became jumpy with listening for the first faint beat of the propellers of an approaching torpedo. Captains and officers of the watch were always tight-strung in anticipation of having to give the emergency orders which might take their ship out of the path of the racing menace.

On this occasion both *Swift* and *Milne* were saved in the nick of time by such vigilance and quick action. In the *Milne* it was fortunate that at the crucial moment the asdic control officer, Lieutenant Collar, was on watch. His ears, well attuned from long practice, never ceased subconsciously listening to the loud-speaker of the asdic on the bridge.

At a moment when all seemed peaceful and quiet he suddenly stiffened and calmly said, 'Torpedo approaching.' Campbell, his captain, stayed not to question or confirm his statement. Leaving Collar to swing the ship to a course parallel to that which he estimated the torpedo to be travelling, he shouted for full speed and gave orders for a depth charge to be dropped to upset the mechanism of the Gnat, if Gnat it was which was approaching.

The ship swerved round under full helm, trembling as power was forced into her engines and shook as the depth charge went off close under her stern. Hearts beat fast on the bridge for the next minute or so until it gradually became clear that Collar's vigilance and quick reactions had led to the torpedo being avoided. Incidents such as this kept nerves at full stretch with no let-up.

The Kola season was now nearing its end as the sun rose higher and stayed aloft longer each day in the Arctic. At least this was the reason given out for the decision not to run summer convoys during 1944. But, of course, the supreme naval undertaking of the war, the landing of British and American armies in

Normandy, was planned for June. Every destroyer, frigate and corvette would be required for this, the greatest combined operation of history. None would be available for Arctic convoys.

There was time for one more round trip yet, however, and on 27th March a large convoy set out comprising forty-eight ships and the U.S.S. *Milwaukee*, being turned over to the Russians under 'lease-lend'. No chances were taken with this convoy. Besides the through and ocean escorts, there were two auxiliary aircraft carriers, *Activity* and *Tracker* and two support groups from the Western Approaches. The whole force was under the command of Vice-Admiral Dalrymple-Hamilton with his flag in the cruiser *Diadem*.

By this time escort carriers had become available to accompany every convoy and the technique of night-flying from the darkened decks had been mastered. This was a development which set the final seal on the defeat of the U-boats in their efforts to attack the convoys on passage even during the dark winter months which had previously been their favoured time. No longer could they cruise in safety on the surface, charging their batteries and getting ahead to a suitable attacking position. There was no rest for them night or day. At any time out of the darkness might come the roar of an aircraft's engines as a Swordfish, guided to the position by its radar, dived to release depth charges or send a salvo of rocket projectiles crashing into the submarine's hull.

But the operation of these aircraft in the darkness and bitter cold of the Arctic night and the enormities of the weather, was a supreme test of skill, endurance and courage. It was no picnic for the aircraft handlers and control teams on the often ice-covered and wildly heaving flight decks, a wind seemingly composed of icicles streaming down their length. For the pilots and observers in their open cockpits, rumbling off into the black loneliness of the night sky, their last contact with a friendly world and warmth gone unless they could put their aircraft back on to the tiny deck they had just left, the prospect was one which only cold courage could face calmly.

Waiting to receive them should their engine falter or if they failed to follow the dimly lit guidance of the 'batsmen' on to the deck on their return was a sea so icy that survival was a matter of minutes only. It was not only the night which brought its hazards. Twelve hours flying and twelve hours maintenance was the routine for the Swordfish, night or day. By day there were still the dangers of fog or snow which might blot out the carrier when petrol was running low in her aircraft aloft. Icing of wings and engines could send the aircraft down to a forced landing in the sea.

And always there was the decision to be made whether the seas were too high, the crazy motion of the carrier too violent for flying. Once in the air there was no going back on the decision and at the end of the patrol there would be waiting the desperate, heart-stopping swoop on to the floundering deck.

The fighters, too, faced these hazards, though not as a rule at night, and in addition they faced aerial combat at great odds in which even minor damage from the enemy's guns might make deck landing impossible. Yet they tore into the enemy's formations with a spirit of selfless courage that time and again brought a cheer to the throats of the watching seamen down below.

It was the escort carriers and their airmen that brought to the convoys the immunity from attack from above as well as below the surface which would not have been believed possible in the dark days of 1942.

With such an escort, it was not surprising that the U-boats were completely routed, losing three of their number without ever achieving an attack on either the outward or homeward convoy; while the infuriating 'snooper' aircraft which had always been a part of the scenery on the Kola Run were eliminated by the *Activity*'s fighters one by one as fast as they arrived.

This satisfying success could be said to bring the Kola season to a close, but one more operation was necessary to bring back the large assembly of empty freighters which would otherwise have been locked up, out of circulation, in Russian ports for the summer. There were also the American crew from the *Milwaukee* to bring back and 2300 Russian sailors to man the battleship *Royal Sovereign* and other ships which were to be lent to our ally.

In spite of their previous defeats the U-boats gathered round this large convoy in as great numbers as ever and succeeded in torpedoing one ship out of it but at a cost of three of their number to the Swordfish aircraft from the auxiliary carrier *Fencer*.

With this, the Kola Run closed down for the three mid-summer months. It seemed as though the enemy's efforts had been once and for all defeated. The Arctic voyage had become primarily a test of good seamanship and endurance in face of savage weather and bitter cold.

But though Hitler's Third Reich was about to go down in final defeat, the dying giant's death throes were yet to be reckoned with. Just as the V1s and V2s on land were to pose a problem to which only overrunning of their launching sites would bring a solution, so at sea the new schnorkel-fitted and Gnat-armed U-boats were to give a new lease of life to the enemy's assault on allied shipping which had not been fully countered when military defeat brought an end to their activities. The Kola Run was still to be no picnic when it re-opened later in that year.

19

SCHNORKEL AND GNAT

The tremendous, all-absorbing operations in the English Channel in June and July 1944 make the Arctic convoys seem almost a hum-drum affair. But the exercise of sea-power is more commonly to be found in the slow, unobtrusive, often dull business of protecting merchant convoys than in the occasional pitched battle or the vast intricacy of a combined operation to put armies ashore. Operation 'Overlord' brought only a pause in the otherwise continuous business of taking aid to Russia.

By the beginning of August the naval situation in home waters was no longer absorbing the great majority of the escort forces. Escort carriers, too, were available in greater numbers so that daylight voyages to Russia could be undertaken even if the hard-pressed Luftwaffe decided to take a hand.

Only the *Tirpitz* was a possible serious threat. Still moored in Altenfiord and attended by five destroyers, strenuous efforts had been made by the Germans to get her battleworthy after the damage done to her by the midget submarines and by Fleet Air Arm attacks in the spring. It was possible they had succeeded. It was therefore arranged for further Fleet Air Arm attacks to be synchronized with the passage of the first convoy in August.

This was numbered J.W. 59 and was composed of thirty-three merchant ships, a Rescue ship and eleven Russian submarine chasers. Strongly escorted by a cruiser, two carriers and eighteen destroyers and frigates, the U-boats had no success whatever against it. With a double screening line around it, a support group in the 'deep field' and the carrier aircraft able to fly the clock round, it was much too tough a nut for the submarines to crack.

Once again it was the loss of an escort which gave the enemy his only satisfaction when the frigate *Kite*, commanded by Lieutenant-Commander A. N. G. Campbell, was hit by two torpedoes. Sinking very quickly it was some time before a rescuer could arrive on the scene, by which time all but seventeen of her company had succumbed to the cold and more died after being taken aboard another frigate.

But in spite of this success, the U-boat command must have been bitterly disappointed at the balance sheet. For all their Gnats and new boats, they lost three of their number during the passage of this convoy and another during the voyage of the return convoy R.A. 59.A.

However, it was by no means a one-sided fight when escorts hunted one of them – the *Mermaid, Keppel, Peacock* and *Loch Dunvegan* of the support group, for instance. A patrolling Swordfish had directed them to the position in which two U-boats had been seen to dive. Hurrying to the spot they reduced speed as they neared it and set their asdics to search. The explosion of a Gnat and a white spout of water in the wake, shaking the *Keppel* from keel to truck as though by a giant's hand, left no doubt that they were in the right area.

But probe as they would, no echo came back from the sound beam of the asdics. Fifty minutes went by and *Mermaid* and *Loch Dunvegan* were ordered away to see if they could have better luck with the second U-boat known to be near by. Hardly had they set off than *Mermaid* got a contact and held it. The U-boat commander, no doubt realizing that he was fairly caught in the asdic beam, loosed a Gnat which missed, then another Gnat. But Lieutenant-Commander Mosse of the *Mermaid* was taking every precaution. The second torpedo also failed to home on to its target.

Then contact was lost. Cursing the Arctic water conditions, Mosse and Commander Wheeler, R.N.R., of the *Loch Dunvegan* cast this way and that to regain it. Hope was running low when, to everyone's astonishment, a conning tower momentarily broke surface 5000 yards away. It will never be known what mistake by the U-boat's crew led to this fatal disclosure of its position; for both ships were now able to get really close, where contact could be held and send down depth charge after depth charge on the luckless submarine.

We can only imagine the scene down below as each attack brought further damage, leaks developing and lights going out as the boat rocked and shuddered to the blast of the explosions. Then at the sixth attack the end must have come for in the frigates a violent underwater explosion was heard and felt after which oil came welling to the surface.

But this was not enough evidence to claim a certain kill, for the Germans had learnt to put out oil and even bits of false debris to induce the hunters to call off their attacks. More depth charges were sent down on the spot whence the oil could be seen to be coming. Eighteen hours after the U-boat had dived the frigates gave up and shaped course to rejoin the convoy, confident at last that they had indeed been successful, but still lacking the evidence which a prudent Admiralty demanded before assessing a hunt as a kill. But in due course it became known that *U344* had indeed paid the penalty for its mistake.

Three of these same ships, *Mermaid, Peacock* and *Keppel*, this time in conjunction with *Whitehall* and with the aid of a Swordfish from the *Vindex*, were the executioners of the only U-boat to risk approaching the return convoy R.A. 59.A. On this occasion, after persisting in their attacks for twelve hours, they had the satisfaction of seeing wreckage come to the surface and gruesome but irrefutable evidence of a kill in the shape of human flesh. There was no quarter given or asked in the grim struggle between U-boat and escort – nor could there be. It was kill or be killed and devil take the hindmost.

The record of these summer months of 1944 was one of heavy loss to the German U-boat command by no means compensated for by the occasional torpedoing of an escort. The enemy could not go on accepting this state of affairs. As had long been anticipated, with the arrival of more schnorkel-fitted boats, the Captain of U-boats in Norway decided to concentrate them in the Kola approaches. So long as submarines were forced to surface at frequent intervals to charge their batteries, their employment in inshore waters was impossible. But now that they could use their diesel engines and remain submerged they could haunt the focal points of shipping with little risk of detection until they betrayed themselves by an attack.

Thus as the ocean passage became more and more secure, the business of seeing the convoy and the valuable aircraft carriers safely into harbour became more difficult and hazardous. It was with convoy J.W. 61 in late October that this new situation was first evident. A very strong escort with no less than three carriers found small employment during the voyage. But when the two support groups were sent ahead to sweep the approaches to Kola they found the sea alive with U-boats. By dint of feverish activity, the frigates kept the submarines too occupied with their own preservation to hinder the safe arrival of the merchantmen and the carriers. But try as they would the asdic operators could wring no information out of the seemingly sound-proof Arctic waters, and no U-boats were sunk.

The combination of poor asdic conditions, schnorkels and Gnats had swung the advantage heavily on to the side of the Germans. Had their U-boat commanders been of the same calibre as those who had decimated the convoys in the early years of the war the situation would have been serious indeed. But the rapid expansion of the U-boat arm and its earlier heavy losses had inevitably led to a great many boats being sent to sea with inexperienced and scantily trained crews. Furthermore, though morale was to remain high in some submarines to the end, the clear indications of approaching defeat must have robbed others of the incentive to take any risks.

On the British side improved anti-submarine weapons were helping to redress the balance, in particular one known as the 'Squid'. This was fitted in many of the escort frigates and consisted of a four-barrelled mortar which could simultaneously hurl four depth-charge projectiles some hundreds of yards ahead of the ship. With the aid of an improved asdic set which would give an estimation of the target's depth, a submerged submarine could now be bombarded with considerable accuracy from a distance. The necessity to run over the target to deliver an attack as with depth charges – and so lose contact at the crucial moment – was eliminated. It was a deadly weapon once contact with a U-boat was established.

But even so, so long as water conditions deadened the asdic's sound beam, the advantage still lay with the submarine. By flooding the sea area off the Kola Inlet with escorts at the appropriate moment it was at least possible to ensure the safe passage in and out of the merchant ships. Throughout the mid-winter months not one was lost; but casualties amongst the escorts were numerous and narrow escapes legion.

The first to suffer was the frigate *Mounsey*, damaged by a Gnat as the off-shore waters of Kola were being swept for the passage of R.A. 61. She was able to struggle back to harbour on her own. But when the destroyer *Cassandra* was torpedoed in the bow while performing the same service for R.A. 62, her salvage entailed a notable feat of seamanship and endurance.

It was early on 11th December, still black dark and with a rising wind, when *Cassandra* was hit in the bows as she was patrolling her station on the outer screen. Mess decks were wrecked by the explosion and there were many killed and wounded. But the blow had not been a mortal one for the ship. Her captain, Lieutenant Leslie, was determined to get her back to harbour.

As other ships of her group arrived to help, attempts were made to get alongside to take off the wounded; but already there was half a gale blowing and the weather was worsening steadily. The attempts had to be abandoned. Leslie then tried to make for harbour going astern on his engines; but in the increasing wind and sea and with the damaged bow affecting her manoeuvrability, *Cassandra* could do no better than shape a course which would have taken her to enemy territory.

The frigate *Bahamas* next arrived to take her in tow stern-first. Through the night of storm and snow squalls the tow continued as best it might without parting the viciously whipping wire hawser, while *Cassandra*'s consorts patrolled defensively around. Yet when a break in the overcast at dawn permitted star sights, it was found that the gale had driven the two ships thirty miles further to seaward.

By now the condition of the wounded was pitiful. Morphia

had run out; gangrene threatened. Drugs, anti-gangrene and anti-tetanus preparations were therefore sent over by heaving line and the tow continued. The gale was at last subsiding and slow headway was being made. Finally a Russian tug arrived to take over for the last lap into Kola. *Cassandra* was saved and with her many wounded men who would otherwise have had no chance of survival.

It might be thought that considering that the area where these torpedoings were taking place comprised the home waters of the Russian Northern Fleet at Polyarnoe, the Russians themselves would bestir themselves to drive off the U-boats. Submarine chasers built in America for them had been delivered in considerable numbers but they did little but rush about ineffectively. From Russian airfields near by, air patrols could have made life unbearable for the U-boats, but these were impossible, protested the Russians, because there were so many fishing boats off the coast which might be confused with U-boats.

Rear-Admiral Rhoderick McGrigor, who commanded many of the escorts of the convoys at this time, never missed an opportunity to chide the Russians on their lack of offensive spirit, but in vain. It was an inescapable fact that the Russians lacked all flair for naval warfare at that time, whatever they may have developed since. The success of the Arctic convoys owed almost nothing to the efforts of those for whose benefit they were run.

However, at the turn of the year, the Royal Navy could look with a good deal of satisfaction, if not complacency, at results so far. The vicious weather was still the enemy foremost in the minds of escorts and merchantmen alike. This is not surprising when one reads the experiences of the return convoy R.A. 63 of which that veteran of the Kola Run, Rear-Admiral Boucher was Commodore.

A gale with recorded windspeeds of eighty knots swooped on it. Great rollers forty-five feet in height charged down the wind, their crests streaming away before them in flying spume till the air was as thick with it as fog. Black darkness for nearly the whole of each twenty-four hours did nothing to lessen the terror of the tempest.

The carrier *Vindex*, with green seas sweeping her flight deck, was hove-to with half the escorts. The remainder held on to scattered groups of the convoy where the harassed masters were having to deal with shifted cargoes, machinery defects and deck damage. Many of the freighters were American 'Liberty' ships, with a tendency to split their welded seams. At least one of them was kept together by a system of wire hawsers lashed fore and aft round its hull and kept taut by bottle screws. Somehow they survived.

By the time the cyclone had passed on, leaving a blizzard out of the north in place of the south-westerly gale, the ships of the convoy were scattered far and wide. To gather them together again, the senior officer of the escort asked the Admiralty to direct them to the harbour of Thorshavn in the Faeroes. Here, wonderful to relate, they all arrived in safety though sorely battered. While the escorts felt their way in turn through the flying snow to the tanker to replenish their nearly empty fuel tanks, others patrolled the undefended entrances to the anchorage against U-boat attack.

At last when all was ready, the problem arose as to how to give the order to sail to the disorganized congregation of ships dispersed over the wide anchorage and shrouded in the continuous, impenetrable snowfall. Once again it was from Whitehall that this was most easily accomplished and in due course the sorely-tried convoy set forth again to complete its voyage.

With increasing daylight in February, the Luftwaffe made a last effort to stage a come-back. Formations of twelve and twenty-four Ju. 88s tried to attack the outward J.W. 64; but fighters from the carriers made them pay heavily and they failed to score any success. It was still in Russian waters that the real danger lay. The last ship of this convoy was torpedoed as she shaped up to enter Kola Inlet and was only saved from total loss by being beached.

By the time the return convoy, R.A. 64, was ready to sail on 17th February, there was no doubt that a number of U-boats was waiting outside for it. Three days before, two ships coming from Archangel to join it had been sunk at the entrance. Admiral McGrigor therefore sent out as many escorts as possible on the previous day to swamp the area and keep the enemy harassed and jumpy.

In calm, bitterly cold weather, the frigates, working in pairs, quartered back and forth operating their asdics but with little hope of achieving anything, so invariably bad were the water conditions in that area. Through the eerie 'sea-smoke', the low-lying drifting mist which was a common feature of calm weather in the Arctic, their snow-covered shapes weaved and zigzagged, 'Cats' rattling astern to exorcise the Gnats. So certain did it seem that success was impossible that when at one o'clock in the morning an excited asdic operator in the *Lark* shouted 'Contact' and then classified it as a submarine, the frigate's captain, Commander Hedworth Lambton, refused for a time to believe that it could be so. The echo must be off the bottom, off fish, off anything but a U-boat, he felt sure.

Once convinced, however, Lambton treated the contact as the precious and delicate thing it was. There was to be no rough-and-ready attack with depth charges which might not be immediately lethal and on conclusion of which the contact would undoubtedly vanish again. *Lark*'s consort, *Alnwick Castle*, was the proud possessor of a Squid. Called in by Lambton to take over the contact and attack, Lieutenant-Commander Stonehouse, R.N.R., the *Alnwick Castle*'s captain, appreciated the need for a single knock-out blow. With infinite patience and care he stalked his prey. In the two ships the watchers scarcely dared to breathe as the frigate crept slowly forward. Then, as the range came right, the four mortars of the Squid gave their staccato cough. The projectiles sailed away, invisible in the dark, to splash into the water ahead in a diamond pattern.

It seemed an age while the projectiles were sinking down to their set depth. Then four hard detonations shook the two ships. Four upsurges of white foam were dimly visible. All eyes stared hopefully at them. Suddenly, with a cascade of white water pouring from its flanks, a U-boat surfaced full in view – and fired a recognition flare! It was not the correct allied signal in force, but it was only a day out of date.

As the *Lark*'s four-inch and Oerlikon guns slammed shells into the submarine, Hedworth Lambton's emotions were by no means happy. Could this be a Russian submarine foolishly diving where it should not have been? That it should have given a wrong recognition signal was not at all un-Russian. But there was little time to cry over spilt milk, if spilt milk it were, for the submarine was already throwing its bows into the air before sinking and its crew were on deck yelling surrender. A moment later all was over as it slid stern first under the water to the triumphant cheers of the frigates' crews.

Meanwhile a boat from the *Alnwick Castle* had splashed into the water to rescue as many as possible of the crew. Within minutes of the disappearance of the submarine the boat was on the spot, but so murderous was the Arctic cold that but one man was found alive.

Still uncertain whether a 'Well Done' or a 'Tut-tut' would be his reward for the morning's work, Lambton signalled to Stonehouse, 'Does your prisoner speak German or Russian?' Only when the reply came back 'German' could the captain of the *Lark* join wholeheartedly in his crew's jubilation.

They were not to rejoice for long, however. The Germans were evidently enraged at their previous failures and making a dead set at R.A. 64 and its escorts. It was the *Lark* which was to be the first to suffer as a Gnat found its mark in her.

As the torpedo exploded the ship leapt bodily in the water. The shroud of snow covering her was thrown high into the air where it mingled with the oily soot similarly thrown up from the funnel to shower down in a noisome mixture.

The crew of the *Lark* had more reason than most to resent being torpedoed. For many of them it was a year, to the day, since they had been sunk in *Lark*'s sister ship *Woodpecker*. No doubt there were mutters amongst them of 'Why does it always have to happen to me?' On the other hand their previous experience perhaps stood them in good stead for by skilful damage control they kept their ship afloat and she was eventually towed to safety at Murmansk.

The next victim was a ship in the convoy from which the crew was rescued. But then came real tragedy as the corvette *Bluebell*, torpedoed in the magazine, blew up, leaving but one survivor. However, this ended the tale of U-boat success against R.A. 64. The German Air Force made a big effort to improve on the U-boats' score when more than twenty torpedo-carrying Ju. 88s made a spirited attack on this convoy, but admirable discipline in the convoy which enabled two emergency turns to be made in the nick of time caused every torpedo to be avoided, though many exploded inside the convoy against ships' wakes or as they broke surface in the heavy seas running at the time.

But one merchant ship was yet to be sunk by aircraft from this convoy. Heavy weather had scattered the ships but all had been gathered in again except one, the *Henry Bacon*. Nineteen Ju. 88s coming across her straggling astern of the main body had the doubtful honour of sinking this solitary, unprotected ship.

The losses in and around R.A. 64 were a bad setback. Yet so far as U-boat attacks was concerned, given the inability or unwillingness of the Russians to keep their own waters clear of enemy submarines and the poor performance of the asdic, it is really surprising that the Germans did not have far greater success. The schnorkel and the Gnat posed a problem to which a solution could not easily or quickly be found. The nervous strain on the anti-submarine forces was continuous and exhausting. There was no let-up for them while in coastal waters which the U-boats now haunted.

They could have no faith in their asdics there and the make-shift antidotes to the homing torpedo were shown to be far less than sure in their effect. The shattering concussion of a torpedo might come, unheralded, at any hour of the day or night. Waiting to receive its victims was a sea so bitterly cold that survival in it was a matter of a few minutes only.

Yet morale remained remarkably high. During their brief stays in harbour, in the absence of any amenities provided by their Russian hosts, the crews found ways to entertain themselves. On several occasions when the turn-round permitted, regattas were held – hilarious affairs as the great majority of the warships' companies were 'Hostilities Only' and had seldom had an oar in their hands.

Christmas in the sombre surroundings of North Russia might be thought to offer little outlet for gaiety. But 'Boggy' Fisher, captain of *Musketeer*, berthed at the pier in Vaenga Bay with *Opportune* was determined that tradition should not be flouted. In genial spirits after dinner, he and Johnny Lee-Barber of

Opportune mustered a party to go carol-singing at the R.N. Auxiliary Hospital. Carrying candle lanterns they set off hopefully through the snow-covered countryside though not entirely sure where the hospital lay.

They had not gone far when they found themselves halted by a silent, sinister and strictly unamused Russian sentry. Undeterred, they swerved away to try another route only to come against another bulky overcoated figure nervously fingering the trigger of his rifle. As sentry after sentry was encountered, fully prepared to shoot the mad 'bourgeois', enthusiasm waned and the party plodded sadly back to their ships, their carols and their flickering lanterns making an affecting scene had there been anyone to appreciate it.

It was also 'Boggy' Fisher who, with Hedworth Lambton, at that time commanding the destroyer *Westcott*, organized a midwinter regatta for an escort force berthed in Polyarnoe. There were three days in harbour to be passed. Two would be given to practice for any crews who entered for the various races. On the third the regatta would be held during the few hours of daylight.

The response was astonishing. No one wanted to be left out, so that races for every possible category of rating and for the officers had to be arranged. For the next two days Polyarnoe harbour was full of whalers and dinghies being propelled – it could hardly be called 'rowed' – by crews of cooks and stewards, stokers and radar operators, electricians and writers with tremendous zest and total lack of skill or style, perhaps fortunately hidden by darkness and falling snow for much of the time, and occasionally shot at by Russian sentries if they strayed too far towards the harbour entrance.

On the third day the regatta was duly held with a 'tote' being run in the *Westcott*, which was heavily patronised. Amidst scenes of hilarious enthusiasm, no less than twenty-four races were run, the crews cheered to the echo as they covered the half-mile course in a wild flurry of windmilling oars and shouted imprecations.

There is a moral to be drawn, no doubt, from this refusal to be 'got down' by the miserable conditions in North Russia. Certainly it was this sort of attitude which robbed the enemy of the fruits of his material advantages at this time in the field of submarine warfare. A fearless offensive on his part might have cost the allies unacceptable casualties and brought the Arctic convoys to a halt. But in spite of losses amongst the escorts, the U-boats never achieved the ascendancy which their new weapons could have brought them. The convoys continued to run to the very end.

* * *

The story of the Kola Run is nearing its end. But although in the spring of 1945 the end of the war with Germany was well in sight the Nazi fanatics in Berlin refused to admit defeat or to contemplate surrender. Even those in control of affairs who saw the writing on the wall were frantically anxious that it should not be to the Russians that surrender should be made. Every convoy of war material successfully delivered to the Russians accelerated the advance of the Red hordes. The U-boats were therefore kept firmly to their task to the last moment.

So when J.W. 65 made the voyage to North Russia in March, though it suffered no interference on passage, it found the usual submarine concentration waiting for it off the Kola Inlet. In spite of every precaution possible, two freighters and the frigate *Lapwing* were torpedoed and sunk.

Rear-Admiral Cunningham-Graham and Captain Cazalet, the two senior officers of the escort, were infuriated at these losses in sight of their destination. For the return convoy they devised a ruse to outwit the U-boats. It was decided to sail the convoy at midnight on the 23rd/24th March in three columns instead of the usual two so that the ships would clear the entrance more quickly. Instead of sending out hunting groups a long time before, they were only to start operations two hours ahead of the convoy. Then when the merchantmen started to sally forth, four destroyers would go along the old standard route at high speed, dropping depth charges and firing starshell – in fact bustle along as if clearing the path. Meanwhile a new route diverging from the old had been swept and the convoy would proceed along this one.

The stratagem was highly successful, and by the time the U-boats woke up to it the convoy was clear away to sea and had no further trouble.

One more convoy each way was to run before VE Day.

Though no merchant ships were torpedoed from them, the war in the Arctic came to an end with a last fierce fight between escorts and U-boats. The outward convoy J.W. 66 had safely eluded any submarines which may have been lying in wait for them, but by the time R.A. 66 sailed from Kola the enemy was outside in full force.

The first indication was when a torpedo narrowly missed the frigate *Alnwick Castle*. Then Russian Catalina aircraft on patrol came, for the first and last time, into action, attacking three separate U-boats, though without success. The frigate *Loch Insh* was the first to score as a perfectly placed pattern of projectiles from her 'Squid' brought *U307* frothing to the surface to be plastered with gunfire before sinking again, leaving fourteen survivors to be made prisoner.

All was going very well, it seemed. But then it was the enemy's turn to hit back. The frigate *Goodall* was suddenly rent by a devastating blast as a torpedo hit her in the forward magazine, disintegrating her forecastle and folding back her bridge structure against the funnel. It seemed certain at first sight that she must rapidly sink. Her two neighbours *Farnham Castle* and *Honeysuckle* dropped carley rafts alongside her for survivors.

But when it became apparent that the *Goodall* had survived even the loss of a third of her length, the *Honeysuckle* nosed her bows alongside the *Goodall*'s quarter to embark the remnants of her crew. At that moment the already calamitous situation became critically worse as fire broke out. Oil fuel gushing from the *Goodall*'s rent tanks had been spreading over the surface of the water. It now met the flickering flame of a calcium flare attached to a life raft which set it ablaze. The flames spread quickly back to the ship and soon the wreck itself was burning, surrounded by a sea of fire.

In spite of the heat and danger to his own ship, Lieutenant McKilligan, R.N.R., kept the *Honeysuckle* at her rescue work, while his First Lieutenant, Sub-Lieutenant Bell, R.N.Z.N.V.R., gallantly boarded the *Goodall* in an attempt to extricate any wounded remaining amidst the wreckage of the bridge. But the heat and flames drove him back and McKilligan finally backed away with his own paintwork ablaze.

Meanwhile the *Farnham Castle* and some Russian submarine-chasers had picked up from the water those who had abandoned ship. But the loss of life was tragic, only forty-four of the crew being saved.

It was with heavy hearts that the escorts returned to the fight with their hidden enemy. *Goodall* was to be avenged, however. Before the night was out the frigates *Loch Shin* and *Cotton*, with the Russian *Anguilla*, were to account for perhaps the very U-boat responsible.

With this the fight came to an end. The convoy had passed on in safety, the last Arctic convoy before VE Day. By the time the next J.W. convoy sailed, Russian armies, transported perhaps in vehicles brought to them via the Kola Run, had beaten down the last resistance in Berlin. Shells which had helped to reduce the German capital to rubble had travelled the long journey over the roof of the world to Murmansk and Archangel and thence by God knows what meandering, chaotic Russian transport system to the front.

They were but a drop in the ocean, sneered the Russians, compared to their real needs. The enemy did not think so, however. To the very end they directed their utmost energies to stopping the Arctic convoys, for they had come to realize that the material they carried could well be the deciding factor on the eastern front. The *Scharnhorst* was sent to her doom by Doenitz's exhortation to 'strike a blow for the gallant troops on the eastern front by destroying the convoy'.

Vice-Admiral Ruge, a distinguished German writer on naval affairs, has said,

Between August 1944 and April 1945, the 250-plus ships on the Arctic run carried over a million tons of war material. The weapons, equipment and vehicles allowed the Russians to equip a further sixty motorized divisions which gave them not only numerical but material superiority at focal points of the battles. Thus the Anglo-American sea-power also exerted a decisive influence on the land operations in Eastern Europe.

It was fortunate for the Allies that such appreciation of the situation was not made earlier in the war by the Germans. More than double this number of ships had reached North Russia before the period reviewed by Ruge. They had brought aid to the Russians at a time when they were fighting with their backs to the wall, the rumble of enemy gunfire shaking the windows of Moscow itself.

Had Hitler not been obsessed by the idea that an invasion of Norway was intended, against which his surface fleet had to be carefully preserved, the Arctic must have witnessed other naval disasters on the scale of P.Q. 17 and a stoppage of the convoys.

Finally, though the official Russian attitude with regard to the Arctic convoys during the war was one of almost contemptuous lack of appreciation, the words of Mr. Maisky, wartime Soviet Ambassador in London, will serve as a tribute to the courage and endurance of the allied seamen of merchant ships and men-of-war who travelled the Kola Run, many leaving their bones on the bed of the Arctic seas:

> The Russian convoys are a northern saga of heroism, bravery and endurance. This saga will live for ever, not only in the hearts of your people but also in the hearts of the Soviet people, who rightly see in it one of the most striking expressions of collaboration between Allied governments without which our common victory would have been impossible.

* * *

So the Arctic Ocean reverted to its immemorial, empty waste of wild waters. Bear Island and Jan Mayen have become once again simply names on maps and charts. The great icebergs drift southwards to their dissolution all unseen. The mighty gales waste their demoniac forces on thin air and ship-less seas.

Long may it remain so.

Convoy	Commodore	Port and date of sailing		Sailed	Returned to harbour. Weather, damage, etc.
Dervish	Capt. J. C. K. Dowding, D.S.O., R.D., R.N.R.	Hvalfjord	21.8.41	7	
PQ.1	Capt. T. Ridley (Master, S.S. *Atlantic*)	,,	29.9.41	10	
PQ.2		Scapa	17.10.41	6	
PQ.3		Hvalfjord	9.11.41	8	1
PQ.4		,,	17.11.41	8	
PQ.5		,,	27.11.41	7	
PQ.6		,,	8.12.41	7	
PQ.7		,,	26.12.41	2	
PQ.7B		,,	31.12.41	9	
PQ.8	Capt. R. W. Brundle (Master, S.S. *Harmatris*)	,,	8.1.42	8	
PQ.9		,,	1.2.42	7	
PQ.10		,,	1.2.42	3	
PQ.11	? (Master, S.S. *Kingswood*)	Loch Ewe	6.2.42	13	
PQ.12	Capt. H. T. Hudson, R.D., R.N.R.	Reykjavik	1.3.42	16	
PQ.13	Capt. D. A. Casey, C.B.E., D.S.O., D.S.C., R.D., R.N.R.	,,	20.3.42	19	
PQ.14	Capt. E. Rees, D.S.C., R.D., R.N.R.*	,,	8.4.42	24	16
PQ.15	Capt. H. J. Anchor, O.B.E., R.D., R.N.R.	,,	26.4.42	25	
PQ.16	Capt. N. H. Gale, D.S.O., R.D., R.N.R.	,,	21.5.42	35	1
PQ.17	Capt. J. C. K. Dowding, D.S.O., R.D., R.N.R.	,,	27.6.42	36†	2
PQ.18	Rear-Adm. E. K. Boddam-Whetham, D.S.O. (ret.)	Loch Ewe	2.9.42	40	

* Killed in action, 16.4.42.

Lost	Arrived	Port and date of arrival		Remarks
—	7	Archangel	31.8.41	Trial convoy.
—	10	,,	11.10.41	
—	6	,,	30.10.41	
—	7	,,	28.11.41	1 ship returned; ice damage.
—	8	,,	28.11.41	
—	7	,,	12.12.41	
—	{ 2	Murmansk	20.12.41	
	{ 5	Molotovsk	23.12.41	
1	1	Murmansk	12.1.42	1 sunk by U-boat.
—	9	,,	11.1.42	
—	8	,,	17.1.42	1 torpedoed; towed to Murmansk. H.M.S. *Matabele* sunk by U-boat.
—	7	,,	10.2.42 }	Joined up and sailed together from Reykjavik.
—	3	,,	10.2.42 }	
—	13	,,	23.2.42	
—	16	,,	12.3.42	Capital ship support. H.M.S. *Shera* capsized.
5	14	,,	31.3.42	2 bombed and sunk; 2 sunk by U-boat, 1 by surface craft. H.M.S. *Trinidad* torpedoed; German destroyer *Z.26* sunk.
1	7	,,	19.4.42	16 ships returned to Iceland, owing to ice and weather; 1 sunk by U-boat.
3	22	,,	5.5.42	3 torpedoed by aircraft and sunk. O.R.P. *P.551* (95 miles out of position) sunk by escort; H.M.S. *Punjabi* with battle fleet sunk in collision.
7	27	{ ,,	30.5.42 }	1 returned to Iceland, damaged; 5 bombed; 1 torpedoed by aircraft; 1 by U-boat.
		{ Archangel	1.6.42 }	
23†	11	{ 4 ,,	11.7.42 }	1 grounded; 1 returned to Iceland, ice damage; 23 sunk,† (10 bombed,† 3 torpedoed by aircraft, 10 by U-boats). Figures do not include 3 rescue ships, 1 of which was bombed and sunk.
		{ 6 ,,	25.7.42 }	
		{ 1 Molotovsk	28.7.42 }	
13	27	Archangel	17.9.42	3 sunk by U-boats; 10 by torpedo bombers.

† Including 1 R.F.A. oiler. Oilers are included when they carried a cargo or part cargo of oil for Russia.

Convoy	Commodore	Port and date of sailing		Sailed	Returned to Harbour. Weather, damage, etc.
JW.51.A	Rear-Adm. C. E. Turle, D.S.O. (ret.)	Loch Ewe	15.12.42	16†	
JW.51.B	Capt. R. A. Melhuish, R.I.N. (ret.)	,,	22.12.42	14	
JW.52	Vice-Adm. Sir Malcolm L. Goldsmith, K.B.E., D.S.O. (ret.)	,,	17.1.43	14	1
JW.53	Rear-Adm. E. W. Leir, D.S.O. (ret.)	,,	15.2.43	28	6
JW.54.A	Capt. B. B. Grant, R.D., R.N.R.	,,	15.11.43	18	
JW.54.B	Capt. E. C. Denison, M.V.O., R.N. (ret.)	,,	22.11.43	14	
JW.55.A	Capt. W. J. Mills, R.D., R.N.R.	,,	12.12.43	19	
JW.55.B	Rear-Adm. M. W. S. Boucher, D.S.O. (ret.)	,,	20.12.43	19	
JW.56.A	Capt. I. W. Whitehorn, R.N. (ret.)	,,	12.1.44	20	5
JW.56.B	Capt. M. J. D. Mayall, R.D., R.N.R.	,,	22.1.44	16	
JW.57	Capt. R. D. Binks, O.B.E., R.D., R.N.R.	,,	20.2.44	42	
JW.58	Capt. J. O. Dunn, R.D., R.N.R.	,,	27.3.44	49	1
JW.59	Capt. G. H. Creswell, C.B., D.S.O., D.S.C., R.N. (ret.)	,,	15.8.44	33	
JW.60	Capt. J. Smith, R.D., R.N.R.	,,	15.9.44	30	
JW.61	Rear-Adm. M. W. S. Boucher, D.S.O. (ret.)	,,	20.10.44	29	
JW.62	Capt. E. Ullring, R.NOR.N.	,,	29.11.44	30	
JW.63	Rear-Adm. M. W. S. Boucher, D.S.O. (ret.)	,,	30.12.44	35	
JW.64	Capt. E. Ul'ring, R.NOR.N.	Clyde	3.2.45	26	
JW.65	Capt. W. C. Meek, R.D., R.N.R.	,,	11.3.45	24	
JW.66	Capt. Sir Roy K. Gill, K.B.E., R.D., R.N.R.	,,	16.4.45	22	
JW.67	Capt. G. E. Sutcliffe, R.N. (ret.)	,,	12.5.45	23	
40				811	33

Lost	Arrived	Port and date of arrival		Remarks
—	16†	Kola Inlet 25.12.42 Molotovsk 27.12.42	}	
—	14	Kola Inlet 3.1.43 White Sea 6.1.43	}	H.M. Ships *Achates* and *Bramble* sunk by surface ships: German destroyer *Friedrich Eckholdt* sunk.
—	13	Kola Inlet 27.1.43		1 returned to Iceland through lack of speed.
—	22	Kola Inlet 27.2.43 White Sea 2.3.43	}	6 returned to Iceland owing to weather.
—	18	Kola Inlet 24.11.43 White Sea 28.11.43	}	
—	14	Kola Inlet 2.12.43 White Sea	}	
—	19	Kola Inlet 20.12.43 White Sea 22.12.43	}	
—	19	Kola Inlet 29.12.43 White Sea 31.12.43	}	*Scharnhorst* sunk by covering forces, 26.12.43.
3	12	Kola Inlet 28.1.44		Convoy put in to Akureyri owing to weather; 5 returned; 3 sunk by U-boats.
—	16	Kola Inlet 1.2.44		H.M.S. *Hardy* sunk by U-boat.
—	42	Kola Inlet 28.2.44		H.M.S. *Mahratta* sunk by U-boat.
—	48	Kola Inlet 5.4.44		1 ship returned to Iceland; ice damage.
—	33	Kola Inlet 25.8.44 White Sea 27.8.44	}	H.M.S. *Kite* sunk by U-boat.
—	30	Kola Inlet 23.9.44 White Sea 25.9.44	}	
—	29	Kola Inlet 28.10.44 White Sea 20.10.44	}	
—	30	Kola Inlet 7.12.44 White Sea 9.12.44	}	
—	35	Kola Inlet 8.1.45 White Sea 8.1.45	}	
—	26	Kola Inlet 13.2.45 White Sea 15.2.45	}	
2	22	Kola Inlet 21.3.45		Two merchant ships and H.M.S. *Lapwing* sunk by U-boats off Kola.
—	22	Kola Inlet 25.4.45 White Sea 28.4.45	}	
—	23	Kola Inlet 20.5.45 White Sea 22.5.45	}	

58(1) 720

† In addition 5 ships were sunk in Kola Inlet after arrival by aircraft or mines.

Convoy	Commodore	Port and date of sailing		Sailed	Returned to Harbour Weather, damage, etc.
QP.1	Capt. J. C. K. Dowding, D.S.O., R.D., R.N.R.	Archangel	28.9.41	14	
QP.2		,,	2.11.41	12	
QP.3		,,	27.11.41	10	2
QP.4		,,	20.12.41	13	2
QP.5		Murmansk	13.1.42	4	
QP.6	Capt. Davitt (Master, *Empire Redshank*)	,,	24.1.42	6	
QP.7		,,	12.2.42	8	
QP.8		,,	1.3.42	15	
QP.9	Capt. H. T. Hudson, R.D., R.N.R.	,,	21.3.42	19	
QP.10	Capt. D. A. Casey, C.B.E., D.S.O., D.S.C., R.D., R.N.R.	,,	10.4.42	16	
QP.11	Capt. W. H. Lawrence (Master, S.S. *Briarwood*)	,,	28.4.42	13	
QP.12		,,	21.5.42	15	
QP.13	Capt. N. H. Gale, D.S.O., R.D., R.N.R.	{ Archangel { Murmansk	26.6.42 27.6.42	12 23 } 35	
QP.14	Capt. J. C. K. Dowding, D.S.O., R.D., R.N.R.	Archangel	13.9.42	15	
QP.15	Capt. W. C. Meek, R.D., R.N.R.	,,	17.11.42	28	
RA.51	Rear-Adm. C. E. Turle, D.S.O. (ret.)	Kola Inlet	30.12.42	14	
RA.52	Capt. R. A. Melhuish, R.I.N. (ret.)	,,	29.1.43	11	
RA.53	Vice-Adm. Sir Malcolm L. Goldsmith, K.B.E., D.S.O. (ret.)	,,	1.3.43	30	
RA.54.A	Capt. W. L. P. Cox, R.N.R.	Archangel	1.11.43	13	
RA.54.B	(Master, ? S.S. *Empire Scott*)	,,	26.11.43	9	
RA.55.A	Capt. B. B. Grant, R.D., R.N.R.	Kola Inlet	23.12.43	22	1
RA.55.B	Capt. E. C. Denison, M.V.O., R.N. (ret.)	,,	31.12.43	8	
RA.56	Rear-Adm. M. W. S. Boucher, D.S.O. (ret.)	,,	3.2.44	37	
RA.57	Capt. M. J. D. Mayall, R.D., R.N.R.	,,	2.3.44	31	

Lost	Arrived	Port and date of arrival		Remarks
—	14	Scapa	9.10.41	
—	12	Kirkwall	17.11.41	
—	8	Seidisfiord	7.12.41	2 returned, owing to weather.
—	11	,,	16.1.42	2 put in to Murmansk.
—	4	Reykjavik	24.1.42	
—	6	U.K.	2.2.42	
—	8	Seidisfiord	22.2.42	
1	14	Reykjavik	11.3.42	1 straggler sunk by surface craft.
—	19	,,	3.4.42	
4	11	,,	21.4.42	1 returned to Murmansk, 2 bombed and sunk, 2 sunk by U-boats.
1	12	,,	7.5.42	1 straggler sunk by surface craft. H.M.S. Edinburgh torpedoed by U-boat, subsequently sunk.
—	14	,,	29.5.42	1 returned to Murmansk.
5	30	{ 16 Loch Ewe 14 Reykjavik }	7.7.42	4 and H.M.S. Niger sunk in British mine-field; 1 damaged and part beached.
3	12	Loch Ewe	26.9.42	3 sunk by U-boats. H.M. Ships Somali and Leda and R.F.A. Grey Ranger sunk by U-boats.
2	26	,,	30.11–3.12.42	Scattered by gales; 2 sunk by U-boats.
—	14	,,	11.1.43	
1	10	,,	8.2.43	1 sunk by U-boat.
4	26	,,	14.3.43	3 (2 stragglers) sunk by U-boats; 1 foundered in gale.
—	13	,,	14.11.43	
—	9	,,	9.12.43	
—	21	,,	1.1.44	1 ship returned to Kola Inlet.
—	8	,,	8.1.44	
—	37	,,	11.2.44	
1	30	,,	10.3.44	1 sunk by U-boat.

Convoy	Commodore	Port and date of sailing		Sailed	Returned to harbour. Weather, damage, etc.
RA.58	Capt. R. D. Binks, O.B.E., R.D., R.N.R.	Kola Inlet	7.4.44	36	
RA.59	Capt. J. O. Dunn, R.D., R.N.R.	,,	28.4.44	45	
RA.59A		,,	28.8.44	9	
RA.60	Capt. G. H. Creswell, C.B., D.S.O., D.S.C., R.N. (ret.)	,,	28.9.44	30	
RA.61	Rear-Adm. M. W. S. Boucher, D.S.O. (ret.)	{ White Sea 30.10.44 { Kola Inlet 2.11.44 }		33	
RA.62	Capt. E. Ullring, R.NOR.N.	Kola Inlet	10.12.44	28	
RA.63	Rear-Adm. M. W. S. Boucher, D.S.O. (ret.)	,,	11.1.45	30	
RA.64	Capt. E. Ullring, R.NOR.N.	,,	17.2.45	34*	1
RA.65	Capt. W. C. Meek, R.D., R.N.R.	,,	23.3.45	25	
RA.66	Capt. Sir Roy K. Gill, K.B.E., R.D., R.N.R.	,,	29.4.45	24	
RA.67	Capt. G. E. Sutcliffe, R.N. (ret.)	,,	23.5.45	23	
35				715*	8

* Excluding 2 sunk off Kola before joining RA.64.

Lost	Arrived	Port and date of arrival		Remarks
—	36	Loch Ewe	14.4.44	
1	44	,,	6.5.44	1 sunk by U-boat.
—	9	,,	6.9.44	
2	28	,,	5.10.44	2 sunk by U-boats.
—	33	Loch Ewe Clyde	9.11.44 10.11.44	
—	28	Loch Ewe Clyde	19.12.44 20.12.44	Torpedo-bomber attacks recommenced.
—	30	Loch Ewe Clyde	21.1.45 23.1.45	
4†	31	Loch Ewe Clyde	28.2.45 1.3.45	1 returned to Kola; 1 sunk by U-boat; 1 (straggler) by torpedo aircraft; 2 sunk before joining convoy off Kola Inlet. H.M.S. *Bluebell* sunk by U-boat.
—	25	Kirkwall Clyde Belfast	31.3.45 1.4.45 1.4.45	
—	24	Clyde	8.5.45	H.M.S. *Goodall* sunk by U-boat or mine.
—	23	Clyde	31.4.45	
29†	680			

† Including 2 sunk off Kola before joining RA.64.

APPENDIX C:

GERMAN SUBMARINES SUNK IN ARCTIC CONVOY OPERATIONS

U-boat	How sunk	Date	Remarks
		1942	
U655	Rammed	24 Mar.	H.M.S. *Sharpshooter* (QP.9)
U585	Depth charge	29 Mar.	H.M.S. *Fury* (PQ.13)
U589	,, ,,	12 Sep.	H.M.S. *Faulknor* (PQ.18)
U88	,, ,,	14 Sep.	H.M.S. *Onslow* (PQ.18)
U457	,, ,,	16 Sep.	H.M.S. *Impulsive* (PQ.18)
U253	,, ,,	23 Sep.	Catalina
		1943	
U644	Torpedoed	7 Apl.	H.M.S. *Tuna* (patrol, S.E. Jan Mayen)
		1944	
U314	Depth charge	30 Jan.	H.M. Ships *Whitehall, Meteor* (JW.56.B)
U713	,, ,,	24 Feb.	H.M.S. *Keppel* (JW.57)
U601	,, ,,	25 Feb.	Catalina (JW.57)
U472	Rocket; gunfire	4 Mar.	Swordfish (*Chaser*), *Onslaught* (RA.57)
U366	,, ,,	5 Mar.	Swordfish (*Chaser*) (RA.57)
U973	,, ,,	6 Mar.	Swordfish (*Chaser*) (RA.57)
U961	Depth charge	29 Mar.	H.M.S. *Starling* (JW.58)
U355	,, ,,	1 Apl.	H.M.S. *Beagle*, Aircraft (*Tracker*) (JW.58)
U360	Hedgehog	2 Apl.	H.M.S. *Keppel* (JW.58)
U288	Depth charge	1 Apl.	Aircraft (*Tracker, Activity*) (JW.58)
U277	,, ,,	1 May	Swordfish (*Fencer*) (RA.59)
U674	,, ,,	2 May	Swordfish (*Fencer*) (RA.59)
U959	,, ,,	2 May	Swordfish (*Fencer*) (RA.59)
U361	,, ,,	17 July	Liberator (patrol)
U347	,, ,,	17 July	Catalina (patrol)
U742	,, ,,	18 July	Catalina (patrol)
U354	,, ,,	22 Aug.	Swordfish (*Vindex*) (JW.59)
U344	,, ,,	23 Aug.	E.G.20: *Keppel, Mermaid, Peacock, Loch Dunvegan* (JW.59)
U394	Rocket: depth charge	2 Sep.	Swordfish (*Vindex*). E.G. 20: *Keppel, Whitehall Mermaid, Peacock* (RA.59.A)
U921	Depth charge	30 Sep.	Swordfish (*Campania*)
U387		9 Dec.	*Bamborough Castle* (RA.62)
U365	Depth charge	13 Dec.	Swordfish (*Campania*) (RA.62)
		1945	
U425	Squid	17 Feb.	E.G.8: *Lark, Alnwick Castle* (off Kola Inlet)
U307	Gunfire	29 Apl.	E.G.19: *Loch Insh* (RA.66)
U286		29 Apl.	E.G.19: *Loch Shin, Anguilla, Cotton* (RA.66)

ALLIED WARSHIPS FROM WHICH ESCORTS FOR CONVOYS WERE FORMED 1941-1945

Anti-Aircraft Cruisers

H.M.S. *Bellona* (Capt. G. S. Tuck, D.S.O.)
H.M.S. *Black Prince* (Capt. D. M. Lees, D.S.O.)
H.M.S. *Diadem* (Capt. E. G. A. Clifford)
H.M.S. *Scylla* (Capt. I. A. P. Macintyre, C.B.E.)

Anti-Aircraft Ships

H.M.S. *Alynbank* (Act. Capt. H. F. Nash)
H.M.S. *Palomares* (Act. Capt. J. H. Jauncey)
H.M.S. *Pozarica* (Act. Capt. E. D. W. Lawford)
H.M.S. *Ulster Queen* (Act. Capt. C. K. Adam)

Escort Carriers

H.M.S. *Activity* (Capt. G. Willoughby)
H.M.S. *Avenger* (Cdr. A. P. Colthurst)
H.M.S. *Campania* (Act. Capt. K. A. Short)
H.M.S. *Chaser* (Capt. H. V. P. McClintock, D.S.O.)
H.M.S. *Dasher* (Act. Capt. C. N. Lentaigne, D.S.O.)
H.M.S. *Fencer* (Act. Capt. W. W. R. Bentinck)
H.M.S. *Nabob* (Act. Capt H. N. Lay, R.C.N.)
H.M.S. *Nairana* (Capt. H. N. Surtees, D.S.O.)
H.M.S. *Premier* (Act. Capt. R. J. Gardiner)
H.M.S. *Queen* (Act. Capt. K. J. D'Arcy, D.S.O.)
H.M.S. *Striker* (Capt. W. P. Carne)
H.M.S. *Tracker* (Act. Capt. J. H. Huntley)
H.M.S. *Trumpeter* (Act. Capt. K. S. Colquhoun)
H.M.S. *Vindex* (Capt. H. T. Bayliss)
        (Capt. J. D. L. Williams)

Destroyers

H.M.S. *Achates* (Lt.-Cdr. A. H. T. Johns)
H.M.S. *Amazon* (Lt.-Cdr. The Lord Teynham)
H.M.S. *Ashanti* (Cdr. R. G. Onslow)
        (Lt.-Cdr. J. R. Barnes)
H.M.S. *Athabaskan* (Lt.-Cdr. J. H. Stubbs, D.S.O., R.C.N.)
H.M.S. *Badsworth* (Lt. G. T. S. Gray)
H.M.S. *Beagle* (Cdr. R. C. Medley)
        (Lt.-Cdr. N. R. Murch)
H.M.S. *Bedouin* (Cdr. B. G. Scurfield, C.B.E., A.M.)
H.M.S. *Beverley* (Lt. R. A. Price)
H.M.S. *Blankney* (Lt.-Cdr. P. F. Powlett, D.S.O., D.S.C.)
H.M.S. *Boadicea* (Lt.-Cdr. F. C. Brodrick)

Destroyers—continued.

H.M.S. *Bramham* (Lt. E. F. Baines)
H.M.S. *Broke* (Lt.-Cdr. A. F. C. Layard)
H.M.S. *Bulldog* (Cdr. M. Richmond, D.S.O., O.B.E.)
H.M.S. *Campbell* (Act. Cdr. E. C. Coats, D.S.O., D.S.C.)
H.M.S. *Cassandra* (Lt. G. L. Leslie)
H.M.S. *Cavalier* (Lt.-Cdr. D. T. McBarnett, D.S.C.)
H.M.S. *Cowdry* (Lt.-Cdr. C. W. North)
H.M.S. *Douglas* (Lt.-Cdr. R. B. S. Tennant)
H.M.S. *Echo* (Lt-Cdr. N. Lanyon)
H.M.S. *Eclipse* (Lt.-Cdr. E. Mack, D.S.C.)
H.M.S. *Escapade* Cdr. E. N. V. Currey, D.S.C.)
      (Lt.-Cdr. E. C. Peake)
H.M.C.S. *Eskimo* (Cdr. E. G. Le Geyt)
H.M.S. *Faulknor* (Capt. A. K. Scott-Moncrieff)
H.M.S. *Foresight* (Cdr. J. S. Salter)
H.M.S. *Forester* (Lt.-Cdr. G. P. Huddert)
      (Lt.-Cdr. J. A. Burnett, D.S.C.)
H.M.S. *Fury* (Lt.-Cdr. C. H. Campbell, D.S.C.)
O.R.P. *Garland* (?)
U.S.S.R.S. *Gremyaschi* (?)
U.S.S.R.S. *Gromki* (?)
U.S.S.R.S. *Gronzi* (?)
H.M.S. *Grove* (Lt.-Cdr. J. W. Rylands)
H.M.C.S. *Haida* (Cdr. H. G. DeWolfe, R.C.N.)
H.M.S. *Hardy* (Capt. W. G. A. Robson, D.S.O., D.S.C.)
H.M.S. *Huron* (Lt.-Cdr. H. S. Rayner, D.S.C., R.C.N.)
H.M.S. *Icarus* (Lt.-Cdr. C. D. Maud, D.S.C.)
      (Lt.-Cdr. E. N. Walmsley, D.S.C.)
H.M.S. *Inconstant* (Lt.-Cdr. W. S. Clouston)
      (Lt.-Cdr. J. H. Eaden, D.S.C.)
H.M.S. *Impulsive* (Lt.-Cdr. E. G. Roper, D.S.C.)
      (Lt.-Cdr. P. Bekenn)
H.M.S. *Inglefield* (Cdr. A. G. West)
H.M.S. *Intrepid* (Cdr. J. H. Lewis)
      (Cdr. C. A. de W. Kitcat)
H.M.C.S. *Iroquois* (Cdr. J. C. Hibbard, D.S.C., R.C.N.)
H.M.S. *Javelin* (Cdr. G. E. Fardell)
H.M.S. *Keppel* (Cdr. J. E. Broome)
      (Cdr. I. J. Tyson, D.S.C., R.D., R.N.R.)
U.S.S.R.S. *Kuibishev* (?)
H.M.S. *Lammerton* (Lt.-Cdr. C. R. Purse, D.S.C.)
H.M.S. *Lancaster* (Act. Cdr. N. H. Whatley)
H.M.S. *Leamington* (Lt. B. M. D. I'Anson)
H.M.S. *Ledbury* (Lt.-Cdr. R. P. Hill)
H.M.S. *Lookout* (Lt.-Cdr. C. P. F. Brown, D.S.C.)
H.M.S. *Mackay* (Lt. J. B. Marjoribanks)
H.M.S. *Mahratta* (Lt.-Cdr. E. A. F. Drought, D.S.C.)
H.M.S. *Malcolm* (Act. Cdr. A. B. Russell)
H.M.S. *Marne* (Lt.-Cdr. H. N. A. Richardson, D.S.C.)
H.M.S. *Martin* (Cdr. C. R. P. Thompson, D.S.O.)
H.M.S. *Matchless* (Lt.-Cdr. I. Mowlam, D.S.O.)
      (Lt.-Cdr. W. S. Shaw)
H.M.S. *Meteor* (Lt.-Cdr. W. J. B. Jewett)
H.M.S. *Milne* (Capt. I. M. R. Campbell, D.S.O.)
      (Capt. M. Richmond, D.S.O.)
H.M.S. *Meynell* (Lt. B. M. D. I'Anson)

Destroyers—continued.

H.M.S. *Middleton* (Lt.-Cdr. D. C. Kinloch)
        (Lt.-Cdr. C. S. Battersby)
H.M.S. *Montrose* (Act. Cdr. W. J. Phipps)
H.M.S. *Musketeer* (Cdr. E. N. V. Currey, D.S.C.)
        (Cdr. R. L. Fisher, D.S.O., O.B.E.)
H.M.S. *Myngs* (Capt. P. G. L. Cazalet, D.S.C.)
H.M.S. *Oakley* (Lt.-Cdr. R. C. V. Thomson)
        (Lt.-Cdr. T. A. Pack-Beresford)
H.M.S. *Obdurate* (Lt.-Cdr. C. E. L. Sclater, D.S.C.)
        (Lt.-Cdr. R. D. Franks, D.S.O., O.B.E.)
H.M.S. *Obedient* (Lt.-Cdr. D. C. Kinloch)
H.M.S. *Offa* (Lt.-Cdr. R. A. Ewing)
H.M.S. *Onslaught* (Cdr. W. H. Selby, D.S.C.)
        (Cdr. Hon. H. A. Pleydell-Bouverie)
H.M.S. *Onslow* (Capt. H. T. Armstrong, D.S.C.; Capt. J. A. McCoy, D.S.O.)
        (Capt. R. St. V. Sherbrooke, D.S.O.; Capt. H. W. S.
        Browning, O.B.E.)
H.M.S. *Opportune* (Cdr. M. L. Power, O.B.E.; Cdr. R. E. D. Ryder, V.C.)
        (Cdr. J. Lee-Barber, D.S.O.)
H.M.S. *Oribi* (Cdr. J. E. H. McBeath, D.S.O., D.S.C.)
H.M.S. *Orwell* (Lt.-Cdr. N. H. G. Austen, D.S.O.)
        (Lt.-Cdr. J. M. Hodges, D.S.O.; Lt-Cdr. J. R. Gower,
        D.S.C.)
O.R.P. *Orkan* (?)
O.R.P. *Piorun* (?)
H.M.S. *Punjabi* (Cdr. Hon. J. M. Waldegrave, D.S.O.)
H.M.S. *Pytchley* (Lt.-Cdr. H. Unwin)
H.M.S. *Quadrant* (Lt.-Cdr. W. H. Farrington)
H.M.S. *Queensborough* (Cdr. E. P. Hinton, D.S.O., M.V.O.)
H.M.S. *Raider* (Lt.-Cdr. K. W. Michell)
H.N.M.S. *St. Albans* (Cdr. S. V. Storheil, R.N.N.)
H.M.S. *Saumarez* (Lt.-Cdr. E. W. Walmsley, D.S.C.)
H.M.S. *Savage* (Cdr. M. D. G. Meyrick)
        (Lt.-Cdr. C. W. Malins, D.S.O., D.S.C.)
H.M.S. *Scorpion* (Lt.-Cdr. W. S. Clouston)
        (Cdr. C. W. McMullen, D.S.C.)
H.M.S. *Scourge* (Lt.-Cdr. G. I. M. Balfour)
H.M.S. *Serapis* (Lt.-Cdr. E. L. Jones, D.S.C.)
H.M.C.S. *Scioux* (Lt.-Cdr. E. E. G. Boak, R.C.N.)
U.S.S.R.S. *Sokrushitelni* (?)
H.N.M.S. *Stord* (Lt.-Cdr. S. Storheil, R.N.N.)
H.M.S. *Somali* (Capt. J. W. Eaton, D.S.O., D.S.C.)
        (Lt.-Cdr. C. D. Maud, D.S.C.)
H.M.S. *Tartar* (Cdr. R. T. White)
        (Cdr. St. J. R. J. Tyrwhit)
H.M.S. *Venomous* (Cdr. H. W. Falcon-Steward)
H.M.S. *Venus* (Cdr. J. S. M. Richardson, D.S.O.)
H.M.S. *Verdun* (Lt.-Cdr. W. S. Donald, D.S.C.)
H.M.S. *Vigilant* (Lt.-Cdr. L. W. L. Argles)
H.M.S. *Virago* (Lt.-Cdr. R. J. White)
H.M.S. *Volunteer* (Lt.-Cdr. A. S. Pomeroy)
        (Lt.-Cdr. G. J. Luther)
H.M.S. *Wells* (Lt. L. J. Pearson)
        (Lt. F. W. M. Carter)
H.M.S. *Westcott* (Cdr. H. Lambton)
H.M.S. *Wheatland* (Lt.-Cdr. R. de l'Brooke)

Destroyers—continued.

H.M.S. *Whitehall* (Lt.-Cdr. P. J. Cowell, D.S.C.)
H.M.S. *Wilton* (Lt. A. P. Northey, D.S.C.)
H.M.S. *Windsor* (Lt.-Cdr. D. H. F. Hetherington, D.S.C.)
H.M.S. *Woolston* (Lt.-Cdr. W. K. Michell)
H.M.S. *Worcester* (Lt.-Cdr. W. A. Juniper, D.S.O.)
H.M.S. *Wrestler* (Lt. R. W. B. Lacon, D.S.C.)
H.M.S. *Zambesi* (Capt. J. H. Allison, D.S.O.)
H.M.S. *Zealous* (Cdr. R. F. Jessel, D.S.O., D.S.C.)
H.M.S. *Zebra* (Lt.-Cdr. E. G. Peake)
H.M.S. *Zest* (Lt.-Cdr. R. B. N. Hicks, D.S.O.)

Minesweepers

H.M.S. *Bramble* (Capt. J. H. F. Crombie, D.S.O.)
           (Cdr. H. T. Rust, D.S.O.)
H.M.S. *Britomart* (Lt.-Cdr. S. S. Stamwitz)
H.M.S. *Gleaner* (Lt.-Cdr. F. J. G. Hewitt, D.S.C.)
H.M.S. *Gossamer* (Lt. T. C. Crease)
H.M.S. *Halcyon* (Lt.-Cdr. C. H. Corbett-Singleton)
H.M.S. *Harrier* (Cdr. A. D. H. Jay, D.S.O.)
H.M.S. *Hazard* (Lt.-Cdr. J. R. A. Seymour)
H.M.S. *Hebe* (Lt. A. J. Gulvin)
H.M.S. *Hussar* (Lt. R. C. Biggs, D.S.O., D.S.C.)
H.M.S. *Jason* (Cdr. H. G. A. Lewis)
H.M.S. *Leda* (Cdr. A. H. Wynne-Edwards)
H.M.S. *Niger* (Cdr. A. J. Cubison, D.S.C.)
H.M.S. *Salamander* (Lt. W. R. Muttram)
H.M.S. *Seagull* (Lt. C. H. Pollock)
H.M.S. *Sharpshooter* (Lt.-Cdr. W. L. O'Mara)
H.M.S. *Speedwell* (Lt.-Cdr. T. E. Williams, R.N.R.)
H.M.S. *Speedy* (Lt.-Cdr. J. G. Brooks)

Sloops and Frigates

H.M.S. *Cygnet* (Cdr. A. H. Thorold)
H.M.S. *Drury* (Lt.-Cdr. N. J. Parker)
H.M.S. *Goodall* (Lt.-Cdr. J. V. Fulton, R.N.V.R.)
H.M.S. *Kite* (Lt.-Cdr. A. N. G. Campbell)
H.M.S. *Lapwing* (Act. Cdr. E. C. Hutton)
H.M.S. *Lark* (Cdr. H. Lambton)
H.M.S. *Loch Alvis* (Lt.-Cdr. E. G. Old, R.C.N.R.)
H.M.S. *Loch Dunvegan* (Cdr. E. Wheeler, R.N.R.)
H.M.C.S. *Matane* (Lt. J. J. Coates)
H.M.S. *Mermaid* (Lt.-Cdr. J. P. Mosse)
H.M.C.S. *Morrow* (Cdr. E. G. Skinner, D.S.C., R.D., R.C.N.R.)
H.M.S. *Mounsey* (Lt. F. A. J. Andrew)
H.M.C.S. *Nene* (Lt.-Cdr. E. R. Shaw, R.C.N.R.)
H.M.S. *Pasley* (Lt. P. R. G. Mitchell)
H.M.S. *Peacock* (Lt.-Cdr. R. B. Stannard, V.C.)
H.M.S. *Bazeley* (Lt.-Cdr. J. W. Cooper, D.S.C., R.N.R.)
H.M.S. *Bentinck* (Lt. P. R. G. Worth)
H.M.S. *Byard* (Lt.-Cdr. J. I. Jones, D.S.O., D.S.C., R.N.R.)

Corvettes

H.N.M.S. *Acanthus* (?)
H.M.S. *Alnwick Castle* (Lt.-Cdr. H. A. Stonehouse, R.N.R.)
H.M.S. *Bamborough Castle* (Lt. M. S. Work, D.S.C., R.N.R.)
H.M.S. *Bergamot* (Lt. R. T. Horan, R.N.R.)
H.M.S. *Bluebell* (Lt. H. G. Walker, D.S.C.)
H.M.S. *Bryony* (Lt.-Cdr. J. P. Stewart, D.C.S., R.N.R.)
H.M.S. *Camelia* (Lt. F. R. J. Maberley, R.N.V.R.)
H.M.S. *Campanula* (Lt.-Cdr. B. A. Rodgers, R.N.R.)
H.M.S. *Denbigh Castle* (Lt.-Cdr. G. Butcher, D.S.C., R.N.R.)
H.M.S. *Dianella* (Lt. J. G. Rankin, R.N.R.)
     (Lt. J. F. Tognola, R.N.R.)
H.N.M.S. *Eglantine* (?)
H.M.S. *Heather* (Lt. W. L. Turner, R.N.R.)
H.M.S. *Honeysuckle* (Lt. H. H. D. McKillican, D.S.C., R.N.R.)
H.M.S. *Hyderabad* (Lt. S. C. B. Hickman, R.N.R.)
F.F.S. *La Malouine* (Lt. V. D. D. Bidwell, R.N.R.)
H.M.S. *Lotus* (Lt. H. J. Hall, R.N.R.)
H.M.S. *Oxlip* (Lt. C. W. Leadbetter, R.N.R.)
H.M.S. *Poppy* (Lt. N. K. Boyd, R.N.R.)
    (Lt. D. R. O. Onslow, R.N.R.)
H.M.S. *Rhododendron* (Lt. L. A. Sayers, R.N.R.; Lt. G. L. F. Melville, R.N.R.)
     (Lt. R. S. Mortimer, R.N.R.)
F.F.S. *Roselys* (Lt. de V. B. Bergeret)
H.M.S. *Saxifrage* (Lt. N. L. Knight, R.N.R.)
H.M.S. *Snowflake* (Lt. H. G. Chesterman, R.N.R.)
H.M.S. *Starwort* (Lt.-Cdr. N. W. Duck, R.N.R.)
H.M.S. *Sweetbriar* (Lt. J. W. Cooper, R.N.R.)

Trawlers

H.M.S. *Ayrshire* (Lt. L. J. A. Gradwell, R.N.V.R.)
H.M.S. *Blackfly* (Lt. A. P. Hughes, R.N.R.)
H.M.S. *Cape Argona* (Lt. E. R. Pato, R.N.R.)
H.M.S. *Cape Mariato* (Lt. H. T. S. Clouston, R.N.V.R.)
H.M.S. *Daneman* (Lt. G. O. T. D. Henderson, R.N.V.R.)
H.M.S. *Lady Madeleine* (Lt. W. G. Ogden, R.N.V.R.)
H.M.S. *Lord Austin* (Lt. O. B. Egjar)
H.M.S. *Lord Middleton* (Lt. R. H. Jameson, R.N.R.)
H.M.S. *Northern Gem* (Skipper Lt. H. C. Aisthorpe, R.N.R.)
H.M.S. *Northern Pride* (Lt. A. L. F. Bell, R.N.R.)
H.M.S. *Northern Spray* (Lt. G. T. Gilbert, R.N.R.)
H.M.S. *Northern Wave* (Lt. W. G. Pardoe-Mathews, R.N.R.)
H.M.S. *Paynter* (Lt. R. H. Nossitter, D.S.C., R.A.N.V.R.)
H.M.S. *Retriever* (Lt.-Cdr. G. E. K. Greeve, R.N.R.)
H.M.S. *St. Elstan* (Lt. R. M. Roberts, R.N.R.)
H.M.S. *St. Kenan* (Lt. J. Mackay, R.N.R.)
H.M.S. *Vizalma* (Lt. R. J. Angleback)

INDEX

249

251

ESCAPE FROM THE RISING SUN

IAN SKIDMORE

'The oily dust fell everywhere, on hungry stragglers searching for their units, on armed deserters who roamed the streets searching for loot, on . . . fear-crazed men fighting their way at the point of a gun or bayonet, pushing women and children aside . . . The dead lay in the streets . . . but no one collected the corpses now.'

Singapore had fallen. The British Army, retreating in disorder before the onslaught of the Japanese shock-troops, had been told to surrender. One man was convinced he could escape.

Geoffrey Rowley-Conwy seized a junk and sailed for Padang. There he joined a group of fellow officers for a desperate escape-bid in a dilapidated sailing boat across the Indian Ocean to Ceylon. 1,500 miles of open sea swept by the fury of the monsoon and patrolled by Japanese fighter planes on the lookout for British survivors.

'One of the best and liveliest escape stories of the Second World War . . . enthralling.'
Times Literary Supplement

GUNNER'S MOON

John Bushby

Ten to One against

In 1941-42, before the tide turned against Hitler's Germany, the odds against aircrew survival in Bomber Command were assessed as ten to one against. In the ill-fated Manchester bomber which bore the brunt of the raids on the Ruhr, the odds against returning alive were even higher.

John Bushby, one of the few survivors from those years, and a member of the legendary 601 Fighter Squadron, flew as rear gunner in the Manchester on almost forty successive operations over Europe.

Now he tells his thrilling story of the night raids across the Channel against heavily defended targets in the industrial heart of Germany, an area ringed with night fighter airfields, protected by the blinding glare of searchlights and flak. A deathtrap for the attacker.